CHEAPER
&
BETTER

CHEAPER & BETTER

Homemade Alternatives
to
Storebought Goods

BY

Nancy Birnes

A SHADOW LAWN PRESS BOOK

HARPER & ROW, PUBLISHERS, New York
Cambridge, Philadelphia, San Francisco, London
Mexico City, São Paulo, Singapore, Sydney

Designed by Shadow Lawn Press

Library of Congress Cataloging-in-Publication Data

Birnes, Nancy H.
        Cheaper and Better.

        "Perennial Library."
        Includes index.
        1. Recipes.   I. Title.
TX158.R54   1987   600   86-45655
ISBN 0-06-096057-4 (pbk.)

87 88 89 90 91 RRD 10 9 8 7 6 5 4 3 2

*Larry Ashmead tells a story of a small willow sewing basket
that was his grandmother's. It was quite old, and dusty;
so he took it outside to rinse it with the hose
and let it dry in the sun.
After a while, an amazing thing happened: the old willow
started to sprout and grow.*

Cheaper & Better
*is dedicated to that
spirit.*

Contents

Acknowledgments

Part of the challenge in researching **Cheaper & Better** has been to find people whose own expertise and experience has enabled them to develop cheaper and better solutions to their problems and within their working environments. By sharing with me their private cheap tricks, recipes, and formulas, they have helped me to make this book a reality.

Accordingly, I wish to acknowledge the contributions of Bill Woodall at Software Specialists, Somerville, NJ; W. David Duthie, Jr. of the Yellow Brick Toad, Lambertville, NJ; and Mike Anglin at Jack's Marine in Shelter Island, NY.

For help in testing, tasting, and approving the final recipes, I would like to thank Laura Hayfield, Antoinette and Don Kiker, Frederick Hayfield, Joan Mullen, Barton and Dee Klein, Geoffrey Birnes, Carleen Birnes, Holly Duthie, W. David Duthie, III; Purr-kins, Nemesis, and Max.

Introduction

According to the title of this book, the recipes described here will show you how to make foods and household items that are both cheaper and better. The concept of "cheaper" is obvious: if you make every item in this book just one time, you will save a total of **$1,656.80** over the cost of those very same items purchased from the grocery store, drugstore, hardware store, or garden center. That's a lot of money, but is it worth it to you? In other words, is it "better"?

For many people, the simple fact that an item is cheaper means that it is better for them. Everybody, it seems, can be ridiculously cheap about certain things. They may save string or the tiniest slivers of soap, perhaps, while at the same time buy an extravagantly priced condiment or costly piece of computer equipment without blanching. Therefore, the wide range of items covered in the following chapters gives you plenty of leeway to experiment and indulge your cheapest tendencies while saving loads of money for private indulgences.

For some people, a homemade item is better because all the ingredients that go into it are known, familiar, and safe. Consider that the food and products you make yourself will not contain any additives to prolong their shelf life or spark up their appearance. Nor will they contain excessive amounts of salt, sugar, or any ingredient a family member may not like or which might cause an allergic reaction. It is becoming obvious that the less we stabilize, chemically alter, or dye the food we eat and the cosmetics we use, the better off we will be, both physically as well as economically.

Obviously, you will save a great deal of money by packaging your food and household items yourself in simple wrappings or in reusable containers. We pay a small fortune for the informative, eye-catching, theft-resistant, and tamper-proof containers that hold the items we buy, and since some of the containers are costlier than their contents, you will have the opportunity to use and reuse those containers you've already purchased to hold your own creations from **Cheaper & Better**.

There's even a measure of built-in convenience when you make it yourself, from scratch, in the quantities you will need.

You can make and freeze a jumbo supply of tomato-based sauce from ingredients you've purchased in bulk at the end of the summer and then make fresh Mexican and Italian dinners all winter long by varying a few spices and side dishes. You can make up shampoo and cleaning solutions in gallon-size containers and eliminate constant and expensive trips to the store for these items. You can even package individual servings of granola snacks, frozen pancake batter, or herbal teas so that breakfast can be simple and quick, yet still inexpensive.

*Of course, all this takes a bit of planning and organization, and that's what **Cheaper & Better** is all about. I've spent over 20 years keeping a house, clipping coupons, learning gourmet and restaurant cooking techniques, and especially, learning how to save money. Over those same years I've tended to two husbands, four kids, five dogs, two cats, four apartments, several houses, one entire Brownie troop, and assorted gerbils, fish, frogs, plants, gardens, and cars. In addition, my parents and grandparents taught me many thrifty habits from the "old country," from the Depression, and from the years during World War II when Victory gardening, scrap collecting, and rationing were the norm.*

*Since those cautionary voices from the past are fainter now, some of the lessons they taught us are in danger of being lost in the din of good and plenty that we hear all about us. The truth is, most of us have less to spend than we would like, so the way we spend our money is more important than ever. On the following pages, I will show you how to create a **Cheaper & Better** way of life for yourself. You will learn how to plan and organize your time for cooking in quantity, for buying in season and in bulk. I will describe how to recognize and save useful containers, what kind of supplies, equipment, and tools you will need, and give you general information about how to complete the recipes which follow.*

It's really not very difficult to learn to save money—a little or a lot—as you will soon see.

A Word About the Prices

Prices change. They change each season, each year, and they are different in every part of the country. In addition, there are weekly specials, free samples, and sales promotions offered on various products.

However, in calculating the prices for **Cheaper & Better***, I've not used sale items, specials, or seasonal produce bargains. Nor have I used any coupon cents-off deals in my calculations. Whenever possible, I've avoided using store or generic brands for products because these items vary dramatically in price from state to state. By using nationally recognized name brands whenever possible, both for the ingredients as well as for the comparable purchased prices, you can probably find the same item, at roughly the same price, at a store near you.*

I've gathered prices from many different kinds of stores: huge supermarkets, garden centers, variety, toy, and hardware stores, in Pennsylvania, New Jersey, and New York, as well as from smaller specialty shops in those same states. The Price Finder pamphlet that the Grand Union supermarkets makes available to consumers is especially helpful in checking and double checking prices.

Since most of the prices were gathered in 1986, you can add a bit to the cost of things to account for inflation. Therefore, rather than try to duplicate the exact prices I've used in my calculations, you should plan on your own costs being even higher than those reported here.

If you are able to take advantage of seasonal opportunities to buy plentiful produce and pantry staples such as flour, cornmeal, and dairy products in bulk and if you have a means to store your food, you will certainly realize greater savings than I've reported here. And if you routinely shop for store brands, specials, and generic items, especially when creating your own mixes, flavorings, beauty, and laundry products, you will save even more.

The price I've listed in the price box for each recipe always compares the price of the basic or core recipe to a comparable purchased item, unless otherwise noted. The **Variations** *that I've listed at the end of many recipes are merely additional things you can do to enhance your finished* product, and I haven't calculated the costs of the ingredients used in the variants as part of my basic price.

Throughout **Cheaper & Better** you will notice many cross references to certain recipes. An item like **Vanilla Bean Extract, Soft Soap, Basic Chocolate Sauce**, or **All-purpose Cleaner** might be mentioned time and again as one of the ingredients in a recipe. These items can be replaced by a similar store-bought item and your recipe will still turn out just fine. But, if you are interested in getting the most savings possible for each recipe, you should make up your own supply of the cross-referenced item and use it in place of the purchased brand.

Here is an explanation of the information in a typical price comparison box:

(a) Cost of making the amount noted under **Yield**.

(b) A typical size of the purchased product.

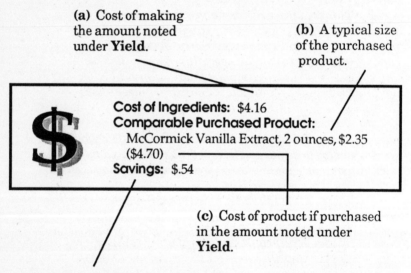

Cost of Ingredients: $4.16
Comparable Purchased Product:
    McCormick Vanilla Extract, 2 ounces, $2.35
    ($4.70)
Savings: $.54

(c) Cost of product if purchased in the amount noted under **Yield**.

(d) Difference between **(a)** and **(c)** which represents your savings.

You should notice that the quantities or yields from the various recipes are almost always greater than the amount you would purchase packaged for you in a store brand. Therefore, to realize your savings and to make sure that your hard work and valuable time have not been spent in vain, it is important that you plan to package, apportion, and otherwise store your creations in amounts that are suitable to your use.

A Word About Containers

Which brings us, undeniably, to the subject of containers. Deciding that you will be responsible for your own packaging and the eventual storage of the items you make is a new responsibility that you must undertake if you intend to save money making things for yourself.

It's extra work, pure and simple, to wash, remove labels, and find the storage space for jars, boxes, crocks, plastic tubs, and fancy tins. I happen to find it enjoyable and fun to save interesting containers that turn out to be exactly the right size for an unusual item or an eventual homemade gift for a friend. In fact, I can't resist buying unusual cruets, baskets, small wooden cheese boxes, and old-time tins when I see them at flea markets or antiques stores, and I have an enviable collection. I will even confess to paying a lot of extra money for an item that is packaged in a way that I can use or reuse the original container. I am a sucker for fancy French crocks, commemorative tin canisters, cute little basket-covered bottles, and pretty cosmetic and perfume bottles.

Therefore, it's no great problem for me to find pantry and closet storage space for my collection of containers, but if you are just beginning to cook or create beauty or cleaning items in quantity for yourself, you might be daunted by the challenge. Here are some tips and recommendations about what to collect for safe, productive storage for your **Cheaper & Better** projects.

☞ *Plastic Gallon Jugs*

You will need some of these for many of the items in Chapters 7 and 9 for cleaning and gardening solutions. In some cases, it is advisable to use the jug one time only for a particular solution and then throw it out when empty. In all cases, I advise that you clean the jug thoroughly with soap and water and let it drain completely. Then store the jugs with their lids kept separately nearby rather than on the jug. You can store clean jugs in a giant plastic garbage bag in the garage. I think I've come up with an especially clever way to store a few of them: I fill them with clean tap water and put them in the freezer. Since our power goes out in storms several times a year, I feel secure knowing that I will have a fresh supply of drinking water if the power is off for a long time, and meanwhile the frozen water keeps the rest of the items in my freezer colder longer. If my freezer gets too full, I remove a jug or two, let it thaw, and water my plants.

When filling any jug with something you've made, be sure to label it correctly—either with a permanent marking pen or with a paper label that you secure with cellophane tape or cover with clear nail polish, thinned-out white glue, or spray fixative so that the information will not run off when wet. Label the contents as to ingredients, use, and date, and put the jug up and out of the way of young children.

☞ Plastic Spray and Pump Containers

These containers are invaluable for your own versions of sprays, lotions, condiments, salves, and creams. If you haven't already begun to buy things packaged in these kinds of containers, you should begin to do so. Once you've used the original contents, you should take the container apart and soak the spray or pump mechanism in warm soapy water, dry thoroughly, and store the tops and containers separately.

The spray-type container used for window cleaner or some hair sprays will take the place of aerosol containers for your own cleaners, room fresheners, and hair spray. The pump-type used for hand lotion and liquid soap can hold your own versions of these products as well as condiments and children's paints.

☞ Glass Jars

A supply of glass jars that you've saved from pickles, spaghetti sauce, relishes, mayonnaise, and peanut butter will come in handy as you create your own versions of these items. Save only jars that are sturdy and lids that are clean and not rusted; clean the jars and lids by washing in hot soapy water or your dishwasher, and store the jars and lids separately.

When you are ready to fill the jars with food or lotions, you should first place them in a large kettle of water to simmer, not boil, for 20 minutes to sterilize them. Place the lids in the water as well, but do not screw them on the jars while they are in the simmering water. Remove the jars from the water with tongs or a clean towel, fill and cover them, and store as described in the individual recipes. No recipe in **Cheaper & Better** instructs you to can any item, because canning should only be done with the jars, lids, and rubber rings intended for that purpose. Jars you've saved from purchased foods may be too thin and they might actually shatter during the canning process. If you are interested in learning to can your food, check the **Resource** section, page 390, for reference.

In addition to smaller jars, you will need larger, gallon-size, glass jars—some with wide openings—for the recipes for homemade liqueurs in Chapter 5. Some of these jars should be dark glass; gallon wine jugs are perfect. Purchase new corks from a wine-making store or craft shop (or see **Resources**, page 392) for bottling your own liqueurs and vinegars.

☞ Miscellaneous Containers

A drawer or box set aside for unusual containers or interesting items in general is a good idea to develop if you would like to learn how to save money the old-fashioned way. The theory behind keeping such a collection is that you will never know when you might need something from the drawer or when something that seemed too nice to throw away will suddenly become useful.

Many serendipitous occurrences have resulted from my finding exactly the right container for an item. The makings for **Live Organic Disco Lights**, page 358, had to be gathered quickly to capture the ingredients, and it's handy to have a large, wide-mouth jar or two on hand.

I've calculated the savings on most items in **Cheaper & Better** as if you'd specifically purchased all the materials needed; in truth, you will save a great deal of money if you go to the trouble of saving rubber bands, soap bits, crayon ends, cookie crumbs, Popsicle sticks, pumpkin seeds, citrus peels, rose petals, coffee grounds, onion skins, ruined floppy disks, milk cartons, empty thread spools, corn husks, and seed pods from the garden. It's a simple choice: these items can form an endless parade of good, recycled parts and pieces that will dance and do tricks if you're imaginative and save a place for them, or they will neatly march out of your life and into the garbage if you're not.

Chapter 1

Pantry Stockers

The items in the **Cheaper & Better** pantry are very nearly the exact duplicates of those things we keep around the kitchen and in the refrigerator for cooking, such as spices, condiments, sauces, and butters.

In addition, a well-stocked pantry will include jellies, jams, pickles, salad dressings, and cereals; while a well-stocked freezer, at least in my house, has a supply of tomato sauces and fruit preserves that recapture some of the warm bounty of summer in the harsh, blowy days of winter.

Salt Substitutes
> *Spicy Lemon Mix*
> *Sea Salt Seasonings*
> *Sesame Seasoning Salt*

Poultry Seasoning
Curry Powder
Firehouse Hot Chili Powder
Scented and Spiced Sugars
> *Citrus and Spice Sugar*
> *Lemon and Mint Sugar*
> *Vanilla Sugar*
> *Rose Sugar*

Cinnamon Sugar
Silly Sparkles
Vanilla Bean Extract
Creamed Wheat Cereal
Homemade Familia
Granny's Granola
Sweetened Condensed Milk
Fresh Mayonnaise
Homemade Cream Cheese
Country Butter
> *Whipped Butter*

Crunchy Croutons
> *Mexican-flavored Croutons*
> *Italian-flavored Croutons*
> *Cheesy Soup Croutons*

Healthy Bread Crumbs
> *Italiano Bread Crumbs*
> *Sweet Crumbs*

Garlic in Oil
> *Onion in Oil*

Dried Minced Vegetables
> *Frozen Minced Vegetables*

Seafood Cocktail Sauce

Chinese Duck Sauce

Chinese Mustard Sauce

Tangy Mustard
> *Spicy Horseradish Mustard*
> *Hot Peppery Mustard*

Homemade Tomato Catsup

Tangy Barbecue Sauce

Bleu Cheese Salad Dressing

Classic French Salad Dressing

Great Seasonings Salad Dressing Mixes

Green Goddess Salad Dressing

Italian Salad Dressing

Thousand Island Dressing

Basic Tomato Sauce

Caruso Spaghetti Sauce

Gazpacho-style Sauce

Primo Primavera Sauce

Quick Maple Syrup
> *Blender Sweet Syrup*

Sweet Berry Syrups
> *Blueberry Syrup*

Basic Chocolate Sauce
> *Hot Fudge Sauce*

Butterscotch Sauce

Peanut Butter
> *Cashew Sesame Butter*

Apple Butter

Freezer Fruit Preserves

Pimientos

Quick Cucumber Pickles

Pickled Beets

Pickled Onions

Salt Substitutes

There are several ways to try to cut down on your salt intake if, like me, you have a low tolerance for heavily salted foods. Spirited combinations of spices are one way, using a salt substitute as part of a recipe is another, and the easiest way to get used to the taste of less salt is to try a substitute that leaves a little salt in, as in the last two recipes.

Whether you use fresh or dried herbs, a mortar and pestle is a good way to grind the spices fine enough to sprinkle through a shaker. Or you can whirl the slices in a blender until you have a fine mix.

Spicy Lemon Mix

1/4 cup Dried Minced Onion (page 25)
1/4 cup Dried Minced Green Pepper (page 25)
1/4 cup Dried Minced Celery (page 25)
5 cloves garlic, chopped
2 tablespoons grated lemon peel
2 tablespoons chopped dried parsley
2 tablespoons basil
1 tablespoon oregano
1 tablespoon savory
1 teaspoon marjoram
1 teaspoon coriander
1 teaspoon cumin

1. Combine all ingredients and whirl in the blender until chopped fine—about 1 minute. Stop and scrape sides of the blender often because mixture will be a bit sticky at first. Store spice in a tightly capped shaker jar and use in place of salt in meat and main-course recipes and on salads.

Sea Salt Seasonings

1/2 cup sea salt
2 tablespoons paprika
1 teaspoon parsley flakes
1 teaspoon basil
1 teaspoon oregano
1 teaspoon thyme

1 teaspoon black pepper
1 teaspoon marjoram
1 teaspoon celery seed
1 teaspoon garlic powder
1/2 teaspoon Curry Powder (page 5)
1/2 teaspoon cayenne

1. Combine all ingredients in the blender; blend until herbs are finely ground and well combined. Store in a tightly covered jar on the pantry shelf. Seasoning will keep well for up to 6 months.

Sesame Seasoning Salt

3/4 cup sesame seeds
1/4 cup sea salt
1 teaspoon paprika
1 teaspoon pepper
1 teaspoon chives, chopped

1. Cook and stir sesame seeds in a large skillet over medium heat until light brown. Stir in salt and cook 5 minutes more, stirring constantly. Cool.

2. Place sesame seed mixture and the rest of the spices in blender; whirl for 1 minute or until mixture is finely ground. Store in an airtight container for up to 6 months.

Yield: 11 ounces

Cost of Ingredients: $2.85
Comparable Purchased Product: Mrs. Dash, 2.5 ounces, $1.69 ($7.43)
Savings: $4.58

Cheap Trick ....✂....

One easy way to cut down on salt is to switch your salt and pepper containers—put salt in the pepper shaker and less salt will come through the smaller holes. You will automatically cut your salt intake by half.

Poultry Seasoning

*This combination of spices is terrific in chicken salad
and in many of the pasta and rice recipes in Chapter 2 that are
meant to accompany chicken as a main course.*

      2 tablespoons sage
      2 tablespoons thyme
      2 tablespoons marjoram
      2 tablespoons savory
      2 tablespoons rosemary

1. Mix all spices together and grind with a mortar and pestle
or process for 1 minute in a food processor or blender.

2. Store in a tightly closed container on the pantry shelf for up
to 6 months.

Yield: 5 ounces

Cost of Ingredients: $8.29
Comparable Purchased Product:
    McCormick Poultry Seasoning, 1.25 ounces,
    $1.83 ($8.60)
Savings: $.31

Curry Powder

*Here is a very authentic curry powder that is much fresher
tasting than the kind that has been on the store shelf for
months.*

      2 tablespoons cumin seeds
      2 tablespoons cardamom seeds
      2 tablespoons coriander seeds
      1/4 cup ground turmeric
      1 tablespoon dry mustard
      1 teaspoon cayenne pepper

1. Preheat oven to 200 degrees.

2. Pour the cumin, cardamom, and coriander seeds into a glass or enamel baking dish and warm in the oven for 20 minutes.

3. Grind the seeds in the blender on high speed. Add turmeric, dry mustard, and cayenne pepper. Mix until all ingredients are well blended.

2. Store in a tightly capped container. Seasoning will keep for 1 year on the pantry shelf.

Yield: 8 ounces

Cost of Ingredients: $7.47
Comparable Purchased Product:
  McCormick Curry Powder, 1.25 ounces, $1.35
  ($8.64)
Savings: $1.17

Firehouse Hot Chili Powder

If you like your chili fiery hot, you can vary this recipe to include a bit more cayenne and use hot, rather than mild, chili peppers—but label it accordingly. This powder will have a better consistency if you use a mortar and pestle to grind the peppers and coarser spices.

6 tablespoons paprika
2 tablespoons turmeric
1 tablespoon dried mild or hot chili peppers
1 teaspoon cumin
1 teaspoon oregano
1/2 teaspoon cayenne
1/2 teaspoon garlic powder
1/2 teaspoon salt
1/4 teaspoon ground cloves

1. Mix all ingredients and grind to a fine powder using a mortar and pestle, or process in your food processor or blender. Spice will keep for up to 6 months on the pantry shelf.

To Use:

      This powder is somewhat more pungent and fresher tasting than a packaged brand, so use a bit less.

Yield: 5.5 ounces

Cost of Ingredients: $2.40
Comparable Purchased Product:
   McCormick Chili Powder, 2.10 ounces, $1.75
   ($4.58)
Savings: $2.18

Scented and Spiced Sugars

*These delicately colored and lightly scented sugars are an excellent accompaniment to **Herb Teas**, page 174, and are delicious sprinkled on buttered toast or pancakes in the morning. Try these sugars to flavor fresh fruit, especially bananas, and to top off applesauce or sliced peaches. For the strongest taste, use freshly grated citrus peel and freshly ground spices, if you have a spice grinder.*

Citrus and Spice Sugar

     1 cup sugar
     1 tablespoon grated orange peel
     1 teaspoon grated lemon peel
     1/2 teaspoon cinnamon
     1/4 teaspoon nutmeg
     1/4 teaspoon ginger

1. Preheat oven to 200 degrees.

2. Mix all ingredients in a shallow baking pan. Heat in the oven for 15 minutes, stirring occasionally. Cool.

3. Pour mixture into blender and whirl on low speed until ingredients are blended and sugar is ground fine. Stored in a tightly closed container, sugar will keep for up to 6 months.

Yield: 9 ounces

Lemon and Mint Sugar

1 cup sugar
1 tablespoon dried mint leaves or 4 to 5 fresh leaves
1 tablespoon grated lemon peel

1. Preheat oven to 200 degrees.

2. Mix all ingredients in a shallow baking pan. Heat in the oven for 15 minutes, stirring occasionally. If you are using fresh mint, heat an additional 10 minutes or until leaves are crunchy. Cool.

3. Pour mixture into blender and whirl on low speed until ingredients are well blended and sugar is ground fine. Stored in a tightly closed container, sugar will keep for up to 6 months.

Variations:
    Other herbs you might try combining with sugar are anise, lemon verbena, or rose-geranium leaves.

Yield: 9 ounces

Vanilla Sugar

To make this recipe a little more economical, you might consider using the expensive vanilla beans first to make **Vanilla Bean Extract,** *page 12, and then after a few weeks, remove them from the extract and add them to the sugar. Then you will have two lovely vanilla-flavored items in your kitchen pantry for the price of the vanilla beans.*

2 cups sugar
2 vanilla beans

1. Place the sugar in an airtight canister or jar with a tightly fitting cover. Using kitchen shears or sturdy scissors, cut the vanilla bean into three or four pieces, working directly over the jar or container so that all the little black seeds will drop into the sugar.

2. Cover and store for 2 to 4 weeks before using. Remove the

beans and whirl in the blender for 1 minute if you have lumps in the sugar. Additional plain sugar may be added to the container as you use the Vanilla Sugar until you notice that the scent and flavor are gone.

Yield: 16 ounces

Rose Sugar

1 cup sugar
1 fragrant rose

1. Pour the sugar into a clean glass jar with a tight-fitting lid. Bury the rose in the sugar and place the jar in full sunlight. Shake the jar every other day for 2 to 3 weeks.

To Use:
You can use this sugar in place of regular sugar in many recipes—the sugar will seem a bit sweeter.
*This sugar is delightful sprinkled on fresh or brandied fruit or served with one of the **Herb Teas** on page 174.*
*Dust freshly made chocolate or pound cake with the sugar through a fancy doily or try some in **Spiced and Fancy After-dinner Coffee**, page 178.*

Variation:
If you would like to try a powdered vanilla or rose sugar, simply place 1 cup of flavored sugar, without the beans or blossoms, into your blender with 1 teaspoon cornstarch and blend on high speed for 2 minutes or until sugar is a fine powder. Let the mixture rest for a week or two before using to make sure the cornstarch flavor is absorbed.

Yield: 9 ounces

Cost of Ingredients: $.56
Comparable Purchased Product:
   McCormick Rainbow Festive Package, 2.5 ounces, $.83 ($2.98)
Savings: $2.42

Cinnamon Sugar

This particular pantry stocker is considered a necessity in certain families. My kids tell me they feel safe and secure knowing it is in the closet, and they love to sprinkle it on hot buttered toast or an English muffin. Since you can smell the heavenly aroma the minute it's sprinkled on, it's easy to descend on the kitchen at just the right moment, swoop down, and take a big bite out of the bread before anyone knows you've struck.

**2 cups sugar
5 tablespoons cinnamon**

1. Stir sugar and cinnamon together until completely mixed. Store in a clean spice jar with a shaker top for up to 6 months.

Ideas:

Shake this mixture over just about any food when your sweet tooth acts up: oatmeal, buttered toast, dusted over whipped cream, in coffee—these are just for starters.

*Try it also in tea, for French Toast (see **Ooh-la-la Butter**, page 104), on puddings (page 86), on ice cream (pages 139 to 141), yogurt (page 121), over jelly (page 50), and dusted over any fruit pie, especially pumpkin.*

Variations:

*Reduce the cinnamon by 1 tablespoon and add 1 tablespoon allspice or 1 tablespoon nutmeg. For more exotic mixes, see **Scented and Spiced Sugars**, page 7. For a colorful mix for parties or holidays, see **Silly Sparkles**, page 11. For a silky taste, try **Vanilla Sugar**, page 8.*

Yield: 8 ounces

Cost of Ingredients: $1.58
Comparable Purchased Product:
   McCormick Cinnamon Sugar, 3 ounces, $1.13
   ($3.01)
Savings: $1.43

Cheap Trick.........................✂.....

Fill pretty jars quickly and easily with fancy sugar by punching a hole in the bottom of a paper cup to use as a funnel. Then tie a bow with ribbon or yarn, add a label telling how to use the sugar, and you have an instant gift.

Silly Sparkles

*To make these colored sugars, first refer to the recipe for **Nature's Colors** on page 367 to create the colors. Since you are making a food item, choose the familiar edible substances for colors over flowers or herbs, which are best left for coloring craft items. For example, dyes made from beets, cabbage, berries, onion skins, or spinach are preferable to those made from grass, moss, or coffee grounds. Choose the colors you like and don't worry about the flavors mixing with the sugar. Once all the liquid or juice from the flavor has evaporated, the sugar will still taste like sugar.*

3 cups sugar
1 cup Nature's Colors (page 367)

1. Preheat oven to 150 degrees.

2. Stir sugar and dye together and spread the mixture in a shallow baking pan. Place the sugar in the oven for 20 minutes, stirring every 5 minutes. Remove when the liquid has evaporated. Cool.

3. Store sugar in a closely covered jar or canister.

Yield: 24 ounces

Cost of Ingredients: $.44
Comparable Purchased Product:
    Sterling Green Crystal Sugars, 4 ounces, $.83
    ($4.98)
Savings: $4.54

Vanilla Bean Extract

This interesting brew is very much like the liquid we call vanilla, and yet it is special. It isn't as potent, but it is smooth and vanilla-flavored, and I use it in the other recipes in **Cheaper & Better** *that call for just a touch of vanilla.*

> **1/2 cup brandy**
> **3 or 4 vanilla beans**

1. Chop vanilla beans into small pieces, being careful not to lose any of the bean or the little black seeds.

2. Drop the pieces into a clean jar and cover with the brandy. Cover with a tight-fitting lid and keep in a dark place, shaking every third day or so.

3. Extract will be ready in about 2 weeks. A touch more brandy can be added if the beans still seem potent. Mixture can be added to indefinitely.

To Use:
> *Use just as you would regular vanilla extract, but taste to make sure the brandy flavor is not too strong.*

Yield: 4 ounces

Cost of Ingredients: $4.16
Comparable Purchased Product:
   McCormick Vanilla Extract, 2 ounces, $2.35
   ($4.70)
Savings: $.54

Cheap Trick ....

Sprinkle a musty-smelling ice chest with some baking soda and close the lid for an hour. Then rinse with clean water and wipe with a soft cloth dampened with a teaspoon of Vanilla Bean Extract. Your ice chest will smell wonderful between picnics.

Creamed Wheat Cereal

Get the cracked bulgur wheat for this recipe from the health food store, or from a well-stocked baking section of your grocery store. It's easy to make the freshest tasting cereal from these simple ingredients.

3 cups uncooked cracked bulgur wheat
1/2 cup wheat germ

1. Grind wheat by placing 1/4 cup at a time in your blender or food processor. Process until the wheat is powdered. Store powder in an airtight container on the pantry shelf, or in the refrigerator or freezer in warm weather, for up to 6 months.

To Use:
Combine 3 1/2 tablespoons of powdered wheat with 1 1/2 cups cold milk in a saucepan. Add a dash of salt and quickly bring the mixture to a boil, stirring constantly. Lower the heat and simmer for 5 minutes; remove from heat, cover, and let sit for a few minutes before serving.

Hint:
To save time in the morning, measure the cereal, milk, and salt into the pan as you are doing your evening chores. Leave the mixture in the refrigerator overnight; cook for 5 minutes on the stove, or 2 minutes in the microwave.

Variations:
Serve this, and other cooked cereals, with a dot of butter, a sprinkle of brown sugar, and light cream for a very rich treat.
Or, sprinkle chopped apple, cinnamon, and 2 tablespoons apple cider on the cereal.

Yield: 26 ounces

Cost of Ingredients: $1.80
Comparable Purchased Product: Nabisco
Cream of Wheat, 14 ounces, $.99 ($1.83)
Savings: $.09

Homemade Familia

*This is a Swiss version of granola, with the emphasis on fruits and nuts. It is a little softer tasting than granola, and you can serve it the Swiss way, by mixing milk, yogurt, or juice into the cereal and letting it absorb the liquid before eating (see **Variations**) or the American way, by pouring the milk over and eating just like regular cereal.*

*Try making up a bowl to test each way and see which one you like best. Also, as in **Granny's Granola** on page 15, you can vary the ingredients to suit what you or your family prefers to eat, as long as the proportion of liquid to dry ingredients remains constant.*

> **6 cups instant-style rolled oats**
> **2 cups of any combination of the following: shredded wheat, whole wheat flakes, or millet flakes**
> **2 cups wheat germ**
> **1 cup chopped walnuts**
> **1 cup chopped almonds or hazelnuts**
> **1 cup chopped dates**
> **1 cup chopped dried fruits: apples, bananas, or pears**
> **2 cups raisins**
> **1 cup instant nonfat dry milk**

1. To obtain the proper consistency of this cereal, you must use a food processor or the quick chopping action of your blender. In a large bowl, combine the oats, wheat, and wheat germ. Run the grains through your food processor in 1-cup batches for just a few seconds. Return processed grains to the bowl and stir thoroughly to mix.

2. Combine the nuts, dried fruit, and dry milk and run through the food processor in 1-cup batches until thoroughly chopped but not overly mushy. Continue adding the processed fruits and nuts to the bowl. Add spoonfuls of wheat germ or oats if the fruit-nut and dried milk mixture feels too sticky in the processor.

3. When all the ingredients are processed, mix them lightly. Store in a covered jar or canister in the refrigerator for up to 2 months, or in a tightly closed container on the pantry shelf if the weather is not too hot or humid. Do not freeze.

Variations:

To try this cereal the Swiss way, mix 1 cup of familia with one of the following:

1 pint cold milk
1 cup **Homemade Yogurt** (page 121)
1 cup orange or apple juice

Stir well and let soak for 10 minutes. Then serve with:
fresh sliced fruit
grated apples
honey
fresh cream or milk

Yield: 9 cups

Cost of Ingredients: $5.18
Comparable Purchased Product: Familia
Swiss Cereal, 12 ounces, $2.39 ($14.34)
Savings: $9.16

Granny's Granola

This is not my own granny's granola, of course. She made us big bowls of pastina in the winter, but this is the kind of cereal I hope my own grandchildren will eat when they come to visit, when they want a change from pastina.

This is the best kind of recipe to let a child help with in the kitchen, as long as you supervise at the cooking stages. It's fun to mix and mix the dried ingredients, and then mix and mix the oil and honey into them. It's also educational to let a child see what good things can go into a breakfast cereal.

4 cups old-fashioned rolled oats
1 cup wheat germ
1/2 cup instant nonfat dry milk
Any combination of the following ingredients to make
a total of 4 more cups:
Chopped nuts or sesame seeds
Sunflower seeds or pumpkin seeds
Dried fruit: raisins, apples, bananas, or dates

1/2 cup shredded unsweetened coconut
1/2 cup vegetable oil or butter
1/2 to 1 cup honey
1 teaspoon Vanilla Bean Extract (page 12)
1 teaspoon cinnamon

1. Preheat oven to 350 degrees.

2. Combine all the dry ingredients in a large bowl and stir thoroughly to mix.

3. Heat the oil and honey slowly until they just begin to simmer. Remove from heat and stir in the vanilla.

4. Stir oil-honey mixture into the dry ingredients, making sure to coat all the dry ingredients well.

5. Turn the mixture out into an oiled shallow baking pan and pat down well. Bake for 20 to 30 minutes. It's a good idea to check the granola every now and then—be careful the top doesn't brown too quickly. Stir carefully and pat down during the baking.

7. When completely cooled, store in a tightly covered jar or canister. If the weather is very warm or humid, keep in the refrigerator; otherwise, this granola will keep for about a month on the pantry shelf. Do not freeze.

Variations:

This recipe can be used as the basis for a crunchy, fruity candy by mixing the cereal with a bit with honey, forming into balls, rolling in **Vanilla Sugar**, page 8, and refrigerating.

Granola also makes an excellent topping for your homemade ice cream, pudding, and yogurt.

Yield: 11 cups

Cost of Ingredients: $8.62
Comparable Purchased Product:
   Kretschmer Granola with raisins, 16 ounces, $1.69 ($9.29)
Savings: $.67

Sweetened Condensed Milk

I've always believed that this convenient pantry item only comes in cans—boiled into them with some sort of magical factory formula. Imagine the fun of making it up fresh when this, and only this, form of milk will do in a recipe.

>2 cups instant nonfat dry milk
>1 1/2 cups sugar
>2/3 cup boiling water
>6 tablespoons sweet butter, melted and slightly cooled

1. Mix the dry milk and sugar together and then slowly add the boiling water. Stir in the melted butter.

2. Whip in a blender or by hand until smooth.

3. Store milk in the refrigerator for 1 week, or freeze the extra for up to 6 months.

Yield: 20 ounces

Cost of Ingredients: $.85
Comparable Purchased Product: Eagle Brand Condensed Milk, 14 ounces, $1.29 ($1.80)
Savings: $.95

Fresh Mayonnaise

There is a bit of a knack required when making your own mayonnaise, but learning the technique is not that hard—it only requires patience—and you will be well rewarded for your time. Just follow the directions carefully, especially Steps 2 and 4, which direct you to add the oil to your egg mixture slowly, literally one drop at a time.

The safest procedure to follow if you are a first-time mayonnaise maker is to use a blender rather than trying to keep up with the pace of hand whisking. Take all your ingredients out of the refrigerator 30 minutes before beginning

*so everything is at room temperature. Also, make your
mayonnaise on a sunny day, with no threat of rain, because the
higher humidity will affect the delicate emulsion.*

> **3 eggs**
> **3 teaspoons hot mustard**
> **1/2 teaspoon salt**
> **1/4 teaspoon cayenne pepper**
> **2 teaspoons honey**
> **3 3/4 cups vegetable, safflower, or peanut oil**
> **9 tablespoons lemon juice or wine vinegar**

1. Put eggs, mustard, salt, pepper, and honey in the blender
with 3/4 cup of the oil. Blend until thoroughly combined.

2. With blender still running, remove lid and very slowly,
drop by drop, add 1 1/2 cups of the salad oil.

3. Blend in the lemon juice or wine vinegar.

4. Again, with the blender still running, add the final 1 1/2 cups
of salad oil, very slowly. The mayonnaise should be
thickening slowly at this point.

5. Store in a covered jar in the refrigerator and use as the base
for the various salad dressings described in this chapter. This
mayonnaise will keep well in the refrigerator for 2 to 4 weeks.

Yield: 18 ounces

Cost of Ingredients: $1.21
Comparable Purchased Product: Hellman's
   8 ounces, $.75 ($1.68)
Savings: $.47

Cheap Trick . . . .✄. . . .

*If you're just learning how to make mayonnaise and your
first batch or two doesn't look good enough to eat, don't throw it
out. It will make a rich, nourishing moisturizer for your hair
or face—simply pat it on, let it stay in place for 10 minutes,
and then rinse off or shampoo as usual.*

Homemade Cream Cheese

It's fun to make your own creamy, very creamy cheese. If your first attempts seem too thick or too thin, try adding some mushrooms or chili sauce to the cheese and serve it as a dip. You will need a kitchen thermometer for this recipe, as well as some cheesecloth.

>**1 gallon whole milk**
>**1 quart cultured buttermilk**
>**1/2 teaspoon salt**

1. Pour milk and buttermilk into a large pan and suspend the thermometer in the milk. Cook over medium heat, stirring occasionally, until the temperature registers 170 degrees.

2. Keep mixture on the heat and keep the temperature of the milk between 170 and 175 degrees. After 30 minutes, the mixture should start to separate into curds (the lumps) and whey (the liquid).

3. Line a strainer with several layers of moistened cheesecloth and set it inside a large bowl or pan to catch the drippings. Use a slotted spoon to lift the curds from the milk mixture and lay them in the cheesecloth. Pour the remainder of the whey through the cheesecloth and save the whey for **Light-skin Bleaching Cream**, page 216.

4. Let curds drain, at room temperature, for 2 to 4 hours. Remove the cheese from the cheesecloth and place in blender with the salt. Blend until creamy.

5. Store cheese in small containers with tight-fitting lids and refrigerate. Cheese can also be frozen, thawed, and then beaten in a blender until creamy.

Yield: 64 ounces

Cost of Ingredients: $2.57
Comparable Purchased Product:
Philadelphia Cream Cheese, 3 ounces, $.49 ($10.45)
Savings: $7.88

Country Butter

*Here is a clever way to stretch margarine, while at the
same time softening and enriching its flavor a bit. My mother
tells me that this was one of the many ways people made do
without butter during World War II. And, except for the small
amount of butter in the buttermilk, you will have a spread that
is relatively low in unsaturated fats, if that is a concern of
yours.*

> **1 pound margarine, softened**
> **1 cup corn oil**
> **1 cup buttermilk**

1.   Whip ingredients together in a food processor or with an
electric mixer. Stored in a tightly covered container in the
refrigerator, this spread will keep well for 1 month.

Idea:

*Use this spread as the basis for any of the **Herb Butters**
(page 105), **Sweet Butters** (page 104), or some of the other savory
butters and spreads listed in the Index. You will save a bit
more than if you used regular butter, but be careful of the
consistency—reduce the corn oil, if necessary.*

Whipped Butter

*If you would like to save even more money, consider
whipping your own butter or butter spreads. You can use your
own **Country Butter** or any purchased butter in this recipe, but
you will need a portable electric mixer because you must keep
the butter extremely cold as you whip, and the only simple way
to do this is to whip the butter directly over ice.*

*First, let the butter warm to room temperature and place it
in a bowl that you have nestled in a bed of ice cubes. Whip the
butter at high speed until it begins to harden again and lighten
in color. Scrape the sides of the bowl often and stop when the
butter begins to stick to the beaters.*

*You can add herbs, spices, honey, or other flavorings
at this point if you wish. Scrape the butter into a crock or plastic
container, cover, and refrigerate. Butter will keep for 3 weeks.*

Yield: 32 ounces

Cost of Ingredients: $.86
Comparable Purchased Product: I Can't
   Believe It's Not Butter, 1 pound, $1.39 ($2.78)
Savings: $1.92

Crunchy Croutons

*If you keep these croutons in a tightly closed container in the refrigerator, you can add new ones to the batch indefinitely (see **Variations**). Use these delicious, crunchy nuggets to stretch out salads, add interest to the tops of soups, as a top layer on scalloped tomatoes, or in all sorts of stuffings for turkey, chicken, and even as the basis for your own **Top-of-the-Stove Stuffing Mix** (page 93).*

*Croutons are one of the time-honored ways to use up any type of bread and muffins you have; other ways include **Healthy Bread Crumbs** (page 23) and **High-Protein Bird Treats** (page 291).*

> **1 cup cubed day-old bread or rolls**
> **2 tablespoons butter, melted**
> **1 teaspoon seasoning: either onion salt, garlic salt, grated cheese, paprika, thyme, Poultry Seasoning (page 5), or tarragon**

1. Preheat over to 250 degrees.

2. Stir the seasoning of your choice into the melted butter.

3. Toss the flavored butter with the cubed bread, making sure each piece is coated. Place in shallow baking dish.

4. Bake for 10 to 15 minutes, shaking the pan at least once during cooking to ensure that all the bread is crisp and lightly browned.

5. Store in a covered container in the refrigerator for up to 2 months, and replenish with the different version of croutons described here. Shake vigorously before dipping a portion out of the container to distribute all the different flavors.

Variations:

   Cook 4 slices of bacon until crispy, remove bacon to
paper toweling to drain and measure out 1/4 cup bacon grease.
Return the 1/4 cup grease to frying pan and add the bread cubes.
Cook over low heat, stirring , until the cubes are browned and
slightly crispy. Crumble bacon and toss together with the
cubes.

   Add 1/2 cup of lightly browned chopped onions, green
peppers, or chopped celery to the cubes and then cook as
directed.

Mexican-flavored Croutons

1/2 cup cubed bread
1/2 cup nacho chips, crumbled
1 tablespoon Mexican Seasonings Mix (page 103)
2 tablespoons corn oil

Italian-flavored Croutons

1 cup cubed bread
1/2 teaspoon oregano
1/2 teaspoon garlic powder
1/2 teaspoon basil
2 tablespoons olive oil

Cheesy Soup Croutons

1 cup cubed bread
1/4 cup Parmesan or Cheddar cheese, grated
2 tablespoons butter

1. Gently toss all ingredients together in a large bowl, spread
in a shallow baking pan, bake, and store as directed in
Crunchy Croutons.

Yield: 8 ounces

Cost of Ingredients: $.24
Comparable Purchased Product: Arnold
   Seasoned Croutons, 6 ounces, $1.09
Savings: $.85

Healthy Bread Crumbs

These bread crumbs are healthy, both for your body and your wallet. If you use all sorts of bread that comes your way, you will invariably have a dandy mixture of whole wheat, rye, and various other interesting grains. It's always a good idea to get into the habit of saving the ends and bits of breads to use in recipes and to give to the birds.

2 cups stale bread

1. Preheat oven to 250 degrees.

2. Arrange bread in a single layer in a shallow baking pan. Bake for 20 minutes to crisp. Cool.

3. Break into small pieces and feed, slowly, into a blender or a food processor. Store crumbs in an airtight container. Crumbs will keep for several weeks on the pantry shelf and indefinitely in the freezer. You can continue to replenish your supply as you collect stale bread. Stir the new bread crumbs into the old to mix.

Italiano Bread Crumbs

2 cups Healthy Bread Crumbs
1/4 cup Parmesan cheese, grated
2 tablespoons parsley
1 teaspoon oregano
1 teaspoon basil
1 teaspoon garlic powder

1. Combine all ingredients and store in an airtight container in the refrigerator for up to 2 months.

Sweet Crumbs

2 cups cookies, crackers, sweet buns, or dry cake
1 tablespoon brown sugar

1. Grind the cookies and crackers in a blender for 1 minute or until you have a fine-textured crumb. Store in an airtight container in the refrigerator or freezer for up to 2 months.

2. Replenish your supply and stir any new crumbs thoroughly into the existing mixture.

Yield: 20 ounces

 Cost of Ingredients: $1.37 for Italian version
Comparable Purchased Product: Arnold
   Italian Bread Crumbs, 15 ounces, $1.35 ($1.80)
Savings: $.43

Garlic in Oil

This recipe miraculously keeps garlic tasting fresh almost forever. It's an efficient way to store garlic, especially if you use it infrequently. Use the finest, purest olive oil you can afford, and if you want a special treat, use the garlic- or onion-flavored oil in your favorite Italian recipes as well.

1 to 10 bulbs garlic
Olive oil to cover

1. Peel and slice garlic. You can also finely mince the garlic slices or force them through a garlic press if you prefer. Place garlic in a sterilized glass jar and add just enough olive oil to cover.

2. Refrigerate, tightly covered, for up to 6 months.

To Use:
   Use as you would fresh garlic: approximately 1/2 teaspoon Garlic in Oil equals 1 clove fresh garlic.

Onion in Oil

1 cup minced onion
Olive oil to cover

1. Place onion and olive oil in a sterilized glass jar, cover, and store in the refrigerator for up to 6 months.

Idea:
> You can add bits of finely chopped green or red pepper, parsley, or scallions to the onion jar if you like the flavors mixed. This is an excellent way to save the last bits of a pepper or scallion.

Yield: 8 ounces

Cost of Ingredients: $.72
Comparable Purchased Product: William
   Sherrel Natural Garlic in Oil, 8 ounces, $1.59
Savings: $.87

Dried Minced Vegetables

Here is a handy way to use up celery before it becomes all limp and uncouth in the refrigerator, or to store away a nice harvest of peppers. I always buy celery, scallions, and carrots with the best of intentions, but whenever I need some in a recipe, they are usually too far gone to slice.

Drying a batch of vegetables is an easy way to keep them chopped and handy when you need them. Freezing chopped, uncooked vegetables is another way to store them for cooking, and if you use them without thawing, the vegetables will reconstitute rather well.

1 to 2 cups vegetables, finely chopped: onions, mushrooms, red or green peppers, scallions, or celery

1. Preheat oven to 120 degrees.

2. Spread finely chopped vegetables in a thin layer on a cookie sheet. Dry in oven until crisp. The drying time will vary, depending on amount of moisture in the air and in the vegetables. Plan on leaving the tray in the oven for at least 12 hours, stirring occasionally.

3. Cool and store immediately in a sterilized dry glass or metal container with a tight-fitting lid for up to 6 months in the pantry.

Variations:
      To dry citrus skins, place a roomy basket on a sunny
windowsill and drop your peels from oranges, tangerines,
lemons, limes, and grapefruit into it. Toss the peels
occasionally and when they are completely dry, you can break
them up a bit for use in **Sweet Potpourri**, page 282, or you can
grind the dried peels in the blender and use them for **Oatmeal-
citrus Scrubbing Grains**, page 209.
      To dry corn, husk and clean ears of corn and then
steam or blanch for 3 minutes. Drain, cut kernels from the cob,
and dry as for the vegetables on page 25. When fully dry, the
corn should be hard and brittle.

To Use:
      Pour 2 cups boiling water over 1 cup dry corn and
simmer, covered, for 1 hour.

Hint:
      If you want to conserve energy, try drying the
vegetables in the sun. Pick a dry sunny day and place the tray
in full sunlight. Cover loosely with cheesecloth or arrange a
screen above the trays. The trick is to ensure air circulation
and the drying effect of the sun, and at the same time to protect
the vegetables from insects and critters. Take the trays in at
night and repeat the drying process for 1 to 3 days, or until
vegetables are thoroughly dried.
      If you use the sun-drying method, place the food in the
oven at 125 degrees for 1 hour or store the food in the freezer for
24 hours before using to kill any insect eggs which may be
invisible, but there.

Frozen Minced Vegetables

   You can wash and chop your vegetables and place them in a
single layer on a cookie sheet or in a cake pan. Cover with
plastic wrap and freeze until firm. Store the vegetables in a
freezer container or plastic bag suitable for the freezer.

To Use:
      Use the frozen vegetables **only** for cooking and drop
them while still frozen into soups and stews, or use them for
braising.

Yield: 8 ounces

Cost of Ingredients: $1.99
Comparable Purchased Product: Nouvelle
   Garni Chopped Mushrooms, .75 ounce, $1.89
   ($20.16)
Savings: $18.17

Seafood Cocktail Sauce

*This mild sauce is perfect for dipping shrimp, clams, or oysters, and you can spice it up with any of the **Variations** if this version tastes too wimpy.*

>1 cup Homemade Tomato Catsup (page 31)
>1/3 cup lemon juice
>1 tablespoon Worcestershire sauce
>1 tablespoon grated onion
>1 tablespoon grated green pepper

1. Combine all ingredients, mix well, and allow to rest for at least 1 hour so the ingredients will blend and mellow.

2. Chill thoroughly before serving.

3. Store in the refrigerator in a sterilized glass jar for up to 6 months. This sauce will not freeze well.

Variations:
   For a spicier sauce, add 1 teaspoon Tabasco sauce to the mixture before chilling.
   For an even kickier sauce, add 1 teaspoon horseradish along with the Tabasco, and then stand back.

Yield: 12 ounces

Cost of Ingredients: $.77
Comparable Purchased Product: Heinz
   Cocktail Sauce, 12 ounces, $.99
Savings: $.22

Chinese Duck Sauce

*Use this recipe, along with the recipe for **Chinese Mustard Sauce** which follows, for dipping. Items to be dipped can include breaded chicken bits, crispy raw vegetables, or the rest of all those fried noodles you get from the takeout.*

> 1/2 cup plum jam
> 2 tablespoons applesauce
> 5 tablespoons cider vinegar
> 1 teaspoon brown sugar

1. Stir the applesauce into the plum jam and then add the vinegar and sugar. Vigorously mix the ingredients in a bowl with a wire whisk.

2. Serve sauce at room temperature. Store in a covered jar in the refrigerator; it will keep for 6 months.

Yield: 8 ounces

Cost of Ingredients: $.82
Comparable Purchased Product: Far East Duck Sauce, 8 ounces, $1.27
Savings: $.45

Chinese Mustard Sauce

*Use this sauce along with **Chinese Duck Sauce** for an authentic beginning to any Chinese meal—just like in the restaurant.*

> 4 tablespoons dry mustard
> 6 drops peanut or corn oil
> 4 teaspoons vinegar

1. Combine all ingredients and stir thoroughly. If the paste is too thick for dipping, add a few more drops of vinegar until it is the consistency of thick cream.

Variations:

> For a stronger, more pungent flavor, try substituting sesame oil for the peanut or corn oil.
> To add real bite to the sauce, a drop or two of Tabasco or Chinese hot vinegar will do the trick.

Yield: 4 ounces

Cost of Ingredients: $.39
Comparable Purchased Product: Far East Chinese Mustard, 4 ounces, $.85
Savings: $.46

Tangy Mustard

The ingredient that imparts the tang to the following different mustards varies from recipe to recipe. You might like the zip of horseradish over the bite of cayenne—try the versions listed here and invent your own from these ideas.

These mustards also make fantastic gifts, either alone or in combination with other spices and cheeses. Plan ahead for gift giving by saving pretty containers and crocks for the mustards, but do not freeze these mixtures.

Spicy Horseradish Mustard

1 cup dry mustard
3/4 cup white wine vinegar
1/3 cup water
1/4 cup sugar
3 tablespoons brown sugar, lightly packed
2 teaspoons onion salt
1 teaspoon caraway seeds
2 eggs
1 tablespoon horseradish

1. Combine all ingredients except eggs and horseradish in the top of a double boiler. Cover and let stand for 5 hours at room temperature before cooking so that the flavors will blend.

2. In a separate bowl, lightly beat the eggs and stir them into the mustard mixture. Cook the mixture slowly over low heat, stirring constantly for 10 minutes or until the mixture thickens.

3. Stir in the horseradish, remove from heat, and cool for 10 minutes. Pour into a sterilized jar and refrigerate for 24 hours before using. Mustard will keep in the refrigerator for up to 3 months.

Hot Peppery Mustard

> 2/3 cup beer
> 1/2 cup dry mustard
> 2 tablespoons water
> 1 tablespoon sugar
> 2 teaspoons white wine vinegar
> 1 teaspoon salt
> 1 teaspoon cayenne pepper
> 1/2 teaspoon turmeric
> 1/2 teaspoon ginger
> 1 egg

1.   Combine all ingredients except egg in the top of a double boiler. Cover and let stand for 3 hours at room temperature.

2. In a separate bowl, lightly beat the eggs and stir them into the mustard mixture. Cook the mixture slowly over low heat, stirring constantly for 10 minutes or until the mixture thickens.

3. Remove the mustard from the heat and cool for 10 minutes. Pour into a sterilized jar and refrigerate for 24 hours before using. Mustard will keep in the refrigerator for up to 3 months.

Variations:
> Try adding 2 tablespoons of **Great Seasoning Salad Dressing Mix**, page 34, to one of the mixtures before stirring in the egg.
> Replacing the sugar with the same amount of honey will give a smooth, different flavor.

Yield: 16 ounces

Cost of Ingredients: $3.80
Comparable Purchased Product: Massey & Morrison American Herb Mustard, 8 ounces, $2.89 ($5.78)
Savings: $1.98

Homemade Tomato Catsup

This catsup is thick and rich, just like the kind in the store. The good news here, however, is that you never run out if you freeze the extra. If you like your catsup in a squeeze or pump container, consider something unusual to hold your condiments—maybe a clean soap dispenser or hand lotion container—as long as you label it clearly, and as long as you know your family has a sense of humor.

> **4 pounds tomatoes**
> **1 large onion, chopped**
> **1 teaspoon ground cloves**
> **1 teaspoon salt**
> **1 teaspoon allspice**
> **1 cup vinegar**

1. First prepare your tomatoes by peeling them: Put a large pan of water on to boil and when the water is hot, drop 2 or 3 tomatoes in at a time and leave them in the water for a minute, or until you see the skins begin to split. Then remove them to a bowl or strainer until they are cool enough to handle. Peel and chop the tomatoes over a bowl to catch all the juices.

2. Simmer tomatoes and onion in a heavy saucepan until tender—about 10 minutes.

3. Puree the cooked onion-tomato mixture in a blender or food processor and return to saucepan. Add spices and vinegar and simmer, uncovered, *very* slowly for 1 1/2 hours or until the mixture is reduced in volume by about a third. Stir frequently.

4. Cool and pour into containers. Let cool before storing in the refrigerator for up to 4 months or the freezer for 9 months.

Yield: 48 ounces

Cost of Ingredients: $2.24
Comparable Purchased Product: Heinz
   Squeeze Catsup, 28 ounces, $1.79 ($2.88)
Savings: $.64

Tangy Barbecue Sauce

*I am always amazed at how good this sauce tastes,
especially when it is made up fresh and used to cover chicken
parts for roasting. I've used it on ribs with equal success.*

>   2 onions, sliced
>   2 green peppers, sliced
>   1 cup chopped celery
>   1/4 cup vegetable oil
>   1 cup Homemade Tomato Catsup (page 31)
>   1 cup water
>   1/4 cup lemon juice
>   3 tablespoons Worcestershire sauce
>   2 tablespoons brown sugar
>   2 tablespoons vinegar
>   2 tablespoons mustard

1. In a large skillet, gently brown the onion, green pepper, and
celery in the oil.

2. Stir in the rest of the ingredients and simmer uncovered for
20 minutes. Cool and store in a sterilized glass jar in the
refrigerator. Sauce will keep well for 6 to 8 months.

To Use:
>   *You can use this sauce exactly as you would a
commercial brand, or you can shorten your cooking time by
browning a meat such as chicken or ribs right along with the
vegetables in Step 1. Add the rest of the ingredients, cover, and
cook for several hours, or until the meat is fork-tender. Bottle
and reuse any extra sauce.*

Yield: 26 ounces

Cost of Ingredients: $1.68
Comparable Purchased Product: Kraft
   Onion B-B-Q Sauce, 18 ounces, $1.49 ($2.15)
Savings: $.47

Bleu Cheese Salad Dressing

This version is a favorite with those strange folk who like bleu cheese, because it is absolutely full of big chunks of the stuff. I have to hold my breath while I make this, but everyone who eats it seems to love it, so I take their word.

> **1/2 teaspoon salt**
> **1/4 teaspoon freshly ground pepper**
> **2 ounces bleu cheese, coarsely crumbled**
> **1 1/3 cup Fresh Mayonnaise (page 17)**

1. Slowly and smoothly whisk the spices into the mayonnaise until the mixture is thoroughly combined.

2. Gently stir in the crumbled bleu cheese, being careful not to break it up too much.

3. Store in a covered jar in the refrigerator for 3 to 6 months. Do not freeze.

Hint:
> *Try serving some of this salad dressing as a side dip, with any spicy barbecued foods: chicken, ribs, or beef.*

Yield: 16 ounces

Cost of Ingredients: $1.48
Comparable Purchased Product: Wishbone
   Chunky Bleu Cheese Salad Dressing, 8 ounces,
   $.99 ($1.98)
Savings: $.50

Classic French Salad Dressing

The ingredients in this dressing can be varied, of course, to suit your tastes. Many people would prefer more mustard, for example. I recommend using only the best extra-virgin olive oil for the lightest taste.

> 1/2 cup olive oil
> 1 tablespoon red or white wine vinegar
> 1/2 teaspoon dry mustard
> 1/2 teaspoon sugar
> 1/2 teaspoon salt
> 1/4 teaspoon pepper
> 1/2 teaspoon parsley
> 1/2 teaspoon basil

1. Place oil, vinegar, mustard, sugar, salt, and pepper in blender. Blend at high speed for 30 seconds, add herbs and blend for 15 seconds. Store in a sterilized glass jar, tightly covered, in the refrigerator. Dressing tastes best if used within a week, but it will keep in the refrigerator for up to 4 weeks.

Yield: 5 ounces

Cost of Ingredients: $.38
Comparable Purchased Product: Taste of Nature French Dressing, 12 ounces, $1.49 ($.62)
Savings: $.24

Great Seasonings Salad Dressing Mix

*Keep this mix on your pantry shelf to combine with wine vinegar or one of the **Herbal Vinegars**, page 148, and oil. The flavors will vary widely depending on the herbs in the different vinegars, but you will have a whole range of dressings with one seasoning mix.*

1/4 cup grated Parmesan or Romano cheese

1 tablespoon paprika
2 teaspoons garlic powder
2 teaspoons celery seeds
1 teaspoon sesame seeds
1/2 teaspoon salt
1/2 teaspoon pepper

1. Mix ingredients, label, and store in a tightly closed container.

2. This mix will keep on the pantry shelf for 1 to 2 months and in the refrigerator for 6 months.

To Use:

Combine 2 teaspoons Great Seasonings Salad Dressing Mix, 1/4 cup vinegar, and 2/3 cup vegetable oil in a jar; cover and shake well.

Transfer to a pretty cruet for serving.

Ideas:

Add 1 tablespoon Great Seasonings Salad Dressing Mix to 1/4 cup **Fresh Mayonnaise**, page 17, for a creamy herbal dressing.

Or try adding 1 tablespoon mix to 1/4 cup sour cream or **Homemade Yogurt**, page 121, for a tangy herbal dip. A few tablespoons of **Tangy Mustard**, page 29, will add additional spice.

Yield: 5 ounces

Cost of Ingredients: $1.60
Comparable Purchased Product: Good Seasons Salad Dressing, .75 ounces, $.63 ($4.20)
Savings: $2.60

Green Goddess Salad Dressing

The ingredients in this recipe can be varied to suit your tastes. Try different kinds of vinegar—perhaps one of your own **Herbal Vinegars**, page 148.

1 cup Fresh Mayonnaise (page 17)
1 teaspoon Garlic in Oil (page 24)
1/2 teaspoon dry mustard
3 tablespoons tarragon vinegar
3 tablespoons minced chives
1/4 cup minced parsley
1/2 cup sour cream
Salt and pepper to taste

1. Combine all ingredients and allow to rest, refrigerated, for 4 hours; store in a tightly closed container for up to 3 months.

Yield: 14 ounces

Cost of Ingredients: $1.59
Comparable Purchased Product: Kraft Green Goddess Dressing, 8 ounces, $.99 ($1.73)
Savings: $.15

Italian Salad Dressing

If you mix this dressing in the blender or food processor to save time, don't bother grating the onion first.

2 cups vegetable oil
1 cup wine vinegar
1/4 cup sugar
1 teaspoon oregano
1 teaspoon basil
1 teaspoon celery seed
1/2 cup grated onion

1. Combine all ingredients in a sterilized glass jar, cover, and shake; store in the refrigerator for 6 months.

Yield: 26 ounces

Cost of Ingredients: $1.35
Comparable Purchased Product: Kraft Italian Dressing, 14 ounces, $1.89 ($3.51)
Savings: $2.16

Thousand Island Dressing

This dressing will fool your kids into thinking they've got a fast-food hamburger if you spread it on their burgers between the cheese, pickle, onion, lettuce, and tomato on the sesame-seed bun.

> **2 hard-boiled eggs, chopped**
> **1/3 cup green pickle relish, drained**
> **1 cup Fresh Mayonnaise (page 17)**
> **1/2 cup chili sauce**

1. Mix all ingredients and store in a tightly closed container in the refrigerator. This salad dressing will keep for up to 1 month.

Yield: 15 ounces

Cost of Ingredients: $1.23
Comparable Purchased Product: Kraft Thousand Island Dressing, 8 ounces, $.99 ($1.85)
Savings: $.62

Basic Tomato Sauce

*This recipe is an ideal way to use up all the bountiful tomatoes of summer, and if you make sauce in quantity when tomatoes are plentiful, the cost-per-unit savings can be enormous. The procedure described is how my grandmother always made her sauce. This meatless version can be improved upon (**Caruso Spaghetti Sauce**, page 39), made quicker still (**Primo Primavera Sauce**, page 41), or made with a summer or Mexican flavor (**Gazpacho-style Sauce**, page 40).*

> **2 cloves garlic, sliced**
> **2 medium onions, chopped**
> **2 small bell peppers, chopped**
> **2 teaspoons olive oil**
> **4 pounds ripe plum or regular tomatoes or two**
> **20-ounce cans Italian plum tomatoes (whole)**

> **1/2 teaspoon salt**
> **1/2 teaspoon ground pepper**
> **1/2 teaspoon sugar**
> **1/2 teaspoon basil**
> **1/2 teaspoon oregano**
> **4 sprigs fresh parsley or 1/2 teaspoon dried parsley**

1. In a large, heavy saucepan, brown the garlic, onions, and green peppers in the olive oil. Stir frequently over low heat until the vegetables are soft and the onion is transparent.

2. If using canned tomatoes, stir them into the oil mixture.

3. If using fresh tomatoes, put a separate pan of water on the stove to simmer while the vegetables are cooking. Drop 3 or 4 tomatoes in at a time, and remove them after a minute or so to a bowl or strainer. As soon as the tomatoes are cool to the touch, peel them over the pot containing the olive oil mixture, discard the peel, and drop in the whole tomato.

3. Taste and add the spices. Simmer, covered, for about an hour and adjust the seasonings.

4. This sauce can be stored, covered, in the refrigerator for about 1 week, or frozen for 3 to 9 months. Glass jars are better to use for storage than plastic, which reacts to the tomatoes over time.

Note:
> *If you don't object to the tomato skins, or are using Italian plum tomatoes, peeling may not be necessary. However, if your sauce is intended for company, small children, or invalids, the tomatoes should be peeled.*

Yield: 32 ounces

Cost of Ingredients: $2.16
Comparable Purchased Product: Aunt Millie's Plain Spaghetti Sauce, 14 ounces, $1.09 ($2.18)
Savings: $.02

Caruso Spaghetti Sauce

*One of the earliest cooking memories I have is of my
mother making this sauce on a Sunday afternoon, with Enrico
Caruso singing a scratchy, tear-filled aria on the living room
phonograph. To duplicate my mother's recipe, use the
procedure described in the **Basic Tomato Sauce** recipe, page 37,
for cooking the vegetables and peeling the tomatoes, or simply
add 2 quarts of **Basic Sauce** to the braised pork.*

*For an authentic Italian flavor, you must use fresh pork as
a flavoring ingredient, as well as the larger quantites of spices
listed. It is a good idea to taste the sauce frequently throughout
the cooking process by dipping in a slice of Italian bread. You
can vary the quantities of the spices to your taste, and, of course,
you could listen to Luciano Pavarotti while you cook, without
significant loss of authenticity.*

> 1 pound pork (ends, rib, or butt)
> 2 teaspoons olive oil
> 5 to 6 cloves garlic, sliced
> 2 medium onions, chopped
> 2 bell peppers, chopped
> Two 4-ounce cans tomato paste
> 4 pounds ripe plum tomatoes or two 20-ounce cans
>   Italian plum tomatoes (whole)
> 1 to 2 teaspoons salt
> 1 to 2 teaspoons sugar
> 1 to 2 teaspoons pepper
> 1 to 2 teaspoons basil
> 1 to 2 teaspoons oregano
> 4 sprigs fresh parsley or 1 teaspoon dried parsley

1. Very slowly brown the pork in a large, heavy saucepan,
turning the meat frequently. Do not add any oil—the meat will
baste in its own juice. When thoroughly browned (about 40
minutes), remove meat, trim and discard visible fat, and dice
meat into 1-inch pieces. Put aside.

2. Pour off most of the remaining pork fat in the pan and save;
add the olive oil and garlic and brown for 2 minutes. Then add
the onions and green pepper, together with 2 tablespoons of the
pork fat, and slowly cook the vegetables until soft.

3. Add 2 cans of tomato paste and 2 cans of water to the vegetables; simmer for 2 minutes. Stir in 1 cup of water and simmer for another 10 minutes.

4. Add peeled fresh or canned tomatoes, the pork, and the spices. Simmer, covered, for 1 to 3 hours.

Variations:
        Add browned crumbled hamburger meat to the sauce at Step 2. Drain the meat on paper towels before adding.
        Add meatballs along with the pork in Step 4.

Yield: 48 ounces

Cost of Ingredients: $5.02
Comparable Purchased Product: Pasta & Cheese, Sauce Bolognese, 15 ounces, $4.99 ($15.96)
Savings: $7.68

Gazpacho-style Sauce

*This is the Mexican-style version of **Basic Tomato Sauce**, page 37. Like its Italian and American counterparts, it can be frozen successfully and then slowly warmed or microwaved for use with tacos, enchiladas, Spanish-style rice, and various chicken and beef dishes.*

        2 medium onions, chopped
        2 small bell peppers, chopped
        2 teaspoons corn oil
        4 pounds ripe plum or regular tomatoes or two
            20-ounce cans Italian plum tomatoes (whole)
            or 4 cups Basic Sauce (page 37)
        1/2 teaspoon salt
        1/2 teaspoon ground pepper
        1/2 teaspoon ground cumin
        1/2 teaspoon chili powder
        1/2 teaspoon oregano
        1/4 teaspoon cayenne pepper

1. Brown the onion and green pepper in the corn oil. Stir frequently over low heat until the vegetables are soft and the onion is transparent.

2. If using canned tomatoes or Basic Sauce, stir into the oil mixture.

3. If using fresh tomatoes, peel them over the pot containing the oil mixture and drop in the whole tomato.

3. Taste and add the spices. Simmer, covered, for about an hour and adjust the seasonings.

4. This sauce can be stored, covered, in the refrigerator for about 1 week, or frozen for 3 to 9 months.

Yield: 32 ounces

Cost of Ingredients: $2.02
Comparable Purchased Product: Crosse & Blackwell, 13 ounces, $1.05 ($2.58)
Savings: $.56

Primo Primavera Sauce

*While my grandmother and my mother each have their tomato sauce recipes (see **Basic Tomato Sauce**, page 37, and **Caruso Spaghetti Sauce**, page 39), my own variation on the theme is this one.*

*Like the other two sauces, it uses up lots of tomatoes in season, but unlike them, it is extremely quick to make. This sauce depends on the freshness of the vegetables and the quality of the cheese you use for flavor. For extra convenience, you can make a huge batch and freeze the remainder, but if you want the sauce to taste fresh when you reheat it, undercook the vegetables before you freeze them (see **Note**, page 42), and top the reheated sauce with a tablespoon or two of freshly grated cheese.*

4 cloves garlic, sliced
2 tablespoons olive oil
1 medium onion, coarsely chopped
2 Italian sweet peppers, chopped
1 cup of chopped vegetables: yellow squash,
   finely slivered carrots, snow peas, or a combination
   of your choice
2 tablespoons butter
4 ripe tomatoes, chopped
1/2 teaspoon salt
1/2 teaspoon ground black pepper
1/2 teaspoon oregano
4 sprigs fresh parsley
1/3 cup grated Parmesan or Romano cheese

1. In a large frying pan, brown the sliced garlic in the olive oil
for 2 minutes. Then add the onion and green pepper and cook
over medium heat, stirring occasionally, for 5 minutes.

2. Add 1 cup assorted chopped vegetables and let steam,
covered, over low heat for 20 minutes.

3. Remove cover, add butter, and cook for an additional 5
minutes before adding the tomatoes and seasonings.

4. Just before serving, swirl the cheese through the vegetable
mixture. Sauce can be served beside buttered noodles, pasta
with garlic and oil, or it can be tossed with plain spaghetti.

Note:
   *If you are making this recipe in quantity for freezing,
cut the cooking times in half to undercook all the vegetables.
Then, without defrosting, slowly reheat the sauce in a 300
degree oven for 40 minutes or microwave on medium power for
10 minutes to finish the cooking process.*

Yield: 32 ounces

Cost of Ingredients: $3.90
Comparable Purchased Product: Pasta &
   Cheese, 15 ounces, $4.99 ($10.64)
Savings: $6.74

Quick Maple Syrup

This recipe does not pretend to taste as good as real maple syrup, which is anything but quick, and anything but cheap. But if your family goes through gallons of the stuff, you will save money by trying this version.

2 cups water
4 cups brown sugar
2 teaspoons maple extract

1. In an enamel or a glass pot, bring water to a rapid boil.

2. Pour in all the brown sugar at once and stir until it is completely dissolved.

3. Remove from heat and stir in the maple extract.

4. Pour into a sterilized jar and let stand for 24 hours at room temperature before using. Store remaining syrup in refrigerator for up to 6 months.

Variation:
 Add 1 teaspoon butter-flavored extract at Step 3.

Blender Sweet Syrup

1/2 cup molasses
1/2 cup honey
1 teaspoon vanilla

1. Combine all ingredients in a blender or food processor until smooth. Add chopped nuts to the syrup as it is blending, if desired.

Yield: 32 ounces

Cost of Ingredients: $1.52
Comparable Purchased Product:
   Cary's Maple Syrup, 8 ounces, $3.15 ($12.60)
Savings: $11.08

Sweet Berry Syrups

*You can use these syrups on **Quick Pancakes**, page 71, **Quick Crepes**, page 69, and as the basis for **Fuzzy Fruit Sodas**, page 169. In addition, they taste wonderful over vanilla ice cream or swirled through **Vanilla Pudding**, page 86.*

Blueberry Syrup

3 cups blueberries
3 cups sugar
1 cup water
1/4 cup lemon juice

1. Wash and drain blueberries. Crush the berries in a bowl, or process for 1 minute in a food processor or blender.

2. Place the puree in an enamel or a glass pan and stir in the sugar and the water. Cook over medium heat for 30 minutes, stirring regularly.

3. Remove from heat and stir in the lemon juice.

4. Strain the mixture through a coffee filter or cheesecloth and pour the syrup into a sterilized jar. Discard the pulp or use it in **Liquid Fertilizer**, page 298. Cool the syrup before using and store in the refrigerator for up to 6 months.

Variations:
Almost any kind of berry can be substituted for the blueberries. You should add half the sugar called for, taste, and add more sugar if you think the berries will need more sweetening.

Yield: 32 ounces

Cost of Ingredients: $4.56
Comparable Purchased Product: Knotts Blueberry Syrup, 12 ounces, $2.99 ($7.97)
Savings: $3.41

Basic Chocolate Sauce

*This basic sauce can be varied in hundreds of ways, depending on your audience and on the fancy ingredients you have on hand. Once you have developed your own chocolate specialties (see **Variations,** for some ideas to start you off), package your special sauce in small, pretty jars and add them to some of the **Gift Baskets** described in Chapter 12.*

2 ounces semisweet baking chocolate
2 tablespoons butter
1/2 cup boiling water
11/2 cups sugar
Dash salt
1 teaspoon Vanilla Bean Extract (page 12)

1. Melt chocolate in a glass or an enamel double boiler.

2. Stir in butter, then boiling water, then sugar and salt. Cook, stirring occasionally, for 15 minutes.

3. Remove from heat; stir in vanilla.

4. This sauce is best when served warm. Either serve immediately after making or reheat in a double boiler for 10 minutes or in a microwave oven for 1 minute on high.

5. To store, pour into sterilized glass jars. Allow sauce to cool before refrigerating. This sauce will keep for 6 months.

Variations:
   Add any of the following flavorings in place of or in addition to the vanilla in Step 2:

   1 teaspoon orange extract or 1/3 cup orange juice
   1 teaspoon mint extract
   1/8 cup crushed strawberries or raspberries, chopped raisins or nuts
   *1 tablespoon **Homemade Crème de Menthe, Coffee Liqueur, Spicy Orange Cordial,** or Grand Marnier (see Chapter 5)*
   1 teaspoon instant coffee

Hot Fudge Sauce

1 cup Sweetened Condensed Milk (page 17)
1 cup sugar
1/4 cup light corn syrup
4 tablespoons butter
5 ounces semisweet baking chocolate, semisweet
1 teaspoon Vanilla Bean Extract (page 12)

1. Combine all ingredients in the top of a double boiler and cook over low heat, stirring all the while, until the mixture is smooth and all the chocolate is melted. Cool and store it in a sterilized glass jar in the refrigerator for up to 4 weeks and let it warm to room temperature before using.

Yield: 16 ounces

Cost of Ingredients: $1.35
Comparable Purchased Product: Mrs. Rich Chocolate Topping, 19 ounces, $1.69 ($1.45)
Savings: $.10

Butterscotch Sauce

This sauce is simple, relatively quick, and will keep for up to 3 months in the refrigerator.

2 cups brown sugar, packed
2 tablespoons flour
1/2 cup butter, melted
1 cup boiling water
2 teaspoons Vanilla Bean Extract (page 12)

1. In an enamel or a glass double boiler, mix sugar and flour together and slowly add melted butter to the mixture. Cooking over low heat until the butter takes on a golden yellow hue.

2. Slowly add the boiling water to the mixture, stirring constantly.

3. Continue stirring and cook for about 6 minutes.

4. Remove from heat; stir in vanilla.

5. Serve warm or cold. To store, pour while still warm into glass jars. Allow to cool before refrigerating. Sauce will freeze well and keep in the refrigerator for up to 3 months.

Yield: 16 ounces

Cost of Ingredients: $1.55
Comparable Purchased Product: My T Fine
    Butterscotch Sauce, 15 ounces, $3.25
Savings: $1.70

Peanut Butter

It is healthier to avoid adding salt to your recipes, especially for those foods that children eat the most, like peanut butter. However, you may find that a small amount of salt, or salted peanuts as the base of this recipe, will make the food taste more like the brands your children are used to. The fresh taste of the peanuts themselves will probably win the salt-lover over, so try the recipe first without the extra salt.

I've described several different ways to mash or pulverize the peanuts into butter, should you want to experiment. The manual methods will yield a nice crunchy spread and if you allow children to help, they will learn a bit about their favorite food.

> **2 cups dry-roasted or raw peanuts, shelled and skinned**
> **1/2 teaspoon salt**
> **1 to 5 drops peanut oil (optional)**

1. Process and mash nuts in any of the following ways:
    Whirl nuts in food processor for 90 seconds, stopping and scraping down sides when necessary.
    Or place the nuts in blender, about 1/4 cup at a time, and puree for 60 seconds.
    Or place nuts on a clean cookie sheet and mash with a

potato masher, moving mashed nuts to the side as you go and adding drops of peanut oil to the mixture as needed.

Or mash and roll the nuts with a rolling pin on a clean cutting board. Scrape mixture into a bowl, and stir in additional oil if the mixture seems too dry.

2. Store peanut butter in a clean jar or covered plastic bowl in the refrigerator. If the oil separates, stir before using. This peanut butter should keep for up to 3 months in the refrigerator.

Cashew Sesame Butter

For another kind of nut butter, you might try this blend of seeds and nuts.

3 tablespoons vegetable oil
2 cups roasted cashews
3 tablespoons toasted sesame seeds

1. Combine ingredients and blend on medium in your blender or food processor; store covered in the refrigerator for up to 2 months.

Idea:
Try adding some additional flavors to your freshly ground peanut butters and swirling them once or twice through to combine but not mix in completely.

A cup of miniature marshmallows or some raisins, jam, or **Basic Chocolate Sauce,** *page 45, would be delicious and could simplify sandwich preparation because all the ingredients for a sweet sandwich are in one jar. You could also add sliced bananas to finish off the sandwich, if desired.*

Yield: 16 ounces

Cost of Ingredients: $1.19
Comparable Purchased Product: Skippy
   Creamy Peanut Butter; 12 ounces, $1.45 ($1.93)
Savings: $.74

Apple Butter

My family likes a very rich, very spicy apple butter, so the spices in this recipe may seem too heavy for those used to a milder butter. You might want to try the recipe with half the cinnamon, cloves, and allspice and taste to see if you want to add more.

> 8 pounds ripe apples
> 2 cups apple cider
> 3 cups brown sugar, firmly packed
> 3 tablespoons cinnamon
> 1 teaspoon allspice
> 1 teaspoon ground cloves

1. Peel, core, and slice the apples. Place apples in a large saucepan, pour the apple cider over them, and cook over low heat until they are tender. Stir frequently and make sure the apples don't stick and burn.

2. When apples are soft, remove them from the heat and cool. To strain and mash them, you can either press them through a sieve or place the apples and juice in a food processor and whirl them until you have a smooth mixture.

3. Return the pureed apples and juice to a large saucepan and add the spices. Cook over low heat, stirring constantly, until mixture begins to bubble and thicken. Remove from heat after 30 minutes and cool.

4. Pour apple butter into sterilized glass jars, cover, and store in the refrigerator. Or, leave some room for expansion in the jars and freeze. Apple Butter will keep for 2 to 4 weeks in the refrigerator and up to 9 months in the freezer.

Variations:

Try the same recipe, but substitute pears or peaches for the apples, and instead of apple cider, use a mixture of 2 cups water and 1/2 cup lemon juice. Use half the spices, or spice to your taste.

Yield: 13 cups

Cost of Ingredients: $5.93
Comparable Purchased Product: Taste of Nature Apple Butter, 18 ounces, $2.29 ($13.48)
Savings: $7.55

Freezer Fruit Preserves

When you freeze your fruit jams and preserves, you save yourself all the trouble of hot-water canning, adding paraffin, and making sure the seals are secure. If you have a lot of freezer space, you can enjoy a very fresh-tasting preserve.

4 cups strawberries
8 cups sugar
1 1/2 cups water
2 tablespoons fruit pectin
2 tablespoons lemon juice

1. Clean berries, place in a large bowl, and crush them a bit. Add sugar and stir gently to mix. Let berries stand for 10 minutes.

2. In a saucepan, combine water and pectin and bring to a boil. Boil for 1 minute, stirring constantly.

3. Pour water-pectin mixture over the strawberries and stir to mix and to mash the berries a bit more. Stir in the lemon juice.

4. Pour the fruit into freezer containers or sterilized glass jars, leaving room for expansion. Cover and let sit at room temperature overnight.

5. Refrigerate one jar for immediate use if desired and freeze the other containers. Preserves will keep for up to 9 months in the freezer.

Variations:
   Many other fruits can be made into quick freezer preserves. For example, try freezing freshly crushed blueberries, raspberries, or cranberries and chopped lemon.

Yield: 10 cups

Cost of Ingredients: $4.48
Comparable Purchased Product: Smuckers
  Strawberry Preserves, 18 ounces, $1.79 ($5.96)
Savings: $1.48

Pimientos

*Most people are used to seeing pimientos in the center of
their cocktail olive or as a cheery red accent to macaroni
salad. This has always been a mystery food to me—I used to
think there were pimiento plants, when actually they are
simply sweet peppers or, as in this recipe, marinated sweet
peppers. Try using green peppers for a slightly different taste
and a decidedly different look.*

> **4 large red peppers**
> **1 cup white vinegar**
> **1 cup water**
> **1/2 cup sugar**
> **4 garlic cloves, chopped**
> **2 teaspoons oil**
> **1 teaspoon salt**

1. Wash peppers, remove inner seeds and membranes, and
slice into inch-wide strips. Cover peppers with boiling water
and let them soak for 5 minutes. Drain.

2. Combine vinegar, water, and sugar in a glass or an enamel
pan and bring to a boil. Simmer mixture for 5 minutes, remove
from heat, and add garlic, oil, and salt.

3. Place peppers in a sterilized quart-size glass jar and pour
the vinegar mixture over them to cover. Store pimientos in
refrigerator for 2 weeks before using. Pimientos will keep for
several months in the refrigerator.

Yield: 32 ounces

Cost of Ingredients: $1.55
Comparable Purchased Product: Osage
  Sliced Pimientos, 2 ounces, $.39 ($6.24)
Savings: $4.69

Quick Cucumber Pickles

The secret to crisp cucumber pickles is to salt the sliced pickles and onions and press out as much liquid as you possibly can during the first stages of preparing this recipe. You do this by weighting the cucumbers with a heavy object and letting them drain overnight.

You will be amazed at the amount of liquid that runs off the cucumbers in the morning. Then the cucumber will absorb the vinegar and give you a satisfying crunch when you bite into it.

It's a great convenience to use your food processor for slicing the cucumbers and onions. If you use one, alternately add the pickles and onions as you slice so that the two vegetables will be thoroughly mixed.

8 cups peeled and sliced cucumbers
2 cups sliced onions
3 tablespoons salt
1 cup sugar
1/2 cup white vinegar
2 tablespoons dill

1. Mix cucumber and onion slices and place them in a colander. Place the colander in a larger bowl, salt the cucumber and onion slices thoroughly and mix to distribute salt evenly.

2. Cover the slices with a clean kitchen towel or cheesecloth and place one or two heavy cans on top to press down on the slices. Refrigerate overnight.

3. Drain the cucumber-onion mixture and transfer the slices to a glass or ceramic bowl. Mix together the sugar, vinegar, and dill and pour the liquid over the cucumbers and onions. Stir to thoroughly mix liquid and vegetables.

4. Transfer the cucumber mixture to sterilized glass jars. Cover and store in the refrigerator for up to 2 months.

Yield: 10 cups

Cost of Ingredients: $3.36
Comparable Purchased Product: Vlasic
Sweet Butter Chip Pickles, 22 ounces, $1.39
($5.05)
Savings: $1.69

Pickled Beets

*Although this is an excellent way to take care of a bumper crop of beets from your garden, you can also use canned beets in this recipe. When you finish precooking the beets, check the recipe for **Nature's Colors**, page 367, for ideas on using the beautiful red beet juice or see the **Idea** on page 54 or another way to use the juice.*

> 2 cups thinly sliced beets
> 1/2 cup white vinegar
> 1/2 cup water
> 1/2 cup sugar
> 1 teaspoon salt
> 1/2 teaspoon pepper

1. If you are using fresh beets, peel and retain the skins for **Nature's Colors**. Precook the beets by covering with water and simmering in a saucepan until tender. Cool the beets before continuing with the recipe. If you are using canned beets, there is no need to precook.

2. Combine vinegar, water, sugar, and spices in a non-aluminum saucepan. Bring to a boil, stir until sugar is dissolved, and simmer for 5 minutes.

3. Place the beets in a glass or an enamel bowl and pour the hot marinade over them and allow the mixture to cool to room temperature. Cover the bowl with plastic wrap and refrigerate overnight.

4. Spoon the beets and juice into sterilized glass jars, cover, and store in the refrigerator. Beets will keep for up to 2 months.

Idea:
> You can also use the juice from beet pickles as a liquid for tinting and preserving pickled eggs. Simply hard-boil the eggs, cover with the marinade, and refrigerate overnight before serving or using.

Yield: 25 ounces

Cost of Ingredients: $1.04
Comparable Purchased Product: Greenwood Sliced Pickled Beets, 16 ounces, $.79 ($1.23)
Savings: $.19

Pickled Onions

Try these savory treats as a side dish with a sandwich or pack them into a pretty jar and present them in a gift basket.

> 1 pound small white onions
> 1/4 cup salt
> 2 cups malt vinegar
> 1/4 cup sugar
> 1 tablespoon pickling spice
> 3 whole cloves
> 6 whole peppercorns

1. Without peeling the onions, drop them into a pot of boiling water and boil for 1 or 2 minutes. Drain, rinse in cold water, and peel by cutting a circle around the top, lifting it off, and the pushing the onion out of its skin.

2. Place onions in a glass or a ceramic bowl, sprinkle with the salt, and mix well. Cover bowl with plastic wrap and refrigerate overnight.

3. Combine vinegar, sugar, and spices in a large nonaluminum saucepan. Bring mixture to a boil, stirring until sugar is dissolved, and then simmer for 5 minutes more.

4. Remove onions from the refrigerator, rinse well under cold

running water, and dry on paper toweling. Add onions to the vinegar mixture and simmer for 10 minutes, or until onions can be pierced easily with a knife.

5. Using a slotted spoon, carefully place onions in sterilized glass jars, and then pour the vinegar mixture over them. Cover and store in the refrigerator for 1 week before using. Onions will keep well for up to 6 weeks.

Yield: 20 ounces

Cost of Ingredients: $1.47
Comparable Purchased Product: HP
English Sour Pickled Onions, 9.5 ounces, $2.89
($6.08)
Savings: $4.71

Chapter 2

Convenience Foods

Included in this chapter are a variety of mixes and goodies to create with the mixes for every conceivable occasion, from breakfast to snacking, and from quick and simple dinners for one or two people to company's-coming-in-an-hour.

The convenience and savings come from making these mixes up ahead of time and in large quantities. Further savings will be realized when you use these mixes as a basis for the more complicated recipes in the chapters on **Convenience Foods, Snacks and Sweets,** and **Gourmet and Gift Items.**

Never-fail Pastry Mix
    Pie Crust
    Roll-up Treats
Cookie Mix for the Pantry
    Vanilla Cookies
    Granola Cookies
Instant Brownie Mix
    Fudgie Chewie Brownies
    Peanut Butter Brownies
Biscuit Baking Mix
Quick Rolled Biscuits
    Dropped Biscuits
    Sweet Biscuits
    Sprinkled Biscuits
    Filled Biscuits
    Latvian Biscuits
Quick Dumplings
    Herb Dumplings
    Vegetable Dumplings
Quick Crepes
    Blintzes
Quick Pancakes
    Chocolate Pancakes
    Berry Pancakes
Quick Waffles

Healthy Whole Wheat Baking Mix
  Nutty Whole Wheat Biscuits
  Honey Whole Wheat Muffins
Bran Muffin Mix
  Blueberry Bran Muffins
Cornmeal Baking Mix
Quick Corn Muffins
Freezer Pancake Batter
Cookie-crumb Crust
Basic Cake Mix
Quick Pound Cake
Chocolate Cake Mix
Quick Chocolate Cake
Rolled Refrigerator Cookies
E-Z Gelatin Desserts
Puddings and Pie-filling Mix
  Vanilla Pudding Mix
  Chocolate Pudding Mix
  Butterscotch Pudding Mix
  Coconut Cream Pudding Mix
Instant White Sauce Mix
Fancy Alfredo Mix
Noodle-mania Mix
Macaroni and Cheese Sauce Mix
Wheat Germ and Cornflake Topping Mix
Top-of-the-Stove Stuffing Mix
Seasoned Shake-in-a-Bag Coating Mix
  Shake-in-a-Bag Mix for Chicken
  Sage Shake-in-a-Bag Mix for Pork Chops
  Texas B-B-Q Shake-in-a-Bag Mix for Ribs
  Spicy Shake-in-a-Bag Mix for Shrimp
  Italian-flavored Shake-in-a-Bag Mix
Flavored Rice Mixes
  Onion Rice Mix
  Lemon Dill Rice Mix
  Vegetable Rice Mix
  Spanish Rice Mix
  Creamy Herb Rice
Chili Topping Mix
Bacon Onion Flavoring Mix
Spaghetti Sauce-from-Scratch Mix
Mexican Seasonings Mix

Ooh-la-la Butter
   Sweet Butters
Herb and Flavored Butters
   French Herb Butter
   Italian-flavored Butter
   Mexican-flavored Butter
   Chinese-flavored Butter
   French-flavored Butter
Garlic Butter

Never-fail Pastry Mix

Once your have a batch of pastry mix, you've almost got the secret to making fantastic pie crusts. You will have to practice until you develop a sure touch, but if you follow the steps here, even your very first pie crust will be respectable.

> **6 cups flour**
> **1 tablespoon salt**
> **1-pound can vegetable shortening**

1. Sift flour and salt together into a large bowl.

2. Drop shortening into the mixture by spoonfuls and with a pastry blender or two knives, cut it into the flour mixture until the mixture is crumbly. Stop when the mixture still looks coarse—do not let it become smooth. If you know exactly how the mixture should look, you can perform this step with a food processor, but be careful not to process too long.

3. Store pastry mix in a tightly sealed container on the pantry shelf in medium to cool weather for 1 to 3 months. If the weather is very warm or humid, it is better to keep this mixture in the refrigerator. Let it warm to room temperature and recrumble a bit, if necessary, before using.

Pie Crust

To make a single pie crust, you will need:

> **2 cups Pastry Mix**
> **2 to 3 tablespoons ice water**

1. Toss the mix and ice water gently until the mixture begins to stick together.

2. Turn the dough out onto a floured surface—Formica, marble, or a cutting board—and gently roll out a circle to fit your pie pan. Some people use a pastry cloth or a square of clean muslin to cover the surface they are working on, roll the pastry out right on the cloth, and then lift the cloth and pastry, turn it upside down into the pan, and peel the cloth away.

3. As you lift the dough into the pan, remember that tears can be

repaired with a bit of water and a small piece of dough, or you could remove the holey, inadequate crust, knead it back together and try again. The more you knead, however, the tougher the pie crust will become, so practice until you have a light, sure touch.

Roll-up Treats

Ever since I can remember, my grandmother and then my mother used to make us a delicious goodie from the little bits and pieces of pie crust they made sure they had left over.

Leftover pie crust dough, uncooked and rolled out
1 teaspoon butter, softened
1 teaspoon Cinnamon Sugar (page 10)

1. To make treats for your family, simply spread any leftover pie crust dough with butter and then sprinkle with cinnamon and sugar, cut into strips, and roll up.

2. Bake along with the pie. The oven cooks these little treats in half the time, so when you check on your pie after 10 minutes or so, voila! you have finished Roll-up Treats for impatient children.

Yield: 6 cups mix

Cost of Ingredients: $2.15
Comparable Purchased Product: Flako Pie Crust Mix, 10 ounces, $.79 ($3.79)
Savings: $1.64

Cheap Trick ....

If you fear that you'll never get the hang of rolling out a pie crust that doesn't tear apart, you might try placing a ball of dough into a large-size plastic bag and roll the dough while it's still in the bag. When it's the right size, cut open the bag, remove the top sheet, flip the dough into your pan, and remove the bottom sheet.

Cookie Mix for the Pantry

This is one of the most convenient mixes to have around because the kids can spoon it out, add an egg, and make up fresh cookies while you lounge about. The mix will keep for quite a while in the pantry as long as the weather is crisp and dry. If you make this recipe up in the middle of a long, hot summer or if the weather seems too hot or too humid, make up the cookie batter in quantity and store it, covered, in the refrigerator or cook and then freeze the cookies.

3 cups flour
1 1/2 cups white sugar
1 cup brown sugar, lightly packed
1 teaspoon baking soda
1 teaspoon baking powder
1 cup shortening
3 cups old-fashioned uncooked rolled oats
1/2 cup raisins, chopped dates, peanut butter chips,
    chocolate chips, or chopped walnuts

1.   In a large bowl, sift together flour, sugars, baking soda, and baking powder.

2. Cut in shortening with a pastry blender or two knives until mixture is crumbly. You can use a food processor for this step, but be sure to process quickly and stop quickly, before the mixture is too smooth.

3. Stir in rolled oats and any nuts, chips, or fruits you choose.

4. Store mix in a tightly covered, labeled container. Mix will keep for from 1 to 5 months on the pantry shelf in mild, dry weather. Store in the refrigerator during the hottest summer months.

Vanilla Cookies

2 cups Cookie Mix
1 egg
1 tablespoon milk
1 teaspoon Vanilla Bean Extract (page 12)

1. Preheat oven to 350 degrees.

2. Measure mix into a large bowl and add egg, milk, and vanilla.

3. Stir until all ingredients are well blended and drop by teaspoons onto a greased cookie sheet. Bake for 15 minutes.

Yield: 9 cups mix

Granola Cookies

>   1 1/2 cups Cookie Mix
>   1/2 cup Granny's Granola (page 15)
>   2 eggs
>   2 tablespoons milk
>   1 teaspoon Vanilla Bean Extract (page 12)

1. Mix and bake as for Vanilla Cookies.

Yield: 3 dozen cookies

Cost of Ingredients: $3.67
Comparable Purchased Product: Duncan
   Hines Oatmeal Cookie Mix, 16.5 ounces, $1.79
   ($7.81)
Savings: $4.14

Instant Brownie Mix

Keeping this mix on hand can really help if a chocolate attack comes—trust me—in the middle of the night and you want to go about making brownies quietly, alone, undisturbed. Once you've got the mix waiting there in the pantry, the rest of the job is very quiet.

>   4 cups sugar
>   2 1/2 cups flour
>   1 1/2 cups unsweetened cocoa
>   2 teaspoons baking powder
>   1 1/2 teaspoons salt
>   2 cups shortening

1. Mix dry ingredients together in a large bowl and add shortening by spoonfuls, cutting in with a pastry blender or two knives, or in a food processor.

2. Store mix in a tightly covered container in the pantry. If you have many children around, it might help to label this one "Health Food," to preserve the mix a bit longer. If there are no children, mix will keep for up to 3 months in dry weather.

Fudgie Chewie Brownies

3 cups Instant Brownie Mix
2 eggs
1 teaspoon Vanilla Bean Extract (page 12)
1/4 cup Basic Chocolate Sauce (page 45)
1/2 cup chocolate chips

Peanut Butter Brownies

3 cups Instant Brownie Mix
2 eggs
1 teaspoon Vanilla Bean Extract (page 12)
1/2 cup peanut butter chips

1. Preheat oven to 350 degrees.

2. Combine the ingredients in a bowl, stirring to mix thoroughly. Pour into a buttered 8-inch-square pan and bake for 30 minutes or until a knife inserted in the middle comes out clean.

Variations:

You can also add one or more of the following ingredients to any of the brownie recipes:

> *1/2 cup chopped walnuts*
> *1/2 cup pulverized butter brickle*
> *1/2 cup shredded coconut*
> *1/2 cup chopped dates or raisins*
> *1/2 cup crumbled chocolate candy bar*

Yield: 56 ounces

Cost of Ingredients: $2.67
Comparable Purchased Product: Duncan
Hines Brownie Mix, 23.6 ounces, $1.29 ($3.06)
Savings: $.39

Biscuit Baking Mix

I've used this mix as the basis for several of the recipes that follow, so if you think you will be making lots of pancakes, shortcake, or biscuits in the near future, double or triple the quantity of the basic baking mix. It keeps very well in the pantry and you can use it for a quick finish for a meat or vegetable casserole by simply sprinkling a few teaspoons of the mix on the top before baking—it will sink to the bottom and form a soft pie crust.

10 cups flour
1/3 cup baking powder
1 tablespoon salt
2 cups shortening

1.   Sift dry ingredients together in a large bowl. With two knives, a pastry blender, or your food processor, add the shortening in spoonfuls and cut it in until the mixture is the texture of coarse cornmeal. If you are using a food processor, start and stop it often during processing and watch closely.

2. Keep mix stored in a labeled, tightly closed container. It will keep on the pantry shelf for 1 to 6 months in dry weather. In very hot and humid weather, it's a good idea to keep the mix in the refrigerator.

Ideas:
See the recipes that follow in this chapter for ways to use the basic mix as a dinner or breakfast accompaniment by making:

Quick Rolled Biscuits (page 66)
Quick Dumplings (page 62)
Quick Crepes (page 69)
Quick Pancakes (page 71)
Quick Waffles (page 72)

And check Chapter 3 for ways to use Biscuit Baking Mix for making these quick desserts:
Quick Coffee Cake (page 128)
Quick Biscuit Shortcake (page 129)

Yield: 10 cups

Cost of Ingredients: $2.76
Comparable Purchased Product: Bisquick, 20 ounces, $1.69 ($6.76)
Savings: $4.00

Quick Rolled Biscuits

These simple biscuits are easy to make, and if you don't have any milk on hand, you can use water or reconstituted instant nonfat dried milk. For variety, add fillings of your choice, sweet toppings, or try my Latvian grandmother's special biscuits, (recipe follows), which are absolutely heavenly. Each recipe yields 10 medium-size biscuits.

2 cups Biscuit Baking Mix (page 65)
2/3 cup milk

1. Preheat oven to 400 degrees.

2. Combine mix and milk and beat until smooth. If dough feels too sticky, add more mix (up to 1/4 cup).

3. Turn dough out onto a surface dusted with baking mix or plain flour, roll dough into a ball to coat, and knead gently ten times. Roll dough out to 1/2-inch thickness and cut into 2-inch circles or squares.

4. Place on an ungreased cookie sheet, brush tops with milk to brown, and bake for 8 to 10 minutes.

Dropped Biscuits

2 cups Biscuit Baking Mix (page 65)
1 cup milk

1. Follow Steps 1 and 2 for **Quick Rolled Biscuits**. Mixture will be a bit looser than the dough for regular biscuits. Drop by spoonfuls onto an ungreased cookie sheet and bake for 8 to 10 minutes.

Sweet Biscuits

2 cups Biscuit Baking Mix (page 65)
2/3 cup milk
1/4 cup Cinnamon Sugar (page 10)
2 tablespoons Country Butter (page 20)

1. Follow the instructions for either **Quick Rolled** or **Dropped Biscuits**. Just before baking, brush biscuit tops with melted butter and then dust with cinnamon sugar.

Sprinkled Biscuits

2 cups Biscuit Baking Mix (page 65)
2/3 cup milk
2 tablespoons milk
1/4 cup poppy, sesame, or caraway seeds

1. Follow the instructions for either **Quick Rolled** or **Dropped Biscuits**. Just before baking, brush biscuit tops with milk and then dust with seeds.

Filled Biscuits

2 cups Biscuit Baking Mix (page 65)
2/3 cup milk
2 tablespoons Country Butter, melted (page 20)
1/2 cup chopped vegetables, tuna, or another meat or vegetable filling of your choice

1. Follow the mixing and baking instructions for **Quick Rolled Biscuits**.

2. Before baking, brush one biscuit circle for the bottom with melted butter, add a teaspoon of chopped vegetables, chicken, tuna, or other filling, top with second biscuit circle, pinch sides, brush with milk to seal.

Latvian Biscuits

1 small onion
2 slices bacon
2 cups Biscuit Baking Mix (page 65)
2/3 cup milk
2 tablespoons Country Butter, melted (page 20)

1. Chop onion and bacon into small pieces. Cook them together over low heat until onion is transparent and bacon is soft but not crispy.

2. Meanwhile prepare the dough for **Quick Rolled Biscuits**. Lift onion and bacon from pan and add, without draining, to the dough just before kneading. Proceed as for **Quick Rolled Biscuits**, page 66, brushing the tops with a bit of the bacon grease before baking.

Yield: 10 biscuits

Cost of Ingredients: $.64
Comparable Purchased Product: Pillsbury
 Heat and Eat Biscuits, 10 ounces, $1.49
Savings: $.85

Quick Dumplings

Dumplings are old-fashioned, and yes, they are fattening, but nothing in the world is as comforting as seeing them sitting cozily on the top of stews, broth, or even chili. Try the pretty speckled ones for variety, or when you want to impress yourself.

2 cups Biscuit Baking Mix (page 65)
2/3 cup milk

1. Beat mix and milk together to form a soft dough.

To Use:
 Wait for the right moment to drop the dough by spoonfuls onto the top of stew, soup, or chili: the liquid must be nearly ready to eat, bubbling hot, and gently simmering.

*Drop on the dumpling dough, simmer for 10 minutes,
then cover and cook for 10 minutes more.*

Herb Dumplings

2 cups Biscuit Baking Mix (page 65)
2/3 cup milk
1 tablespoon chopped fresh herbs: parsley, dill, or
   chives
1 clove garlic, minced
1 teaspoon freshly ground black pepper

1. Blend and cook, as above.

Vegetable Dumplings

2 cups Biscuit Baking Mix (page 65)
2/3 cup milk
2 tablespoons finely chopped onion, green pepper, or
   scallions
1 teaspoon freshly ground black pepper

1. Blend and cook, as for **Quick Rolled Biscuits**.

Yield: 12 dumplings

Cost of Ingredients: $.64
Comparable Purchased Product: Bisquick
   Baking Mix, 20 ounces, $1.69 ($1.32)
Savings: $.71

Quick Crepes

*Making crepes can be easy if you already have a batch of
Biscuit Baking Mix in the pantry. You may have to practice a
bit to get the hang of flipping and filling the crepes, but after a
little experimentation, you should be able to make crepes very
quickly. Make sure the pan you use is hot enough to make a
drop of water bounce merrily on the surface, and make sure the
pan is smooth, with no rough spots.*

*Crepes can be filled with various meat stuffings for a quick dinner or brunch, and they are fantastic with sliced fruits for dessert. Top a sweetened crepe with a tablespoon of one of your own homemade liqueurs from Chapter 5 for a fancy, grown-up taste, and check the **Ideas**, here, for additional ways to fill and serve your crepes.*

You can make a big batch of crepes at one time, cool them, and then freeze with a sheet of wax paper or plastic wrap between each one for even quicker suppers and desserts.

> **2 cups Biscuit Baking Mix (page 65)**
> **1 1/2 cups milk**
> **4 eggs**

1.   Combine ingredients and beat until smooth in a blender, food processor, bowl, or shaker container. Mixture will be thin.

To Use:

For each crepe, pour about 1/4 cup of batter into a hot, greased pan. Turn pan until batter covers the bottom and cook over medium heat until golden brown. Loosen edge with a spatula, turn over, and cook the other side until golden brown.

To reheat frozen crepes: either thaw, still wrapped, at room temperature for 1 hour before warming in an oven set to 350 degrees or unwrap and place in a microwave oven on medium for 1 or 2 minutes.

Ideas:

For dinner or brunch crepes, try filling with a spoonful of finely ground tuna, chicken, or turkey salad and top with white sauce.

For a dessert crepe, fill with spiced apples, sweetened cherries, or berries; top with sweetened whipped cream and dust with cinnamon.

Blintzes

> **2 cups Biscuit Baking Mix (page 65)**
> **1 1/2 cups milk**
> **2 tablespoons sugar**
> **1 teaspoon Vanilla Bean Extract (page 12)**
> **4 eggs**

Filling

1 cup Homemade Cream Cheese (page 19)
1/4 cup sour cream
2 tablespoons Vanilla Sugar (page 8)

1. Mix batter and cook, as for **Quick Crepes**, page 69. Fill the crepe while still warm with sweetened cream cheese, top with sour cream, and dust with more sugar.

Yield: 12 crepes (32 ounces)

Cost of Ingredients: $1.07
Comparable Purchased Product: Golden
Brand Blintzes, 15 ounces, $1.69 ($1.35)
Savings: $.28

Quick Pancakes

*Use your **Biscuit Baking Mix** as the basis for these delicious pancakes, and then vary them by following some of the suggestions, here. You can top your pancakes with any of the **Sweet Butters**, page 104, or **Sweet Berry Syrups**, page 44, or simply top with **Homemade Yogurt**, page 121, for a lower-calorie treat.*

2 cups Biscuit Baking Mix (page 65)
1 cup milk
2 eggs

1. Combine ingredients in a blender, food processor, bowl, or shaker container and beat until smooth.

To Use:
For each pancake, pour a small amount of batter into a hot, greased pan and cook over medium heat until bubbles form on the top. Flip and cook until the pancake is golden brown.

Variation:
For thinner pancakes, use 1 egg and 1 1/2 cups milk.

Chocolate Pancakes

2 cups Biscuit Baking Mix (page 65)
3/4 cup milk
1/4 cup Basic Chocolate Sauce (page 45)
1 egg

1. Combine ingredients and cook, as for **Quick Pancakes**. Top with one of the **Sweet Butters**, page 104, whipped cream, or nuts.

Berry Pancakes

2 cups Biscuit Baking Mix (page 65)
3/4 cup milk
1/2 cup berries and juice
1 egg

1. Combine ingredients and cook, as for **Quick Pancakes**. Top with one of the **Sweet Butters**, page 104, **Sweet Syrups**, page 44, whipped cream, or nuts.

Yield: 20 ounces

Cost of Ingredients: $.55
Comparable Purchased Product: Aunt
    Jemima Pancake Mix, 32 ounces, $1.09 ($.68)
Savings: $.13

Quick Waffles

This recipe makes really big waffles that hold together. If you make a double batch of waffles, you can wrap the extra ones and store them in the freezer. Then, for a quick breakfast, pop the frozen waffles into the toaster, toaster oven, or microwave without defrosting.

2 cups Biscuit Baking Mix (page 65)
2 tablespoons vegetable oil
1 egg
1 1/3 cups milk

1. Combine all ingredients and beat until smooth.

2. Pour into the center of a hot waffle iron and close the lid. Bake until steaming stops.

Idea:
    For dessert or Belgian waffles, add 2 tablespoons sugar to the recipe and serve the waffles with an ice cream topping.

Yield: 6 waffles

Cost of Ingredients: $.76
Comparable Purchased Product: Bisquick
    Baking Mix, 20 ounces, $1.69 ($1.35)
Savings: $.59

Healthy Whole Wheat Baking Mix

*This basic mix can be used like the **Biscuit Baking Mix**, page 65, for creating muffins, pancakes, breads, and buns. It is rich and tasty and you can add honey and nuts to some of the recipes for extra flavor.*

> 4 1/2 cups whole wheat flour
> 1 cup instant nonfat dry milk
> 3 tablespoons baking powder
> 2 tablespoons sugar
> 1 teaspoon salt
> 3/4 cup vegetable shortening or oil

1. Mix the dry ingredients in a large bowl and cut in the shortening with a pastry blender or two knives, or in the food processor. If you are using oil, mix with a fork until the oil disappears and the mixture has a coarse texture.

2. Store in a tightly closed container. Mixture will keep on the pantry shelf in dry weather for 2 months. Keep refrigerated in the summer.

Nutty Whole Wheat Biscuits

This recipe will make 15 to 20 small biscuits.

> **2/3 cup water**
> **3 cups Healthy Whole Wheat Biscuit Mix (page 73)**
> **1/2 cup chopped walnuts or pecans**

1.   Preheat oven to 350 degrees.

2.   Combine water and biscuit mix. Stir until mixture becomes a soft dough; add nuts and mix well. Turn out onto a lightly floured board and knead gently ten times.

3.   Roll dough 1/2 inch thick and cut into 2-inch circles. Bake on an ungreased cookie sheet for 15 to 20 minutes, or until golden brown.

Hint:

Flour the rim of a drinking glass and use it to cut out your biscuits if you don't have a biscuit cutter. Or thoroughly clean out a tin can, cut the lids off both ends, and keep it handy as a cutter. This way you can develop a drawerful of different sizes and shapes of cutters for cookies as well as biscuits.

Honey Whole Wheat Muffins

These muffins can be varied in many ways by adding your own favorite goodies in place of the chopped walnuts in this recipe. Try adding dates, **Candied Citrus Peel,** *page 164, or raisins.*

> **2 cups Healthy Whole Wheat Biscuit Mix (page 73)**
> **3 tablespoons honey**
> **1 egg**
> **1/2 cup water**
> **1/2 cup chopped walnuts**

1.   Preheat oven to 350 degrees.

2.   Mix all ingredients at once and stir until thoroughly moistened. The mixture will be lumpy.

3. Fill greased muffin cups two-thirds full and bake for 20 minutes.

Idea:

> *For very fresh muffins when you don't have time to cook, line a muffin tin with paper muffin cups, pour in the batter, cover the tin with plastic wrap and freeze until firm. Remove the cup and batter from the tin and store in a plastic bag. When you're ready to bake, simply pop the frozen muffins back into the tin and add 10 minutes to the cooking time.*

Yield: 48 ounces

Cost of Ingredients: $1.26
Comparable Purchased Product: Aunt Jemima Whole Wheat Pancake Mix, 33 ounces, $1.39 ($2.02)
Savings: $.76

Bran Muffin Mix

> *If you want to include foods with more fiber in your diet, make up a batch of muffins from this baking mix and add them to your breakfast menu. It makes a nice change from simply eating cereal for fiber, and you can spread a tablespoon of honey or **Freezer Fruit Preserves**, page 50, on your warm muffins for added sweetness.*

> **4 cups bran cereal**
> **5 cups flour**
> **1/4 cup baking powder**
> **3/4 cup brown sugar**
> **1 cup vegetable shortening**

1. Mix dry ingredients and cut in shortening with a pastry blender or two knives, or in a food processor. Mix will have a coarse consistency.

2. Store mix in a tightly closed container. It will keep on the pantry shelf for up to 4 months in dry weather. Refrigerate the mix if the weather is hot and humid.

Yield: 9 cups mix

Blueberry Bran Muffins

These muffins freeze very well, so you can make a double batch and defrost the extra ones in the microwave or a warm oven for a nice change on a cold day.

> **1 egg**
> **3/4 cup milk**
> **2 1/2 cups Bran Muffin Mix (page 75)**
> **1/2 cup fresh or frozen blueberries, slightly thawed**

1. Preheat oven to 400 degrees.

2. Stir egg and milk together and add to muffin mix. Stir until mixture is evenly moist. Stir in the blueberries and pour into greased muffin pans and cook for 20 to 30 minutes.

3. If reheating frozen muffins, warm without thawing for 20 minutes at 350 degrees in the oven or for 2 minutes on high power in the microwave.

Yield: 12 muffins

Cost of Ingredients: $1.38
Comparable Purchased Product: Arnold Branola Muffins, 6 muffins, $1.29 ($2.58)
Savings: $1.20

Cheap Tricks . . . . ✂ . . . .

There are lots of ways to add fruit, even fruit you considered too far gone, to your muffins for additional fiber in your diet.

One of my thriftiest tricks is to freeze overripe or brown bananas and use them in cooking. I peel the bananas and mush the fruit into a plastic bag or freezer container. The fruit can be added, while still slightly frozen, into the muffin batter.

Dried-out raisins can be reconstituted by soaking them in orange juice for 30 minutes before adding them to the batter.

Cornmeal Baking Mix

*Similar to the other baking mixes for convenience and
storage, this recipe lets you whip up corn muffins and corn
breads when the mood strikes, because you've already done all
the measuring and gathering of ingredients.*

> 4 cups flour
> 4 cups cornmeal
> 2 cups instant nonfat dry milk
> 3/4 cup sugar
> 1/4 cup baking powder
> 1 teaspoon salt
> 1 cup shortening

1.   Combine dry ingredients and cut shortening in with a
pastry blender or two knives, or mix in a food processor.

2. Store in a tightly covered container in the pantry. Mixture
will keep for 1 to 6 months on the pantry shelf in dry weather.
In hot and humid weather, store in the refrigerator.

Yield: 10 cups

Cost of Ingredients: $2.32
Comparable Purchased Product: Aunt
    Jemima Corn Bread, 10 ounces, $.95 ($7.60)
Savings: $5.28

Quick Corn Muffins

*If you're dieting or your pantry is bare, these muffins can
be made with water instead of milk and the egg may be
omitted.*

> 1 egg
> 1/2 cup milk
> 2 cups Cornmeal Baking Mix
> 1 tablespoon butter, melted

1. Preheat oven to 350 degrees.

2.. Mix egg and milk in a small bowl, stir into mix, and stir in melted butter. Pour into greased muffin tins and bake for 20 to 30 minutes.

Idea:

Corn muffins are delicious split, buttered, and then reheated in the same pan alongside your bacon and eggs.

Variations:

Try adding any of the following ingredients to the basic batter for fancier corn muffins. Or stir one or more of these ingredients into the batter, pour into a buttered loaf pan, and bake at 350 degrees for 30 minutes.

1 teaspoon grated orange peel
1/2 cup chopped nuts
1/2 cup chopped raisins or dates
1/2 cup fresh or frozen berries or chopped apple

Yield: 8 to 10 muffins

Cost of Ingredients: $.69
Comparable Purchased Product: Thomas' Corn Toast-R-Cakes, 7 ounces, $1.09
Savings: $.40

Freezer Pancake Batter

*Although you can freeze any extra batter you might have remaining after making **Quick Pancakes**, page 71, this batter is especially suitable for longer times in the freezer. Freeze this mixture in any kind of container that you can easily pour from, such as a clean milk carton.*

If you set the batter out to thaw the night before, you will have a very convenient breakfast ready to pour and cook. A frozen container of pancake batter can also be packed in a cooler for overnight camping trips and it will be ready to pour in the morning.

2 cups flour
1/2 cup sugar

4 teaspoons baking powder
1/2 teaspoon salt
1/2 cup vegetable shortening
4 eggs
1 3/4 cups milk

1. Sift dry ingredients into a large bowl.

2. Add the shortening to the dry mixture, cutting it in with a pastry blender or two knives until the mixture is coarsely blended.

3. Add the eggs and milk, stirring until smooth.

4. Pour into a container for the freezer and cover tightly. Mixture will keep for up to 12 months.

Variations:
 Add any of the following to the batter before freezing:

  1 cup fresh or frozen berries
  2 teaspoons cinnamon, 2 tablespoons chopped apple
  1/2 cup chopped dates or finely chopped nuts

 Stir before using to evenly distribute fruit.

Yield: 22 ounces

Cost of Ingredients: $1.23
Comparable Purchased Product: Aunt Jemima Pancake Batter for the Freezer, 16 ounces, $1.09 ($1.49)
Savings: $.26

Cookie-crumb Crust

This recipe is most economical if you use up a variety of slightly stale cookies, and it's a good idea to keep a plastic bag in the freezer to accumulate the cookies and the crumbs at the bottom of the cookie jar until you have enough to make a pie

*crust. The traditional type of cookie to use is the graham
cracker, but you can vary the flavor and texture by using just
about any kind of cookie you might have on hand.*

> **2 cups Sweet Crumbs (page 23) or 1 pound cookies**
> **1/4 cup sugar, brown or white**
> **1 teaspoon cinnamon**
> **1/4 cup melted butter, sweet or salted**

1.   If you are making fresh crumbs, grind the cookies up in the
blender or food processor, about 1/2 cup at a time, until you have
2 cups of crumbs.

2. Mix crumbs, sugar, and cinnamon. Stir in the melted butter
and press into a 9-inch pie pan or several small tart pans.

3. Chill the crust for 2 hours before filling and baking or freeze
the crust right in the pie pan, wrapped in plastic freezer wrap,
for up to 6 months. Several crusts can be nested together in the
same freezer bag if you place a layer of plastic wrap between
each pie crust. Do not defrost before filling and baking.

Variation:
> *You can also substitute* **Granny's Granola***, page 15,
finely crushed, for the cookie crumbs. This type of pie crust
works quite well with cheesecake fillings.*

Yield: 1 pie crust or 4 tart shells

Cost of Ingredients: $.53
Comparable Purchased Product: Keebler
   Graham Cracker Crust, 9 inches, $.89
Savings: $.36

Basic Cake Mix

*Store this mix in the refrigerator rather than on the pantry
shelf because it contains butter. It will still be as convenient as
a packaged mix, however, as the recipe for* **Quick Pound Cake**,
page 81, shows.

3 cups flour, sifted
2 1/2 cups sugar
1/2 teaspoon baking powder
1 cup butter
1/2 cup vegetable shortening

1. Sift flour, sugar, and baking powder together. Cut in butter and shortening with a pastry blender or two knives. You can also use your food processor for this step.

2. Store mix in a covered container in the refrigerator and use within the month.

Yield: 60 ounces

Cost of Ingredients: $2.36
Comparable Purchased Product: Betty Crocker Golden Pound Cake Mix, 16 ounces, $1.29 ($4.83)
Savings: $2.47

Quick Pound Cake

*The cakes from the **Basic Cake Mix** are moist and buttery. You can use these cakes as the basis for a delicious strawberry shortcake or add cocoa and make a chocolate cake.*

3 eggs
1/2 cup milk
1/2 teaspoon Vanilla Bean Extract (page 12)
3 cups Basic Cake Mix (page 80)

1. Preheat oven to 300 degrees.

2. Beat eggs until foamy; add milk and vanilla and continue beating.

3. Add dry mixture to eggs, 1/2 cup at a time, beating well after each addition.

4. Pour into a greased 9-inch loaf pan and bake for 1 1/2 hours.

Idea:

For a fruit shortcake, pour batter into a greased 9-inch-square pan and bake for 1 hour 15 minutes. When cool, cut cake into 2-inch squares. Slice each square in half, fill with berries and juice, and replace top half. Cover with sweetened whipped cream.

Variation:

For a chocolate pound cake, add 1/2 cup unsweetened cocoa to the batter before baking.

Yield: 1 cake

Cost of Ingredients: $1.38
Comparable Purchased Product:
    Entenmann's Pound Cake, 12 ounces, $2.19
Savings: $.81

Chocolate Cake Mix

*This mix can be kept handy on the pantry shelf and is very convenient for a quick but rich treat. The basic chocolate cake from your own mix can be varied by the addition of different kinds of icings and fillings. Try spreading 1 cup of **Freezer Fruit Preserves**, page 50, between the layers before frosting, and sprinkle the top with shredded coconut.*

> 6 cups flour, sifted
> 5 1/2 cups sugar
> 1 teaspoon baking powder
> 5 1/2 teaspoons baking soda
> 2 cups unsweetened cocoa
> 2 cups vegetable shortening

1. Sift dry ingredients together. Cut in shortening with a pastry blender or two knives, or you can use your food processor for this step.

2. Store mix in a tightly closed container on the pantry shelf.

Mix will keep for up to 6 months in dry weather. If the weather is hot and humid, keep this mix in the refrigerator.

Yield: 15 cups

Cost of Ingredients: $7.26
Comparable Purchased Product: Duncan Hines Deluxe Devil's Food Cake Mix, 18.25 ounces, $1.29 ($8.48)
Savings: $1.22

Quick Chocolate Cake

You can substitute 2 tablespoons of one of the berry cordials from Chapter 5 for 2 tablespoons of the water in this recipe, and you can add some of the **Basic Chocolate Sauce**, *page 45, to the filling or frosting.*

5 cups Chocolate Cake Mix (page 82)
1 cup water
1 teaspoon Vanilla Bean Extract (page 12)
3 eggs

1. Preheat oven to 350 degrees.

2. Shake the container of cake mix before measuring and spoon the mix lightly into the measuring cup.

3. Mix in the water and vanilla, using an electric mixer or beat by hand, using 300 strokes. Add eggs one at a time, beating well after each addition.

4. Pour into two well-greased 9-inch layer pans and bake for 25 to 30 minutes.

Idea:
    Make 2 dozen cupcakes from the recipe and let children decorate by swirling the cupcakes into a mixture of **Homemade Cream Cheese**, *page 19, softened and whipped with*

1/2 cup milk and 1/2 cup sugar, or dust the tops of the cakes with confectioner's sugar or one of the **Scented and Spiced Sugars** *(page 7).*

Yield: 1 layer cake, 21 ounces (about 24 cupcakes)

Cost of Ingredients: $2.91
Comparable Purchased Product:
Pepperidge Farm Chocolate Layer Cake, 11.5 ounces, $1.79 ($3.26)
Savings: $.35

Rolled Refrigerator Cookies

The basic dough you create for these cookies can be varied to make chocolate or spice cookies by changing the flavorings. Try new and exciting combinations yourself, depending on what you have on hand. You can also frost and decorate these cookies for holiday treats.

> **1 cup vegetable shortening**
> **1 cup sugar**
> **2 eggs**
> **1 tablespoon Vanilla Bean Extract (page 12)**
> **3 cups sifted flour**
> **1/4 teaspoon salt**
> **1 teaspoon baking powder**
> **4 tablespoons milk**

1. In a food processor or an electric mixer, cream shortening with sugar, then add eggs and vanilla and continue mixing until mixture is smooth and creamy.

2. Sift flour, salt, and baking powder together and add to the creamed mixture alternately with the milk.

3. Divide dough into three or four batches and form each batch into a roll. Wrap in plastic, wax paper, or aluminum foil and refrigerate. Dough will keep for up to 2 months in the refrigerator and 6 months in the freezer.

To Use:

    To make approximately 2 dozen cookies:

1. Preheat oven to 350 degrees.

2. Remove dough from the refrigerator 30 minutes before using
or from the freezer 4 hours before using. Remove wrappings
and slice into 1/2-inch thick rounds. Slice the rounds in half or
in quarters.

3. Place on an ungreased cookie sheet and bake for 10
minutes. Store unused dough in the refrigerator.

Variations:

    *For chocolate cookies, add 1 square unsweetened
chocolate, melted, to the mixture.*

    *For chocolate chip cookies, add 1/2 cup semisweet
chocolate bits to the recipe.*

    *For peanut butter cookies, add 1/2 cup **Peanut Butter**,
page 47, to the recipe and reduce the shortening by 1/4 cup.*

    *For butterscotch nut cookies, add 1/4 cup nuts and 1/2 cup
butterscotch chips to the recipe.*

    *For spicy cookies, mix 1 teaspoon cinnamon, 1
teaspoon allspice, and 1 teaspoon nutmeg into the mixture.*

Yield: 5 cups

Cost of Ingredients: $1.54
Comparable Purchased Product: Pillsbury
    Cookie Mix, 20 counces, $2.09 ($4.18)
Savings: $2.64

E-Z Gelatin Desserts

    *You wouldt't necessarily make an unflavored gelatin
dessert to save money—the savings aren't immense—but your
own mix is convenient, with controlled amounts of sugar and
coloring, and this version has the additional benefit of real
fruit juice for nutrition. Any kind of fruit juice can be
used—fresh, frozen, or canned—except for pineapple juice,
which must be used canned.*

1 envelope unflavored gelatin
1 3/4 cups fruit juice
1 cup sugar

1. Place gelatin in a pan and pour 1/2 cup of the fruit juice over the gelatin to soften. Warm the gelatin-juice mixture over low heat for 2 to 3 minutes, stirring constantly, until the gelatin dissolves.

2. Remove from the heat and add the rest of the juice and the sugar. Pour into dessert dishes and chill until firm.

Variations:
You can add all sorts of fruit bits to your gelatin desserts to make them more interesting, and you can also make fluffy versions:
For a fruity mousse, try folding whipped cream into the gelatin when it's partially set—after about an hour in the refrigerator.
For a simple gelatin whip, remove the gelatin from the refrigerator when it is partially set, whip at high speed with an electric mixer, and pour the frothy mix into dessert dishes and put them back into the refrigerator until set.

Yield: 16 ounces

Cost of Ingredients: $.17
Comparable Purchased Product: Jell-O
  Wild Strawberry, 3 ounces, $.43 ($2.93)
Savings: $2.12

Puddings and Pie Fillings

The basic mix will make twenty batches of pudding, divided into four servings of 1/2 cup each. I've given instructions for making a basic pudding from the mix, as well as some suggestions for fancier, richer puddings from the same mix.

Vanilla Pudding Mix

3 cups instant nonfat dry milk

4 cups sugar
1 teaspoon salt
3 cups cornstarch
1 vanilla bean

1. Mix the milk, sugar, salt and cornstarch until the ingredients are well blended. Cut the vanilla bean into several large pieces and stir them into the mix, seeds and all. Store mix in an airtight canister or a closely covered jar.

To Use:

Stir the mix in the canister before measuring out 1/2 cup mix into a saucepan. Add 2 cups milk and cook over low heat, stirring, until mixture thickens and comes to a boil.

Continue stirring for 1 minute, remove from heat, and pour into individual serving dishes. Pudding will thicken further as it cools.

Variation:

*For a richer tasting pudding, try cooking as directed and after taking the pudding off the heat, stir in an egg lightly beaten with 1/2 teaspoon nutmeg, 1/2 teaspoon **Vanilla Bean Extract**, page 12, and 1 tablespoon sweet butter into the pudding. Cover and let sit for a minute or two, uncover and stir, and then pour into the individual serving dishes.*

Chocolate Pudding Mix

2 1/2 cups instant nonfat dry milk
5 cups sugar
3 cups cornstarch
1 teaspoon salt
2 1/2 cups unsweetened cocoa

1. Mix all the ingredients until they are well blended. Store mix in an airtight canister or a closely covered jar.

To Use:

Stir the mix in the canister before measuring out 2/3 cup of the mix into a saucepan. Add 2 cups milk and cook over low heat, stirring, until mixture thickens and comes to a boil.

Continue stirring for 1 minute, remove from heat, and pour into individual serving dishes. Pudding will thicken further as it cools.

Variation:

Cook as directed, but add 1 teaspoon **Vanilla Bean Extract**, page 12, and 1 tablespoon sweet butter to the pudding as it cooks.

For a chocolate-mocha flavor, add 1 tablespoon instant coffee to the pudding mix before cooking.

Butterscotch Pudding Mix

2 cups instant nonfat dry milk
5 cups brown sugar, firmly tightly packed
3 cups cornstarch
1 teaspoon salt

1. Mix all the ingredients until they are well blended. Store mix in an airtight canister or a closely covered jar.

To Use:

Stir the mix in the canister before measuring out 1/2 cup mix into a saucepan. Add 2 cups milk and 4 tablespoons butter and cook over low heat, stirring, until mixture thickens and comes to a boil. Continue stirring for 1 minute, remove from heat, and pour into individual serving dishes. Pudding will thicken further as it cools.

Variation:

Add 1/2 cup chopped peanuts to the pudding when you take it off the heat.

Coconut Cream Pudding Mix

3 cups instant nonfat dry milk
4 cups sugar
1 teaspoon salt
3 cups cornstarch
1 1/2 cups shredded, unsweetened coconut
1 teaspoon coconut extract

1. Mix the milk, sugar, salt, and cornstarch together until the ingredients are well blended.

2. Whirl the coconut and the coconut extract in a blender or food processor for 1 minute. Add coconut mixture to the cornstarch mixture. Store mix in an airtight canister.

To Use:

Stir the mix in the canister before measuring out 2/3 cup mix into a saucepan. Add 2 cups milk and cook over low heat, stirring, until mixture thickens and comes to a boil. Continue stirring for 1 minute, remove from heat, and pour into individual serving dishes. Pudding will thicken further as it cools.

Yield: 10 cups

Cost of Ingredients: $2.79
Comparable Purchased Product: Jell-O
Pudding and Pie Mix, 3.3 ounces, $.49 ($11.87)
Savings: $9.08

Instant White Sauce Mix

I was very proud of myself when I first learned how to make a perfect white sauce with no lumps in it. I realize now that it's not such a big accomplishment—all you have to remember is to add the liquid to the dry ingredients, stirring all the while, never the other way around, and you will have smooth, lump-free sauces.

2 cups instant nonfat dry milk
1 cup flour
1 teaspoon salt
1 cup vegetable shortening or butter

1.   Mix the dry ingredients and cut the shortening in with a pastry blender or two knives, or with a food processor.

2. Store mixture in a tightly closed container. If you are using butter, store the mix in the refrigerator; vegetable shortening will keep on the pantry shelf in dry weather for up to 6 months.

To Use:

In general, use 1/2 cup mix for every 1/2 cup liquid unless you are adding more dry ingredients, such as cheese. In that case, increase the liquid until the sauce is the consistency you like.

Variation:

*To make a **chicken or turkey gravy**, remove the chicken or turkey from the pan in which it has been frying or baking and leave the pan on low heat. Sprinkle 3 tablespoons mix over the drippings in the pan, add 1/2 cup milk, slowly, mixing with a spirited circular motion to loosen any bits of meat clinging to the pan. Cook over low heat for 10 minutes.*

Yield: 27 ounces

Cost of Ingredients: $.76 if made with shortening; $1.57 if made with butter
Comparable Purchased Product: Durkee White Sauce Mix, 1 ounce, $.63 ($17.01)
Savings: $15.44

Fancy Alfredo Sauce Mix

*Make a batch of **Instant White Sauce Mix** using butter instead of vegetable shortening for this delicious, rich version of a classic Alfredo-type sauce. You can use fettuccine noodles for this dish because they are wide and flat and hold all the tasty sauce, and you can add cooked Italian sausage, crumbled or sliced, to the sauce before serving.*

> 1/2 cup Instant White Sauce Mix (page 89)
> 2 to 4 cloves garlic, pressed
> 1/2 cup grated Parmesan or Romano cheese
> 1 cup light cream

1. Assemble the ingredients and have them ready to mix in with hot pasta just before serving. Cook and strain the pasta and return it to the large pan used for boiling. Turn off heat.

2. One by one, add the ingredients, mixing and tossing well after each addition. Serve immediately.

Yield: 8 ounces

Cost of Ingredients: $3.84
Comparable Purchased Product: Pasta 'n Cheese Alfredo, 15 ounces, $4.99
Savings: $1.14

Noodle-mania Mix

*There are lots of different mixes on the market now for spicing up and flavoring noodles, pasta, and spaghetti. I love them all, and once I had ten or so of them in my pantry at one time. This mix, along with its **Variations**, saves you money, time and, in my case, pantry space.*

> **1 cup instant nonfat dry milk**
> **2 tablespoons grated Romano or Parmesan cheese**
> **1/3 cup Dried Minced Onion (page 25)**
> **1 tablespoon garlic powder**
> **1/2 teaspoon salt**
> **1/2 teaspoon white pepper**

1. Combine ingredients and store in a tightly closed container. Mix will keep for 4 months in the pantry.

To Use:
    Combine 1/4 cup mix with 2 tablespoons melted butter and 1/4 cup milk. Toss with pasta.

Variations:
    Add 1/4 cup grated Cheddar cheese in place of the Parmesan cheese for a different taste. Or try tossing the pasta and mix with 1/2 cup braised snow peas, 1/2 cup carrot slivers, and 1/2 cup pignolia nuts for a tasty main course pasta salad.

Yield: 12 ounces

Cost of Ingredients: $1.46
Comparable Purchased Product: French's Pasta Toss Alfredo, 3 ounces, $1.89 ($7.56)
Savings: $6.10

Macaroni and Cheese Sauce Mix

*Make **Instant White Sauce Mix** with butter instead of vegetable shortening and use elbow macaroni for this recipe.*

> 1/2 cup Instant White Sauce Mix (page 89)
> 1/2 cup grated Cheddar cheese
> 1 cup milk

1. Combine ingredients and immediately pour over hot elbow macaroni. Toss well.

Yield: 10 ounces

Cost of Ingredients: $.83
Comparable Purchased Product: Kraft Deluxe Macaroni and Cheese Dinner, 14 ounces, $1.19 ($.85)
Savings: $.02

Wheat Germ and Cornflake Topping Mix

This mix adds a pleasant crunch and more interest and nutrition to the vegetables, meats, or pasta you combine it with.

> 1 cup wheat germ
> 1 cup crushed cornflakes
> 1 tablespoon parsley flakes
> 1 teaspoon paprika
> 1/2 teaspoon dry mustard
> 1/2 teaspoon tarragon
> 1/2 teaspoon celery salt
> 1/2 teaspoon Dried Minced Onion (page 25)
> 1/2 teaspoon salt
> 1/2 teaspoon pepper

1. Combine all ingredients and store in a tightly covered container on your pantry shelf for up to 4 months.

To Use:

     Combine 1/2 cup topping and 2 tablespoons melted butter and crumble over a tuna, salmon, or cheese-and-noodle casserole.

Yield: 17 ounces

Cost of Ingredients: $1.31
Comparable Purchased Product: Kellogg's
    Cornflake Crumb Topping, 21 ounces, $1.99
    ($1.61)
Savings: $.30

Top-of-the-Stove Stuffing Mix

    Collect pieces and ends of bread until you have accumulated enough for this recipe. Or make it up fresh by buying day-old bread from the supermarket and you will still be saving money. This basic stuffing mix is flavored for chicken, but you can vary the spices for pork or beef.

    6 cups cubed bread
    1 tablespoon parsley flakes
    3 cubes chicken bouillon, crumbled or 3 tablespoons
      chicken bouillon powder
    1/4 cup Dried Minced Onion (page 25)
    1/2 cup Dried Minced Celery (page 25)
    1 teaspoon thyme
    1 teaspoon pepper
    1/2 teaspoon sage
    1/2 teaspoon salt

1. Preheat oven to 350 degrees.

2. Spread bread on a cookie sheet and bake for 8 to 10 minutes, turning a few times to brown evenly. Cool.

3. In a large bowl, toss bread cubes with the rest of the seasonings until the cubes are evenly coated. Store in a tightly closed container in the pantry for 1 to 4 months, or mixture can be kept in the freezer for 12 months.

To Use:

    Combine 2 cups Stuffing Mix with 1/2 cup water and 2 tablespoons melted butter. Stir to toss thoroughly and stir again right before serving. You can rewarm the stuffing in a pan on top of the stove, in the microwave oven, or in a regular oven.

Variations:

    To change the flavor of the basic stuffing mix to accompany different meats, add any of the following spices and flavors to 2 cups of mix:

    *For **pork**, add:*
        1/2 teaspoon sage
        1/4 cup chopped apple
        1/4 cup chopped nuts
    *For **turkey**, add:*
        1/4 cup raisins
        1/4 cup chopped apple
        1/4 cup chopped cranberries
    *For **beef**, add:*
        1/4 cup mushrooms, canned or fresh
        2 tablespoons Worcestershire Sauce

Yield: 7 cups

Cost of Ingredients: $1.44
Comparable Purchased Product:
  Stove Top Stuffing, 6 ounces, $.89 ($8.30)
Savings: $6.86

Seasoned Shake-in-a-Bag Coating Mix

    *You can save money if you make your own shake-em-ups for chicken, chops, ribs, and even for shrimp. Save day-old bread for the crumbs or grind up **Crunchy Croutons** (page 21) or **Top-of-the-Stove Stuffing Mix** (page 93) to add to the crunch. If you do use crumbs that are already spiced, taste the mix after you've blended it with the flour and before you add new spices.*

Shake-in-a-Bag Mix for Chicken

1 cup Healthy Bread Crumbs (page 23)
1/2 cup flour
2 teaspoons onion powder or Dried Minced Onion
(page 25)
2 teaspoons Dried Minced Celery (page 25)
2 teaspoons Poultry Seasoning (page 5)
1 teaspoon garlic powder
1 teaspoon paprika
1/2 teaspoon cayenne
1/2 teaspoon salt
1/2 teaspoon pepper

1. Mix all ingredients and store in a tightly closed container. The mixture will keep on the pantry shelf for 1 to 4 months in dry weather. If the temperature is hot or humid, you can keep the mix in the freezer for 6 to 12 months.

To Use:

Keep a few brown paper bags handy to shake your chicken pieces in—it sounds more satisfying than shaking them in a plastic bag and your family will know you're there in the kitchen, working away.

Have ready:

1/2 cup milk
1 egg, beaten

1. Preheat oven to 375 degrees.

2. Gently beat the milk and egg together in a bowl deep enough for dipping.

3. Cut chicken into serving-size pieces; wash and pat dry with paper toweling. Fill a paper bag with 1 cup of the coating mix.

4. Dip each piece into the milk-egg mixture and then drop a piece of chicken into the bag and shake. Let pieces dry thoroughly before baking.

5. Place chicken in a shallow, lightly greased baking dish and bake for 1 hour or until very tender when you test it with a fork.

Sage Shake-in-a-Bag Mix for Pork Chops

You won't be picking these pork chops up and eating them like fried chicken—this coating is used for extra flavor.

> 1 cup Healthy Bread Crumbs (page 23)
> 1 cup flour
> 4 teaspoons Dried Minced Onion (page 25)
> 1/2 teaspoon salt
> 1/2 teaspoon pepper
> 1/2 teaspoon sage
> 4 pork chops
> 1 apple, sliced

1. Preheat oven to 400 degrees.

2. Mix the crumbs, flour, and seasonings in a shallow bowl. Press pork chops into the coating and pat the coating into the chops. Arrange coated chops in an oiled, shallow baking dish and alternate slices of apple between the chops. Bake covered for 40 minutes; uncover and bake for another 15 minutes.

Texas B-B-Q Shake-in-a-Bag Mix for Ribs

> 2 to 3 pounds ribs
> 2 teaspoons vegetable oil
> 1 cup Healthy Bread Crumbs (page 23)
> 1 cup flour
> 1/4 cup Dried Minced Onion (page 25)
> 2 tablespoons parsley
> 1 teaspoon salt
> 1/2 teaspoon Poultry Seasoning (page 5)
> 1/2 teaspoon garlic powder
> 1/2 teaspoon paprika
> 1/2 teaspoon pepper
> 1 teaspoon Tabasco
> 1 cup tomato juice

1. Preheat oven to 425 degrees.

2. Cut ribs into 2-inch pieces and brush them with a teaspoon or two of vegetable oil. Combine crumbs, flour, and spices in a paper bag; add ribs and shake them in the seasonings. Spread the seasoned ribs in a greased baking dish, and sprinkle the Tabasco sauce on top. Bake uncovered for 45 minutes.

3. Baste the ribs once or twice during the cooking process and cover the baking dish with aluminum foil if the ribs are browning too quickly. Make a sauce from the cooking liquid by adding the tomato juice right after you remove the ribs from the pan.

Spicy Shrimp Shake-in-a-Bag Mix

1 pound medium-size shrimp, peeled
1 cup Healthy Bread Crumbs (page 23)
1 cup flour
4 teaspoons onion powder
2 teaspoons Firehouse Hot Chili Powder (page 6)
1/2 teaspoon garlic powder
1/2 teaspoon basil
1/2 teaspoon thyme
1/2 teaspoon oregano
1/2 teaspoon paprika
1/4 teaspoon cayenne
4 tablespoons butter, melted
1 tablespoon Tangy Mustard (page 29)

1. Preheat oven to 375 degrees.

2. Drop the shrimp into a paper bag filled with the crumbs, flour, and spices. Shake the bag to coat the shrimp, and arrange shrimp in a shallow baking dish.

3. Combine the butter and mustard and dribble the mixture over the shrimp. Bake for 20 minutes.

Italian-flavored Shake-in-a-Bag Mix

1 pound chicken pieces, pork chops, or beef cubes
1 tablespoons olive oil (optional)
1 cup Healthy Bread Crumbs (page 23)
1/2 cup grated Romano or Parmesan cheese
1/4 cup chopped parsley
2 tablespoons oregano
1 tablespoon garlic powder
1 tablespoon
1 teaspoon salt
1/2 teaspoon pepper

1. Preheat oven to 400 degrees.

2. Coat meat with milk and egg, as described on page 95, or brush the meat with olive oil before coating. Combine crumbs, cheese, and spices in a paper bag, drop the meat into the bag. Arrange the meat in a shallow baking pan. Bake 1 hour.

Yield: 18 ounces

Cost of Ingredients: $.84
Comparable Purchased Product: Shake 'n Bake Seasoned Coating Mix for Chicken, 3.5 ounces, $1.39 ($7.14)
Savings: $6.30

Flavored Rice Mixes

These mixes are very simple to mix up and store. They are terrific to have on hand when you need a spicy or flavored addition to a meal, and by varying the liquids you cook with the rice, you can change the flavors of these mixes even more.

I have not used instant or minute rice in these mixes because I don't like the flavor or texture of precooked rice. If you decide you would rather use instant rice, simply substitute it for the uncooked rice and follow the instructions on the rice package for cooking time and amount of liquid you should use.

Onion Rice Mix

4 cups uncooked rice
1 envelope onion soup mix
1/4 cup Dried Minced Onion (page 25)
1 tablespoon parsley
1/2 teaspoon salt

Lemon Dill Rice Mix

4 cups uncooked rice
1/4 cup grated lemon peel
1/4 cup powdered chicken soup base

2 tablespoons dill
1 tablespoon chives
1/2 teaspoon salt

Vegetable Rice Mix

4 cups uncooked rice
1 envelope vegetable soup mix
2 tablespoons Dried Minced Onion (page 25)
2 tablespoons Dried Minced Celery (page 25)
2 tablespoons Dried Minced Pepper (page 25)
1 tablespoon parsley
1 teaspoon salt

Spanish Rice Mix

4 cups uncooked rice
1/2 cup Mexican Seasonings Mix (page 103)
1/2 cup Dried Corn (page 26)
2 tablespoons parsley
1 tablespoon basil

Creamy Herb Rice

4 cups uncooked rice
1/2 cup instant nonfat dry milk
1/4 cup Dried Minced Celery (page 25)
2 tablespoons parsley
2 tablespoons thyme
1 tablespoon marjoram

1. Combine the ingredients specified for each different mix.
Store each different mix in a glass jar or tightly closed
container on the pantry shelf for up to 4 months.

To Use:

*Mix 1 cup of any of the rice mixes with 2 cups of liquid,
either water, juice, broth, or a combination. A tablespoon of
butter or margarine is a nice addition. Place the rice, liquid,
and butter on high heat and bring to a rolling boil.
Immediately reduce the heat to very low, cover, and simmer the
rice for 10 to 15 minutes or until all the liquid is absorbed.*

To cook in a microwave oven, combine the rice, liquid, and butter in a 1 1/2-quart casserole, and heat, uncovered, on high or full power for 12 minutes. Stop and stir once or twice during the cooking. Cover the casserole and let rice stand for 5 minutes before serving.

Variations:
It's easy to make a meal in one pot if you sprinkle a cup of the rice mix around a roast or several meat or fish pieces before baking. Just remember to add 2 cups of liquid, cover, and bake for at least 30 minutes or until meat is tender.

Or, try serving the prepared rice combined with stir-fried vegetables, shrimp, or chopped ham.

When making Spanish Rice, it's a good idea to use tomato juice or sauce as the liquid.

Yield: 32 ounces

Cost of Ingredients: $1.88
Comparable Purchased Product: Lipton
Rice & Sauce, Herb & Butter, 4.5 ounces, $.95
($6.75)
Savings: $4.87

Chili Topping Mix

*A tablespoon of **Mexican Seasoning Mix** is the secret ingredient in this mix. Top chili with the mix, or try some of the **Variations**.*

2 cups crushed taco chips
2 tablespoons Firehouse Hot Chili Powder (page 6)
1 tablespoon Mexican Seasoning Mix (page 103)

1.   Combine all ingredients and store in a tightly covered container on your pantry shelf. Mix will keep for up to 4 months.

To Use:
Crumble 1/2 cup topping over chili. Do not mix in.

Variations:

   Add 1 tablespoon chopped raw onion to the topping, or 1 tablespoon chopped green chili peppers.

   Add 2 tablespoons shredded cheese to the topping and broil for 1 minute.

Yield: 17 ounces

Cost of Ingredients: $1.78
Comparable Purchased Product: Old El Paso Chili Seasoning Mix, 1.62 ounces, $.65 ($6.82)
Savings: $5.04

Bacon Onion Flavoring Mix

This topping saves noodles from a boring fate—try it in salads, too, or as a quick coating or toss for buttered vegetables, especially scalloped tomatoes.

   2 tablespoons bacon bits or imitation bacon bits
   2 cups crushed unsweetened wheat, corn, or rice breakfast cereal
   1 teaspoon Dried Minced Onion (page 25)

1. If you are using fresh bacon, cook 2 slices over low heat until crispy. Drain and crumble.

2. Combine all ingredients and store in a tightly covered container on your pantry shelf if you are using imitation bacon bits and in the refrigerator if you are using real bacon. Mix will keep for up to 4 months.

To Use:

   Combine 1/4 cup of the topping mix with 2 tablespoons melted butter. Crumble over casserole.

Ideas:

   Top plain buttered noodles with the mix for extra flavor and crunch. Toss gently right before serving. This topping is also good with noodles and ground beef.

Toss 1/4 cup of topping in with a plain salad before adding the salad dressing.

Yield: 17 ounces

Cost of Ingredients: $1.92
Comparable Purchased Product: Salad
   Chef Salad Topping, 2.5 ounces, $.69 ($4.69)
Savings: $2.77

Spaghetti Sauce-from-Scratch Mix

This handy little spice mix will transform the simple can of tomatoes into an acceptable spaghetti sauce. If you have more time, you could make up a nice batch of sauce from one of the recipes in Chapter 1. But when time is scarce and dinner is fast approaching, this mix plus some noodles will save the day.

1/4 cup celery salt
1 tablespoon dried basil
1 tablespoon oregano
1 tablespoon dried parsley
1 tablespoons garlic powder
1 tablespoon salt
1 tablespoon sugar
1 tablespoon pepper

1. Combine ingredients and store them in a tightly closed container. Shake before using. Mix will keep for up to 6 months on the pantry shelf.

To Use:
      Combine 1/4 cup of mix with one 8-ounce can tomatoes or tomato sauce. Simmer, covered, for 30 minutes.

Ideas:
      Sprinkle a tablespoon mix onto a bland salad to add texture and flavor, or combine the mix with 1 cup of sour cream for a quick chip dip.

Yield: 4 ounces

Cost of Ingredients: $.54
Comparable Purchased Product: Spatini
  Spaghetti Sauce Mix, 2 ounces, $.89 ($1.78)
Savings: $1.24

Mexican Seasonings Mix

Since my family loves Mexican flavors, this seasoning mix is used constantly at our house on ground beef, mixed with cheese for topping nacho chips, and combined with sour cream for a dip.

> **1 cup Dried Minced Onion (page 25)**
> **1/3 cup beef bouillon powder**
> **1/3 cup Firehouse Hot Chili powder (page 6)**
> **2 tablespoons ground cumin**
> **4 teaspoons crushed red pepper**
> **1 tablespoon oregano**
> **2 teaspoons garlic powder**

1. Combine all ingredients and store in a cool, dry pantry for up to 4 months.

Ideas:
Add 1 tablespoon to recipes calling for a Mexican flavor, or sprinkle liberally on top of foods you want to spice: 1 tablespoon mixed with chopped tomatoes and green peppers makes a tasty dip or filling for tacos.
Add 1 tablespoon to shredded cheese before melting for another dip. Serve with sour cream.

Yield: 16.3 ounces

Cost of Ingredients: $4.42
Comparable Purchased Product:
  McCormick Taco Seasoning, 1.25 ounces, $.51
  ($6.65)
Savings: $2.23

Ooh-la-la Butter

This butter is rich, decadent, and makes a wonderful spread when you feel you need pampering. You can spread this on muffins or bread slices and then broil for a minute or two for a hot, bubbly treat.

> 1/2 cup butter or Country Butter (page 20)
> 1/2 cup honey
> 1/4 cup sugar
> 1/4 cup brown sugar, lightly pressed
> 1 teaspoon cinnamon
> 1 teaspoon vanilla or Vanilla Bean Extract (page 12)
> 1 tablespoon heavy cream

1. Combine ingredients in a food processor or with an electric mixer and whip until the butter is light and fluffy.

2. Store in a tightly closed container for 1 to 2 months in the refrigerator.

Sweet Butters

When the urge for something sweet strikes and you want your spread to be a pretty pastel color in addition to tasting wonderful, try any of the following additions to the basic spread.

> 1/2 cup strawberries or other berries
> 1/2 cup chopped dates, raisins, or other dried fruit
> 1/4 cup orange juice concentrate
> 2 tablespoons orange marmalade
> 1/3 cup whole-berry cranberry sauce

1. Mix and store as for Ooh-la-la Butter.

Yield: 8 ounces

Cost of Ingredients: $1.09
Comparable Purchased Product: Walker's
  Honey Whip, 12 ounces, $1.89 ($1.20)
Savings: $.11

Herb and Flavored Butters

Once you've made up a batch of this mix, store it in the freezer and use it for rice and bread spreads, as well as for vegetable and fish dishes. Since the butter is intended to flavor the food to which it is added, it's a good idea to use the freshest herbs you can find. If you don't have any fresh herbs on hand and would like to use dried herbs or spices, reduce the tablespoon to a teaspoon, taste, and adjust the seasoning to suit. You can also use Country Butter, page 20, to replace the butter in the recipe.

See Ideas for individual serving suggestions. In addition, you can make your own international and foreign-flavored vegetable dishes with these butters. The Variations listed with this recipe will get you started, but you should have your own family favorites before long.

French Herb Butter

1 cup butter, softened
1/4 cup chopped parsley
1 teaspoon lemon juice
1 tablespoon dill
1 tablespoon chopped tarragon
1 teaspoon freshly ground pepper
1/2 teaspoon salt

1. Cream butter in a blender, mixer, or food processor and add each of the ingredients separately, scraping down the bowl and blending well after each addition.

2. There are several ways to save and store the butter. Spread the mixture into a plastic compartmentalized ice cube tray, freeze for several hours, and then transfer the cubes to a plastic bag. Plastic egg cartons also work quite nicely—simply pop the butter out of the used cartons and discard once it is frozen and store in a plastic bag. Or line an 8-inch-square cake pan with wax paper or plastic wrap and spread the butter in an inch-thick layer. Freeze for several hours, cut into inch-size cubes while still frozen, and store in a plastic bag, or place the butter on a sheet of wax paper and roll it into a log, freeze for one hour, and then cut the log into slices. Separate the slices with plastic wrap and return them to the freezer in a plastic bag.

To Use:
>   Boil or steam vegetables as usual and drain. About 10 minutes before serving, toss one of the herbed butter cubes in with the hot vegetables.
>   When broiling fish, place one or more cubes of the butter on the broiling pan and put it under the broiler for 1 minute. Then place the fish on top of the butter mixture, basting well, before broiling.
>   If you are grilling fish, use a strong grade of aluminum foil and wrap 1 cube of the butter mixture in with the fish. Place the package on the grill and cook for 10 to 20 minutes, depending on the size of the fish.

Italian-flavored Butter

      1 cup butter, softened
      1 tablespoon olive oil
      2 cloves garlic, pressed
      1 tablespoon oregano
      1 tablespoon basil
      1 teaspoon freshly ground black pepper
      1/2 teaspoon salt

1. Combine, store, and use as for **French Herb Butter**, page 105, on green beans, fresh boiled spinach, with freshly chopped and steamed tomatoes, onions, and peppers, and with zucchini.

Mexican-flavored Butter

      1 cup butter, softened
      1 tablespoon red pepper sauce
      1 tablespoon Firehouse Hot Chili powder (page 6)
      1 tablespoon cumin

1. Combine, store, and use as for **French Herb Butter**, page 105, on chopped red tomatoes and onions, green beans, chopped lettuce and steamed cabbage, or with corn and chopped red peppers.

Chinese-flavored Butter

      1 cup butter, softened

2 tablespoons soy sauce
1 tablespoon ground ginger
1 tablespoon chopped scallions
1 teaspoon sugar

1. Combine, store, and use as for **French Herb Butter**, page 105, on stir-fried snow peas, water chestnuts, bamboo shoots, carrot slivers, broccoli, cauliflower, beans, and asparagus.

French-flavored Butter

1 cup butter, softened
2 tablespoons white wine
2 tablespoons chopped scallions
2 cloves garlic, pressed
1 teaspoon thyme

1. Combine, store, and use as for **French Herb Butter**, page 105, on freshly steamed baby peas, carrots, new potatoes, asparagus, and cauliflower.

Ideas:

Top your herbed vegetables with grated cheese or 2 tablespoons of **Healthy Bread Crumbs**, page 23. Place under the broiler for 1 minute and serve.

Or whip any of these butters with 1/2 cup cottage cheese and serve it with crackers as a party spread.

Herb butters are an excellent addition to scrambled eggs: mix 1 teaspoon in just before the eggs are set.

Use herb butter in place of plain butter to make a regular white sauce more interesting.

A generous chunk of herb butter can be tucked inside chicken breasts or rolled-up fish fillets before broiling.

Yield: 8 ounces; enough for 8 servings

Cost of Ingredients: $1.32
Comparable Purchased Product: Yellow
    Brick Toad Herb Butter, 3 ounces, $.60 ($1.60)
Savings: $.28

Garlic Butter

This spread is pungent, but convenient. Make sure you keep the container you store it in tightly closed or even the baking soda in your refrigerator will smell like an Italian deli.

1 cup butter, softened
6 cloves garlic, chopped
2 tablespoons finely minced parsley
2 tablespoons chopped onions or scallions
1/2 teaspoon freshly ground black pepper

1. Combine all ingredients, either in the blender, food processor, or by hand, and blend thoroughly.

2. Store in a tightly closed container in the refrigerator for up to 3 months, or freeze for 1 year.

Hint:
   For ease of use, freeze this butter in tiny, one-serving-size portions. A plastic ice cube tray is ideal, or you might drop the mixture, by spoonfuls, onto a baking sheet. Cover with plastic wrap and freeze. After the butter is frozen solid, remove it from its container or pop the mounds off the cookie sheet and store them in a plastic bag.

Ideas:
   *Freshly made or refrigerated, this butter is an ideal spread for Italian bread (see **Savory Buttered Bread Sticks**, page 137) or spread on pita bread.*
   Use a single serving to spruce up cooked vegetables, to flavor cooked meats (especially just before broiling), and for tossing with freshly cooked pasta.

Yield: 8 ounces

Cost of Ingredients: $1.79
Comparable Purchased Product: Lawry's
   Garlic Spread, 4 ounces, $1.25 ($2.50)
Savings: $.71

Chapter 3

Snacks and Sweets

Cravings are satisfied in this chapter without spending a fortune. Included here are things to eat while watching old movies on TV, healthy treats to let children snack on, quick things to grab in place of breakfast, and trail mixes and goodies to pack for the road.

Crunchy Snack Crackers
  Honey Graham Crackers
  Herby Vegetable Crackers
Candy Apples
Caramel Corn
Popcorn Nut Munchy Mixture
Polka-dot Popcorn Balls
Homemade "Cracker Jacks"
Healthy Seed Treats
Silly Saturday Cereal
Granola Rolls
Fruit Nut Balls
Happy Trails Mix
Homemade Yogurt
Toaster Tarts
Old-time Doughnuts
Cream-filled Chocolate Cookies
Quick Coffee Cake
Quick Biscuit Shortcake
Fruit Leathers
Beef Jerky
Cheese Thins
Soft Philly Pretzels
Potato Chips
Bagel Chips
Quick Pizza
Savory Buttered Bread Sticks
Fruity Italian Ices
Quickie Ice Cream
Instant Ice Cream
Honey Gelato

Frozen Fruiti Yogurt
Plain and Fancy Fruiti Pops
Fruit 'n' Cream Pops
Frosted Banana Pops
Peanut Butter Bananas
Frozen Pudding Pops

Crunchy Snack Crackers

These crackers are a quite a bit richer than the kind you can buy, but they are very easy to make and a plastic bag of crackers will freeze nicely for several months.

A basket of these crackers can accompany a pot of your own **Herb Tea**, *page 174, as a welcome gift. Finish by adding* **Sweet Butter**, *page 109, and a sweet note to the basket or to a sick tray, and you have a cheery treat.*

Honey Graham Crackers

2 cups flour
1/2 cup whole wheat or graham flour
1/2 cup brown sugar, packed
1/2 teaspoon cinnamon
1 teaspoon baking soda
1/2 cup shortening
1/2 cup honey
1 tablespoon molasses
1/4 cup vegetable oil
3 tablespoons cold water
1 teaspoon salt

1. Preheat oven to 425 degrees.

2. Combine all ingredients in a medium-size bowl by first blending the dry ingredients and then adding the liquids. Stir to blend well and then stir for an additional 3 minutes.

3. Place half the dough on an ungreased cookie sheet and flatten with a rolling pin into a square, dusting dough with flour if necessary to keep it from sticking to the rolling pin. Leave the dough in place on the cookie sheet for baking. Repeat this process on another cookie sheet with the rest of the dough.

4. Score the dough with a knife into 2-inch squares and prick all over with a fork.

5. Bake for 10 minutes or until brown. While still warm, cut crackers apart, but let crackers finish cooling on the sheet. Store in an airtight container for 4 to 6 weeks.

Herby Vegetable Crackers

2 cups flour
2 teaspoons mixed herbs: parsley, chives, oregano,
    savory, thyme, tarragon
1/4 cup Dried Celery (page 25)
1/4 cup Dried Onion (page 25)
1/4 cup sugar
1 teaspoon salt
1/2 teaspoon baking soda
1/4 cup shortening
1 tablespoon oil
3/4 cup warm water

1. Combine all ingredients except the water in a large bowl, stirring the dry ingredients together first. Slowly add the water, stirring well.

2. Continue to stir until well blended and then add the water, stirring until a smooth dough forms. Divide the dough in half, cover, and let it stand at room temperature for 10 minutes.

3. Preheat oven to 400 degrees.

4. Place half the dough on a lightly oiled baking sheet, flatten with a rolling pin, and roll dough out to the edges of the pan. Use extra flour if needed on the pin and the rolling surface to keep dough from sticking.

5. Cut dough into 1-inch squares and prick dough all over with a fork. Bake for 10 minutes until crisp but not brown; remove to racks to cool. Repeat with remaining dough.

Yield: 5 dozen (32 ounces)

Cost of Ingredients: $1.26
Comparable Purchased Product: New Morning Whole Wheat Honey Grahams, 16 ounces, $1.71 ($3.42)
Savings: $2.18

Candy Apples

Because the syrup for these apples must harden to a clear, crisp candy, a candy thermometer is necessary for this recipe. Have all your ingredients and materials assembled before you begin so that you can work quickly once the syrup is ready.

6 wooden or Popsicle sticks, sharpened
6 large apples
3 cups sugar
1 cup light corn syrup
1 1/2 cups water
1 cinnamon stick
Red food coloring

1.   Insert sticks into the apples and grease a cookie sheet with butter to hold the apples as they harden.

2. Combine sugar, corn syrup, water, and cinnamon in a saucepan and bring to a boil, stirring to dissolve sugar.

3. Continue to cook over medium heat, stirring, until the mixture reaches a temperature of 290 degrees on the candy thermometer. Remove from heat and discard cinnamon stick; stir in the red food coloring.

4. Dip and swirl the apples in the syrup and place on the cookie sheet to harden. When hard, wrap in plastic wrap and store apples in the refrigerator. Apples will keep well for 2 weeks.

Variation:
        Sprinkle flaked coconut on the dipped apples before the candy hardens for a festive, snowy effect.

Yield: 6 apples

Cost of Ingredients: $3.02
Comparable Purchased Product: Country
     Farm Candy Apples, $.75 each ($4.50)
Savings: $1.48

Caramel Corn

This treat is an easy one for kids to help you make. If you decide to make this goodie at holiday time or for a child's party, you can wrap individual balls of the corn in plastic wrap and tie with a pretty bow to give away as favors or tree ornaments.

1 cup brown sugar, lightly packed
1/2 cup butter or margarine
1/4 cup light corn syrup
1/2 teaspoon salt
1/2 teaspoon baking soda
15 cups popped corn

1. Preheat the oven to 200 degrees.

2. Mix the sugar, butter, syrup, and salt in a pan and cook over medium heat until the butter is thoroughly melted and bubbles form around the edge. Take the pan off the heat and stir in the baking soda.

3. Divide the popcorn into 2 large baking pans and pour half the sugar mixture over each, stirring the popcorn as you pour.

4. Bake for 1 hour, stirring every 15 minutes. Cool and store in an airtight container, or in individual servings as described. Mixture will keep well for about 2 weeks.

Variation:
       You can add 1 cup of dry roasted peanuts to the mix before baking, or 1 cup of dried fruit, just after you take the corn from the oven.

Yield: 15 cups

Cost of Ingredients: $1.37 ($1.66 with peanuts)
Comparable Purchased Product: Popcorn
   Sensations Caramel Peanut Popcorn, 10 ounces,
   $2.27 ($27.24)
Savings: $25.57

Popcorn Nut Munchy Mixture

*A big bowl of this popcorn is a wonderful accompaniment to
an old movie on television. If you want the mixture to be on the
sweet side, use plain, dry-roasted peanuts and sweet butter. If
you want a bit of a salty tang to the mixture, use salted butter
and salted peanuts.*

> **12 cups popped corn**
> **1 1/2 cups peanuts**
> **1/2 cup honey**
> **1/2 cup butter**

1. Preheat oven to 300 degrees.

2. Mix popcorn and nuts together in a very big bowl. Warm
honey and butter together over low heat until the butter is
melted. Pour the honey-butter mixture over the popcorn-nut
mixture. Toss to mix well.

3. Spread mixture in a large baking pan and bake for 20
minutes, stirring once or twice during baking. Cool and break
into chunks before serving or storing in an airtight container.
Mixture will keep for 2 weeks on the pantry shelf.

Variation:
        *A mixture of cashews, walnuts, and other nuts of your
choice added to the above recipe will will also taste delicious.*

Yield: 12 cups

Cost of Ingredients: $2.13
Comparable Purchased Product: Franklin
    Crunch & Munch, 13.3 ounces, $.85 ($6.13)
Savings: $4.00

Cheap Trick . . . .

*A low-calorie version of this munchy mixture can be made by
popping your corn, without oil, in a microwave oven. Pour 1/2
cup unpopped kernals into a paper bag, sprinkle in a
tablespoon of Salt Substitute, page 3, and a dash of water.*

Polka-dot Popcorn Balls

Here is another snack recipe that you can use several ways—as a snack, of course, as a holiday trim for your tree, and as a party favor for children. A candy thermometer is handy for cooking the syrup, but you can test it the old-fashioned way, as described in Step 2.

1 cup sugar
1/2 cup light corn syrup
1/3 cup water
1/4 cup butter or margarine
1/2 teaspoon salt
1 teaspoon Vanilla Bean Extract (page 12)
16 cups popped corn
1 cup gumdrops, jelly beans, or candied cherries

1. Combine sugar, corn syrup, water, butter, and salt in a saucepan and cook over medium heat, stirring until sugar is dissolved.

2. Continue to cook without stirring until a candy thermometer inserted in the mixture reads 254 degrees. If you don't have a candy thermometer, the mixture is ready when it forms a hard ball when dropped into a cup of cold water. Remove syrup from heat and add vanilla.

3. Divide popcorn into two large baking pans and pour half of the syrup mixture into each pan. Stir to coat thoroughly.

4. Grease your hands with butter or cooking oil and form popcorn into 4-inch balls while the mixture is still warm. Press gumdrops or other colorful candy firmly onto the surface of the ball. Wrap in clear plastic and tie with a bright ribbon. Balls will keep for 2 to 4 weeks.

Yield: 10 balls

Cost of Ingredients: $1.55
Comparable Purchased Product: Heller Farm Popcorn Balls, $.64 each ($6.40)
Savings: $4.85

Homemade "Cracker Jacks"

A candy thermometer is handy to have for this recipe to test the temperature of the syrup that binds the popcorn and nuts together.

 4 cups popped corn
 1 cup shelled peanuts
 1/2 cup molasses
 1/4 cup sugar

1. Mix popcorn and peanuts together in a large bowl or pan.

2. Cook molasses and sugar together until the mixture reaches a temperature of 235 degrees on a candy thermometer. If you don't have a thermometer, test the syrup by letting some drop from a spoon into a cup of cold water. The syrup is done when it forms a thread as it drops into the water.

3. Pour hot syrup mixture over the popcorn-nut mixture and stir to coat evenly. Cool and break into chunks with a wooden spoon. Stored in an airtight container, mixture will keep well for 4 to 6 weeks.

Yield: 40 ounces

Cost of Ingredients: $1.24
Comparable Purchased Product: Cracker
   Jacks, 3 ounces, $.89 ($11.86)
Savings: $10.62

Healthy Seed Treats

When you carve your Halloween pumpkin, save all the seeds you scoop out—they make delicious treats that are good for you as well as tasty.

 1/2 cup salt
 4 cups water
 2 cups sunflower, pumpkin, melon, or squash seeds,
    cleaned

1. Make a mixture of the salt and water and soak the seeds in the mixture for 12 hours.

2. Preheat oven to 200 degrees.

3. Dry the seeds in paper toweling and place them on an oiled cookie sheet in a single layer. Cook for 30 minutes, stirring the seeds often during the cooking time. Cool and store in an airtight container. Seeds will keep well for 4 to 6 weeks.

Variation:
        You can salt or season the seeds, depending on your tastes, with **Sesame Seasoning Salt**, *page 4, or another combination of your favorite spices.*

Yield: 16 ounces

Cost of Ingredients: $.10
Comparable Purchased Product: Princeton Health Foods Roasted Pumpkin Seeds, 1 pound, $2.29
Savings: $2.19

Silly Saturday Cereal

Make up a batch of this cereal for one of those days when you have a roomful of children and a morning full of cartoons. The cereal is best eaten right away—serve with cold milk and sliced fresh fruit. Extra cereal can be stored in an airtight container for another time or eaten as a snack.

> **1/2 cup Rainbow Drink Mix (page 173)**
> **2 tablespoons honey, warmed**
> **2 cups plain wheat, corn, or rice cereal**
> **1/2 cup chopped dried fruit**
> **1/2 cup miniature marshmallow bits**

1. Combine the Rainbow Milk Mix with the warmed honey. Pour over the cereal and toss until cereal is completely covered. Stir in the fruit and marshmallows. Serve at once.

Yield: 16 ounces

Cost of Ingredients: $2.31
Comparable Purchased Product: General
  Mills Lucky Charms, 14 ounces, $2.19 ($2.50)
Savings: $.19

Granola Rolls

*One of my kids' favorite treats for morning and
lunchtime snacks has always been granola candies—bars,
rolls, chocolate chip, peanut butter, raisin-nut-crunch
versions—they love them all.*

*Here are recipes for these, and other varieties, all using
your own lower-cost homemade granola. If you make these
rolls up in quantity, you can refrigerate the extra ones, but
don't try to freeze them or they will become soggy.*

> **2 1/2 cups Granny's Granola (page 15)**
> **1/2 cup confectioner's sugar**
> **1/2 cup light corn syrup**

1. Mix ingredients together in a large bowl. When granola is
well moistened, shape the mixture into rolls, each about 1 inch
in diameter.

2. Transfer rolls to a baking sheet covered with wax paper or
plastic wrap and refrigerate for 1 hour. Slice rolls into
individual-size pieces when firm and store, wrapped in
plastic, in the refrigerator for 2 to 3 weeks.

Variations:

  *For a different flavor, add 1 cup of chocolate chips,
press mixture into a 9-inch-square cake pan, and cut into
squares when firm.*

  *Or add 1 cup peanut butter to the mixture. Other
additions might be 1 cup raisins, 1 cup nuts, or 1 cup peanut
butter chips.*

  *Try adding 1/2 cup honey and 1 teaspoon **Vanilla Bean
Extract**, page 12, to the granola instead of confectioner's sugar.*

Yield: 25 ounces

Cost of Ingredients: $3.12
Comparable Purchased Product: Quaker
  Chewy Granola, 8 ounces, $2.09 ($6.53)
Savings: $3.41

Fruit Nut Balls

Let a child have a hand, literally, with this recipe. It's fun to mix everything up, and the children can get a whole new appreciation of "candy" if they make up some of their own.

> 2/3 cup Sweetened Condensed Milk (page 17)
> 2 teaspoons Vanilla Bean Extract (page 12)
> 1/4 cup finely chopped nuts
> 1/3 cup shredded unsweetened coconut
> 1/3 cup raisins
> 1/2 cup dried fruit
> 1/2 cup instant-style rolled oats

1. Mix all ingredients together and let the mixture sit for 30 minutes before forming into balls.

2. Preheat oven to 325 degrees.

3. Butter your hands and shape the mixture into small balls. Place on a well-greased cookie sheet and bake for 12 to 15 minutes.

4. Remove from pan before candy is completely cool and place the balls on a wire rack. Cool completely before storing in a tightly closed container. The candy will keep for 2 to 4 weeks.

Yield: 18 ounces

Cost of Ingredients: $2.10
Comparable Purchased Product: Quaker
  Chewy Granola Rolls, 8 ounces, $2.09 ($4.70)
Savings: $2.60

Happy Trails Mix

*Store individual servings of this mixture in plastic sandwich bags and pack one with your child's lunch, or in a camper's backpack for a healthy, high-energy alternative to a candy bar. See **Healthy Seed Treats**, page 117, for how to prepare your own seeds for this mixture.*

> 1 cup sunflower seeds
> 1 cup almonds
> 1 cup hazelnuts
> 1 cup raisins
> 1/2 cup shredded unsweetened coconut
> 2 cups various dried fruits: bananas, pineapple,
>   apricots, apples

1. Mix all ingredients and store the mixture in an airtight container. Make up individual snack packs in plastic bags and store the individual packs in the airtight container as well. The snack mix will keep for 2 to 4 months on the pantry shelf.

Yield: 6 cups (48 ounces)

Cost of Ingredients: $4.30
Comparable Purchased Product: Second Nature Health Trails Mix, 1 ounce, $.99 ($47.52)
Savings: $43.22

Homemade Yogurt

To make yogurt, you must already have a bit of yogurt on hand. You will need yogurt with an active culture—Dannon is one of the best—but if you read the labels carefully, you're sure to find others. Then, after you've made your first batch, keep a small amount of your homemade yogurt plain and unflavored and ready to start the next batch.

A candy or kitchen thermometer is necessary for this recipe, at least the first time around, because yogurt making depends on bringing the milk to a favorable temperature for growing the yogurt culture. If you have a yogurt maker, by all means enjoy using it, but it isn't essential to yogurt making. Since there are several easy ways to keep the milk at the right temperature throughout the process, I've described some techniques here.

4 cups milk, whole or low fat
1 cup instant nonfat dry milk
1/2 cup plain yogurt

1. Heat regular milk to 180 degrees. Check temperature with a kitchen thermometer, and when the milk has reached the right temperature, remove it from the heat and stir in the dry milk.

2. Cool milk to between 105 and 110 degrees and stir in the plain yogurt. Pour the mixture into sterilized glass jars.

3. Incubate yogurt for 4 to 8 hours by trying one of the following several methods. Depending on the method you use, you will have to check a few times during the incubation period to see if the yogurt mixture has reached the consistency of custard. When it has, the yogurt is ready to refrigerate. Yogurt will keep for 2 to 4 weeks in the refrigerator.

Hints:
        To incubate yogurt, you can try one of the following methods, all of which keep the culture at the proper 100-degree temperature:
        Pour the yogurt into the containers that come with your commercial yogurt maker and follow the manufacturer's instructions.
        Place the jars and a thermometer in an insulated picnic cooler, cover carefully with a towel, and close the cooler. Check only once or twice, and add a jar of warm water if the temperature goes down.
        Place the jars, covered with a towel, in a 100-degree oven.
        Place the jars, covered, on a rack in an electric frying pan. Pour in an inch or two of warm water, set the thermostat on the pan to 100 degrees, and cover pan.

To Use:
        Yogurt can be eaten plain, if you have acquired a taste for it, and it is delicious as a substitute for sour cream.

*To flavor yogurt, simply add a teaspoon of honey or a tablespoon of your own **Freezer Fruit Preserves**, page 50. You can add cinnamon, **Vanilla Sugar**, page 8, and any other spices and flavors that suit your fancy.*

*You can also make **Frozen Fruiti Yogurt**, page 141.*

Yield: 32 ounces

Cost of Ingredients: $1.18
Comparable Purchased Product: Dannon Yogurt with fruit, 8 ounces, $.67 ($2.68)
Savings: $1.50

Toaster Tarts

Make these tarts in any of the many flavors that are available to tempt your children for breakfast—strawberry, blueberry, chocolate, peanut butter and jelly, or apple.

3/4 **cup vegetable shortening**
3/4 **cup sugar**
3 **eggs**
3 3/4 **cups flour**
3 **teaspoons baking powder**
1/2 **cup strawberry preserves or Freezer Fruit Preserves (page 50)**
1 **egg yolk beaten with 2 tablespoons light cream**

Frosting

1/2 **cup confectioner's sugar**
1/2 **teaspoon Vanilla Bean Extract (page 12)**
2 **tablespoons milk**

1. Preheat oven to 350 degrees.

2. In an electric mixer or a food processor, cream shortening and sugar together and then beat in the eggs, one at a time.

3. Sift together flour and baking powder and stir into shortening mixture to make a soft dough. Chill for 1 hour.

4. Turn dough out onto a floured surface and roll out 12 rectangles, each 8 by 12 inches.

5. Spread about a tablespoon of preserves over half of each rectangle, staying well within the edge of the pastry. Fold pastry dough over the preserves and trim the edges with a pastry wheel or crimp with a fork to close.

6. Place tarts on a greased cookie sheet and brush with the egg yolk-cream mixture. Bake for 20 minutes. Cool.

7. Stir the vanilla and milk into the confectioner's sugar until you have a thin frosting. Dribble a tablespoon onto the top of each tart or brush frosting on with a pastry brush.

8. Wrap tarts with aluminum foil and store in the refrigerator. They will keep for about 7 days. Tarts can also be frozen for 3 to 4 months.

To Use:

Unwrap a tart and place it in the toaster or toaster oven for 2 minutes if refrigerated and 4 minutes if frozen. Or, unwrap a tart and cook it in the microwave for 1 minute on high if it has been refrigerated and 2 minutes on high if it has been frozen.

Be careful of the frosting, which gets extremely hot and somewhat runny when it is cooked.

Variations:

Try adding coconut and chopped nuts to the filling, and brushing the frosting with cinnamon.

Or, add raisins, dates, and chopped nuts to a sliced apple filling.

*For a chocolate tart, try adding 1 tablespoon of **Basic Chocolate Sauce**, page 45, to the tart and topping it with frosting flavored with 1/4 teaspoon orange extract.*

Yield: 12 toaster tarts

Cost of Ingredients: $2.10
Comparable Purchased Product: Kellogg's
    Pop Tarts, 11 ounces, $1.09 (3.27)
Savings: $1.17

Old-time Doughnuts

*My mother always remembers eating these doughnuts,
brushed with confectioner's sugar, at Christmas. You can
make up some of your own memories with these doughnuts on a
cold, blowy winter night. Serve them while they are still toasty
warm, with hot mulled cider or hot chocolate.*

2 eggs
1 cup sugar
2 tablespoons vegetable shortening
3/4 cup buttermilk
3 1/2 cups sifted flour
2 teaspoons baking powder
1 teaspoon baking soda
1 teaspoon cinnamon
1/2 teaspoon salt
1/2 teaspoon nutmeg
Cooking oil

Coating

1/2 cup Cinnamon Sugar (page 10)
1/2 cup confectioner's sugar or Vanilla Sugar (page 8)

1. Use a food processor or an electric beater to beat eggs until
they are light and fluffy. Beat in sugar and shortening. Stir in
the buttermilk.

2. Sift together the flour, baking powder, baking soda, salt, and
spices. Stir into egg mixture until well combined.

3. Turn dough out onto a floured surface and knead gently four
or five times. Roll dough out to 1/3-inch thickness. Let dough
rest for 30 minutes.

4. Cut out doughnut shapes with a doughnut cutter, or flour and
use the rim of two glasses: a drinking glass for the doughnut
and a shot glass for the holes.

5. Pour cooking oil into an electric skillet or pan to a depth of 2
inches and heat the oil to 375 degrees.

6. Fry doughnuts and holes until brown on one side; carefully turn and fry on the other side. Remove doughnuts and place them on several thicknesses of paper toweling or clean brown paper bags to drain.

7. Pour the cinnamon-sugar and the confectioner's sugar into two separate brown lunch bags and drop doughnuts into one or the other while still warm. Shake and serve.

Hint:
    If you want to substitute plain milk for the buttermilk, increase the baking powder to 4 teaspoons and omit the baking soda.

Yield: Two dozen 3-inch doughnuts

Cost of Ingredients: $1.56
Comparable Purchased Product: Hostess
    Old Fashioned Donuts, 9 ounces, $1.59 ($3.18)
Savings: $1.62

Cream-filled Chocolate Cookies

A cookie like this can cause a sort of obsessive behavior in certain people—they like to take it apart, eat the filling, and then dunk the rest of the cookie in milk. If you know any of those kind of people, you might make a double batch of this cookie, or try adding a double dollop of filling. You can also add a teaspoon of jelly or a drop of mint extract to the filling.

For more authentic-looking cookies, it's a nice idea to impress a fancy design in the top layer of cookie with a butter mold or clean rubber stamp just before baking.

      3/4 cup vegetable shortening
      1/2 cup butter
      2 cups sugar
      1 egg
      2 1/2 cups flour
      1/2 cup unsweetened cocoa

Filling

2 cups confectioner's sugar or Powdered Vanilla
   Sugar (page 8)
1/2 cup sweet butter
2 tablespoons heavy cream
2 tablespoons Vanilla Bean Extract (page 12)

1. Using a food processor or an electric mixer, cream together
the shortening and the butter. Gradually beat in the sugar and
the egg, beating well after each addition, until the mixture is
light and lemon-colored.

2. Sift flour and cocoa together and add to creamed mixture,
blending well.

3. Shape dough into several rolls, each about 1 inch in
diameter. Wrap the rolls in wax paper and refrigerate for
several hours or overnight.

4. Preheat oven to 375 degrees.

5. Unwrap and cut rolls of cookie dough into 1/8-inc- thick
slices. Place on ungreased cookie sheet and bake for 5 to 8
minutes. Cool before adding filling.

6. To make filling, cream confectioner's sugar and butter
together; add cream and vanilla.

7. Create a cookie "sandwich" with two cookies and a generous
dab of filling. Cookies will keep for up to 2 weeks in a cookie
jar and for 4 to 5 months in the freezer.

Yield: 36 ounces

Cost of Ingredients: $4.38
Comparable Purchased Product: Nabisco
   Oreo Cookies, 16 ounces, $2.19 ($4.92)
Savings: $.54

Quick Coffee Cake

Sometimes the urge for something sweet comes over us as we're watching television, and this coffee cake takes no time to whip together. It can also be made even sweeter, depending on the amount of topping you crumble on.

2 cups Biscuit Baking Mix (page 65)
1/2 cup sugar
1 egg
2/3 cup milk
1 teaspoon Vanilla Bean Extract (page 12)

Topping

1/2 cup Biscuit Baking Mix (page 65)
1/2 cup brown sugar, lightly packed
1 teaspoon cinnamon
2 tablespoons butter, softened

1.   Preheat oven to 350 degrees.

2. Combine ingredients for the coffee cake and beat well for 3 minutes with a wire whisk, an electric beater, or in a food processor.

3.   Pour into a well-greased 9-inch-square cake pan. Combine the ingredients for the topping and crumble them on top of the cake batter.

4. Bake for 20 to 25 minutes or until a knife inserted in the middle comes out clean.

Yield: 1 cake

Cost of Ingredients: $1.29
Comparable Purchased Product:
    Entenmanns's Coffee Cake, 16 ounces, $2.29
Savings: $1.00

Quick Biscuit Shortcake

The world seems to be evenly divided between those who like a biscuit-type of shortcake and those who prefer a pound-cake type. Try this one, making sure you don't overcook it, before you commit yourself to the pound-cake version.

2 1/3 cups Biscuit Baking Mix (page 65)
1/2 cup milk
3 tablespoons butter, melted
1/4 cup sugar

1. Preheat oven to 400 degrees.

2. Mix all ingredients, stirring until a soft dough is formed. Turn out onto a surface dusted with the baking mix or plain flour and knead gently for 30 seconds.

3. Roll dough 1/2 inch thick and cut into squares or 3-inch rounds.

4. Bake on an ungreased cookie sheet for 10 minutes, or until golden brown.

To Use:
Split shortcakes, spoon berries or jam between halves and over the top and finish off with sweetened heavy cream, whipped if you'd like.

Yield: 6 shortcakes

Cost of Ingredients: $.74
Comparable Purchased Product: Hostess Dessert Cups, 3 ounces, $.79
Savings: $.05

Cheap Trick . . . . ✁ . . . .

Don't despair if your shortcake falls apart—simply break it up, place the pieces in a bowl with a generous amount of the berries and whipped cream, and call it a trifle. It will still taste fine.

Fruit Leathers

This delicious way to preserve, store, and eat fruit has just recently come back into fashion. Fruit leathers are fun to pull at and to eat, and they are full of flavor. Their light weight and long chewability makes them ideal to pack for hiking and for school lunches. To get the best flavors, it's a good idea to use fruit when it is at a very ripe stage.

2 cups fruit: fresh, frozen, cooked, or canned
1/2 cup sugar or honey

1. Pour the fruit and sweetening into a blender container and puree until you have a very fine pulp.

2. Line a cookie sheet with plastic wrap and tape the edges securely with masking tape. Pour the puree over the plastic wrap, spreading it with a spatula so that it is a uniform thickness of about 1/8 inch.

3. Dry the puree by one of the following methods until the puree is dry on the surface, but still pliable.

4. Remove the leather from the pan, leaving the plastic wrap as a backing. Cut into narrow strips and roll up. Store rolls in an airtight container for up to 8 weeks.

Hints:
        There are several methods for drying food: in the sun, in the oven, with a commercial dryer, or with a convection oven. You can even try using your microwave, but each model has different controls and different wattages, so the results are not entirely predictable.
        To dry in the sun, make sure you've chosen a day with plenty of sun and low humidity. You will need 2 to 3 days of full sun, and you must bring your tray in at night. Cover the tray with cheesecloth to keep insects away from the fruit. When the fruit is dry, place it in a 120-degree oven for 1 hour before cooling and storing.
        If you decide to use a conventional oven, set the temperature at 150 degrees and dry the fruit for between 6 to 12 hours, depending on the type of fruit. To be safe, leave the oven door ajar to check on the fruit and rotate the tray every 2 hours.

If you are using a commercial dehydrator, follow the manufacturer's instructions or dry at 120 degrees for 6 to 8 hours.

If you are using a convection oven, reduce the drying time by 3 to 5 hours. The fruit tray will not have to be rotated either with this method or in the dehydrator because there is ample air circulation.

Variations:

You can add a tablespoon of lemon juice to flavor some of the fruit puree, if you wish, and you can sprinkle the puree spread out in the pan with chopped nuts.

A crushed vitamin C tablet will provide enough ascorbic acid in a peach or pear mixture to keep the fruit from browning.

For raw apple leather, add 1/2 cup apple cider and 1/4 teaspoon cinnamon to 2 cups peeled and cored apples.

Yield: 16 ounces

Cost of Ingredients: $.58
Comparable Purchased Product: Fruit
Roll-Ups, 4 ounces, $1.89 ($7.56)
Savings: $6.98

Beef Jerky

Make up a batch of beef jerky if you want to keep your campers or hikers going for a long while—the concentrated flavor lasts and lasts as you chew, and since the cost of making this treat is so low, you can chew all day for pennies.

> **1 pound very lean beef (chuck or round)**
> **1/4 cup Worcestershire sauce**
> **1/4 cup soy sauce**
> **1 tablespoon tomato sauce**
> **1 tablespoon vinegar**
> **1 teaspoon sugar**
> **1/4 teaspoon Dried Onion (page 25)**
> **1 teaspoon salt**
> **1/4 teaspoon garlic powder**

1. Trim all visible fat from the meat and freeze until firm and solid enough to slice into thin strips. Cut across the grain and make sure that the slices are as thin as you can make them, about 1/8 inch thick. Cut slices into 1-inch-wide strips. Arrange strips in a shallow baking pan.

2. Combine remaining ingredients and pour liquid over strips. Refrigerate overnight or for at least 8 hours.

3. Preheat oven to 140 degrees. Remove meat from the marinade and place the strips on a cake rack over a cookie sheet in the oven. Dry until strips will splinter on the edges—from 18 to 24 hours. Cool completely before wrapping lightly with plastic wrap. Jerky will keep in a closely covered container for 2 to 4 weeks.

Hints:
> Do not try to dry meat in the sun, because you need a consistently higher temperature than the sun can provide. If you use a convection oven, you can reduce the drying time by 4 or 5 hours.

Yield: 32 ounces

Cost of Ingredients: $2.98
Comparable Purchased Product: Slim Jim, 1.42 ounces, $.79 ($17.80)
Savings: $14.81

Cheese Thins

*Try making up a batch of these for a football-watching party and serve them along with a bowl of **Gazpacho-style Sauce**, page 40, for dipping, or as an accompaniment to a hearty bowl of homemade soup.*

> 1 cup flour
> 1 teaspoon salt
> 1/4 teaspoon paprika
> 2 cups grated Cheddar cheese
> 1/2 cup butter

1. Sift flour, salt, and paprika together and stir in cheese.

2. Cream butter in a food processor or with an electric mixer and slowly add the flour mixture, mixing until well blended.

3. Shape mixture into a roll, wrap in wax paper, and chill in refrigerator overnight.

4. Preheat oven to 350 degrees.

5. Slice the chilled dough very thin and place on a greased cookie sheet. Roll and twist the slices into little crescents. Bake for 10 minutes, rotating the cookie sheet, if necessary. Cool and store in a tightly closed container for 1 to 2 weeks.

Yield: 24 ounces

Cost of Ingredients: $1.92
Comparable Purchased Product: Bachman
   Cheese Sticks, 10 ounces, $1.09 ($2.61)
Savings: $.69

Soft Philly Pretzels

These pretzels are one of the first things I remember about growing up—they were soft and chewy, and covered with salt—and some people liked them covered with mustard as well. Decent people, of course, would never put mustard on them, but everyone to her taste. You can reconstitute stale pretzels by sprinkling them with water, placing them in a paper bag, and heating in a 250 degree oven for 10 minutes or a microwave for a minute or two.

> 1 envelope yeast
> 1 1/4 cups warm water
> 1/4 teaspoon sugar
> 2 teaspoons salt
> 4 to 5 cups flour
> 4 teaspoons baking soda
> Coarse salt

1. Dissolve yeast in 1/4 cup of the water and then stir in the rest of the water and the sugar.

2. Pour yeast mixture into a bowl, add salt, and beat in enough flour to make a stiff dough. Knead by hand for 10 minutes, or until dough is smooth and elastic. You can perform this step with a food processor if you run the processor until a ball of dough forms.

3. Add additional flour a tablespoon at a time to keep the dough from becoming too sticky and when the correct consistency is reached, continue to run the processor for another 60 seconds to knead the dough.

4. Place dough in an oiled bowl, cover, and let it rise for 45 minutes or until double in bulk.

5. Turn dough out onto a floured board and shape into pretzel shapes or fat sticks that you twist a few times.

6. Preheat oven to 475 degrees.

7. Bring 4 cups of water to a boil in a large pot and add 4 teaspoons of baking soda to the water. Drop in several pretzels at a time and boil for 1 minute or until they float on the surface of the water. Remove carefully and drain on paper toweling.

8. Place boiled pretzels on a greased cookie sheet and sprinkle with coarse salt. Bake for 10 to 12 minutes, or until golden. Cool and store in a tightly closed container. Pretzels will keep for 2 to 4 weeks.

Yield: 8 to 10 pretzels

Cost of Ingredients: $1.19
Comparable Purchased Product:
Philadelphia Soft Pretzels, $1.00 each
($8.00)
Savings: $6.81

Potato Chips

*Try all different kinds of seasonings to flavor your chips until you find the perfect mixture. You can make a Mexican-flavored chip by using 1 /4 cup of the **Mexican Seasonings Mix**, page 103, and dip the chips into a variety of dips: avocado, sour cream, refried beans.*

> 2 pounds potatoes
> 1/4 cup cooking oil
> 1/4 cup assorted seasonings: salt, onion salt, garlic
>   powder, Firehouse Hot Chili powder (page 6),
>   grated Parmesan cheese

1. Preheat oven to 450 degrees.

2. Scrub potatoes and slice as thin as you possibly can, or slice with a food processor.

3. Oil a large cookie sheet and spread slices out in a single layer. Brush tops of potatoes with cooking oil. Bake for 8 to 10 minutes or until potatoes are a golden brown. Rotate pan, if necessary.

4. Pour 1/4 cup of the seasonings of your choice into a clean paper bag and place chips, while still warm, in the bag and shake.

Yield: 2 pounds

Cost of Ingredients: $1.23
Comparable Purchased Product: Wise
    Potato Chips, 16 ounces, $2.39 ($9.56)
Savings: $8.33

Bagel Chips

Here is the only decent thing to do with any leftover bagels. You have to work fast and slice them up while you still can—otherwise your only recourse with old bagels is to laminate them and use them as large refrigerator magnets or small doorstops.

3 bagels
1/4 cup vegetable oil
1 teaspoon garlic salt

1. Preheat oven to 250 degrees.

2. Slice bagels into very thin 1/4-inch slices. Using a pastry brush, lightly coat both sides of the slice with the vegetable oil.

3. Arrange slices on a cookie sheet and sprinkle with the garlic salt. Bake for 20 minutes, turn once, and bake for 10 minutes more, or until both sides are crisp.

Yield: 16 ounces

Cost of Ingredients: $.85
Comparable Purchased Product: Fred's
Bagel Chips, 8 ounces, $1.55 ($3.10)
Savings: $2.25

Quick Pizza

Here is a handy, thick-crusted pizza so easy to create that even the child who has a hankering for pizza can make it for himself. Add a little sauce, cheese—it's a fine after-school snack.

2 cups Biscuit Baking Mix (page 65)
1/2 cup cold water
1 cup Basic Tomato Sauce (page 37)
1/2 cup shredded mozzarella cheese
1/2 teaspoon oregano
1/2 teaspoon garlic powder
Salt and pepper to taste

1. Preheat oven to 425 degrees.

2. Mix baking mix and water until a soft dough forms. Roll or pat dough into a 12-inch circle or square on an ungreased cookie sheet. Pinch up edge of circle to form a 1/2-inch rim.

3. Spoon tomato sauce over the dough, then the cheese and spices.

4. Bake for 20 to 25 minutes or until crust is golden brown.

Variations:

Never let not having a certain ingredient stop you from making a pizza. Around our neighborhood, some delicious pizza pies have been made from what some would consider to be strange items. For example, try brushing the crust with olive oil and top it with braised broccoli and mushrooms and lots of cheese.

Yield: 1 small pizza

Cost of Ingredients: $1.28
Comparable Purchased Product: Phil's
   Pizza, small, $4.50
Savings: $3.22

Savory Buttered Bread Sticks

This recipe is a good way to use day-old Italian or French bread because you can make it up, wrap in foil, and freeze. When reheated, the bread tastes fresh again.

*You can also vary the kinds of butter you use, from **Garlic Butter** for the traditional garlic bread to **Herb Butter** for a light lunch with soup, to **Ooh-la-la Butter** for a sweet breakfast of quick French toast.*

*Additional **Variations** follow the recipe, and you will probably be inspired to invent more of your own.*

*If you are baking a loaf of **Savory Buttered Bread** that you have frozen, add 15 minutes to the baking time.*

1 large loaf Italian or French bread
1/2 cup prepared butter, softened:
   Garlic Butter (page 108)
   Herb Butter (page 105)
   Ooh-la-la Butter (page 104)

1. Preheat oven to 400 degrees.

2. Slice bread crosswise, leaving bottom crust in one piece.

3. Brush all the butter along the cut sides of the bread, top and bottom. Put bread back together and wrap tightly in aluminum foil.

3. Bake for 15 to 20 minutes. Cut bread into 1-inch-by-4-inch rectangles while it's still warm. Serve immediately.

Variation:

*For French Bread, spread with **Ooh-la-la Butter**, as above, and instead of baking, dip the slices in 2 eggs scrambled with 1/4 cup milk, salt and pepper to taste, and 2 teaspoons sugar. Fry in butter, sprinkle with cinnamon, and serve with maple syrup or one of the **Sweet Berry Syrups** (page 44).*

Yield: 1 loaf

Cost of Ingredients: $2.22
Comparable Purchased Product: Grand Union Garlic Bread, $2.48 per pound.
Savings: $.26

Fruity Italian Ices

You can eat these ices right from the paper cups you've frozen them in, squeezing it up in the cup as the ice melts, or you can freeze them in small plastic cups and eat with a small wooden or plastic spoon.

> 4 cups water
> 2 cups sugar
> 2 cups orange juice
> Juice of 2 lemons

1. Combine water and sugar in a pan and bring to a boil. Boil for 5 minutes over medium heat, stirring occasionally. Cool.

2. Stir in juices and pour mixture into a freezer pan, ice cube tray, or 9-inch cake pan and freeze for 30 minutes.

3. Remove ice from freezer, stir thoroughly, and replace. Repeat after 30 minutes.

4. Remove mixture from the freezer, stir again, and press the ice into paper cups. Cover tops of cups with plastic wrap and freeze until firm.

Variations:
   Try substituting the juice of another fruit for the orange juice, retaining the lemon juice in the recipe. Raspberry, pineapple, and grape juice are delicious.

Yield: 10 ices

Cost of Ingredients: $.88
Comparable Purchased Product: Cetroni's
   Lemon Italian Ice, 36 ounces, $1.79
Savings: $.91

Quickie Ice Cream

This chocolate ice cream is a little quirky—it's not a traditional ice cream, but it's not bad, either. If you don't have an ice cream maker, here is one to try with just a freezer compartment as the basic equipment needed.

   2/3 cup Basic Chocolate Sauce (page 45)
   2 cups Sweetened Condensed Milk (page 17)
   1 cup heavy whipping cream, whipped

1. Stir sauce and condensed milk together and fold in the whipped cream. Pour into a freezer tray, 9-inch cake pan, or ice cube tray and freeze for 30 minutes.

2. Pour the mushy mixture into a blender or whip with an electric mixer for 1 minute. Pour back into tray, cover with plastic wrap, and freeze until firm.

Variations:

    Instead of chocolate sauce, try adding 2/3 cup of **Freezer Fruit Preserves,** *page 50, or try adding 1/2 cup chocolate chips and 1 teaspoon mint extract to the chocolate recipe.*

Yield: 32 ounces

Cost of Ingredients: $2.29
Comparable Purchased Product: Bryer's Ice
    Cream, 1 pint, $1.19 ($2.38)
Savings: $.09

Instant Ice Cream

    Try this treat if you have an antsy child around, or if you feel antsy yourself. The way the mixture changes to ice cream right before your very eyes is very involving and exciting, and of course you must eat the frozen concoction right away or the magic will be lost.

        1/2 cup Homemade Yogurt (page 121)
        2 egg whites
        3 tablespoons sugar
        2 teaspoons lemon juice
        3 cups frozen fruit in small pieces

1. If you have time, chill the blender container by placing it in the freezer for about 10 minutes before beginning. Place the yogurt, egg whites, sugar, and juice in the blender and blend for 1 minute. Keep the machine running and gradually add the frozen fruit until soft ice cream is formed. Serve at once.

Yield: 24 ounces

Cost of Ingredients: $.78
Comparable Purchased Product: Tuscan
    Frozen Yogurt, 15 ounces, $2.09 ($3.34)
Savings: $2.56

Honey Gelato

This is a trendy type of ice cream that is also good for you and, best of all, wonderfully low in calories. A 1/2-cup serving has 70 calories, so you can make up a batch and indulge without guilt.

> 1 envelope unflavored gelatin
> 1/2 cup instant nonfat dry milk
> 2 cups skim milk
> 1/2 cup honey
> 1 teaspoon orange juice
> 1 teaspoon lemon juice
> 2 egg whites

1. Mix gelatin and dry milk in a saucepan. Stir in skim milk, cook over low heat, stirring constantly until gelatin dissolves. Remove from heat.

2. Stir in honey and juices. Pour into a freezer tray, 9-inch cake pan, or ice cube tray and freeze for 1 hour.

3. Pour mixture into a chilled bowl and add the egg whites. Beat at high speed with an electric mixer until mixture is fluffy. Return to freezer container, cover, and freeze until firm.

Yield: 42 ounces

Cost of Ingredients: $1.70
Comparable Purchased Product: Glacé Lite, 16 ounces, $2.05 ($5.38)
Savings: $3.68

Frozen Fruiti Yogurt

*If you are making up a nice batch of creamy **Homemade Yogurt**, page 121, you will undoubtedly have enough on hand to turn into frozen fruit-flavored yogurt pops.*

2 cups plain Homemade Yogurt (page 121)
1 cup fresh or frozen fruit: banana, orange,
   strawberries, raspberries, or a combination
1/4 cup honey

1. Puree yogurt and fruit in a blender, adding honey once the fruit is well blended.

2. Pour mixture into a container for the freezer: an ice cube tray, a shallow plastic container, or 9-inch-square cake pan. Freeze for 30 minutes.

3. Spoon frozen mush into the blender container and whip for 1 minute. Pour mixture into Popsicle molds or paper cups. Freeze for 10 minutes, insert Popsicle sticks, and return to freezer until firm.

Variations:
   Spices and other flavorings can be added as you experiment with fruit and yogurt combinations. For example, try 1/2 teaspoon vanilla, 1/2 teaspoon cinnamon, and 1/2 teaspoon nutmeg whipped up with 1 banana.
   Or, try mixing 6 ounces frozen juice concentrate with 1 cup yogurt and 1 teaspoon vanilla.

Yield: 20 ounces

Cost of Ingredients: $1.08
Comparable Purchased Product: Tuscan Yogurt Pops, 13 ounces, $1.89 ($2.90)
Savings: $1.82

Plain and Fancy Fruiti Pops

The degree of smoothness you want in these pops is entirely your choice. If you are making the pops for very small children, try making a mixture that is on the smooth side; others might prefer a meatier mixture with plenty of fruity chunks.

**1 cup fruit juice
1 cup fresh, frozen, or canned fruit
10 wooden sticks or Popsicle sticks**

1. Mix fruit and fruit juice together in a blender or food processor. You can either puree the fruit completely or simply whirl the fruit and juice to mix thoroughly while leaving some chunks.

2. Pour mixture into Popsicle molds or paper cups to freeze. Freeze until slightly firm, insert Popsicle sticks, and continue freezing until firm.

Fruit 'n' Cream Pops

**1 cup fruit and its juice
1 cup light cream or 1 cup milk mixed with 1/2 cup
   instant nonfat dry milk
1 teaspoon honey
1/2 teaspoon Vanilla Bean Extract (page 12)
10 wooden sticks or Popsicle sticks**

1. Mix together fruit and cream. Whip in honey and vanilla until fruit mixture is well blended.

2. Freeze in a freezer container or an ice cube tray for 40 minutes. Spoon the slightly frozen mixture out into the blender or food processor and blend for 30 seconds. Pour mixture into Popsicle molds or paper cups, insert Popsicle sticks, and freeze until firm.

Variation:
   After the pops are frozen solid, try swirling them into 1 cup **Basic Chocolate Sauce,** *page 45, and eating immediately.*

Yield: 10 Pops

Cost of Ingredients: $.66
Comparable Purchased Product: Dole Fruit
   and Juice Bars, 10 ounces, $1.89
Savings: $1.23

Frosted Banana Pops

Here is another freezer goody that is also good for you. You can set out the ingredients and let your kids assemble these treats all by themselves.

> **6 firm bananas**
> **12 wooden sticks**
> **1 cup Basic Chocolate Sauce (page 45)**
> **1/2 cup shredded unsweetened coconut**

1. Peel bananas, cut in half, and insert a wooden stick to make a banana pop.

2. Dip bananas first in chocolate sauce and then in the coconut to cover. Wrap a plastic bag around the banana, leaving the stick out. Use a twist tie to secure the bag around the stick, and freeze bananas until firm, about 2 hours.

Peanut Butter Bananas

> **6 firm bananas**
> **12 wooden sticks**
> **6 tablespoons Homemade Peanut Butter (page 47)**
> **1/2 cup Sweetened Condensed Milk (page 17)**
> **Chopped nuts or crunchy cereal**

1. Cut bananas in half and place a wooden stick in each banana.

2. Mix peanut butter and milk until mixture is smooth. Roll the bananas first in the milk mixture and then in the nuts or crunchy mixture. Cover with plastic wrap and freeze until firm.

Yield: 6 banana pops

Cost of Ingredients: $.67
Comparable Purchased Product: Concord Freeze 'n Dip Chocolate Coating Kit, 4 ounces, $.69
Savings: $.02

Frozen Pudding Pops

These pops are a summertime favorite at our house. My kids like a mixture of vanilla and chocolate swirled together with lots of chocolate chips.

1/2 cup Pudding Mix (page 86)
1/2 cup light cream
10 wooden sticks or Popsicle sticks

1.   Prepare pudding according to instructions and just before cooling, stir in the light cream. Pour into small cups or Popsicle molds and freeze until slushy about 1 hour. Insert sticks and freeze until firm.

Variations:
        *To make a marbled pop, swirl 1/2 cup **Basic Chocolate Sauce**, page 45, into vanilla pudding just before freezing. Don't mix the sauce in completely. Add chocolate chips, nuts, or butter-brickle chips if desired.*

Yield: 10 pops

Cost of Ingredients: $.94
Comparable Purchased Product: Jell-O
     Pudding Pops, 12 ounces, $2.49
Savings: $1.55

Chapter 4

Gourmet and Gift Items

These are the seasonal and specialty food items that cost the most in both time and money. Whether you find a small jar of brandied peaches in a gourmet shop and want to recreate the item or whether you carefully prepare the same recipe your grandmother lovingly created, these are the treats that make worthwhile gifts and lasting memories.

Raspberry Vinegar
Herbal Vinegar
Mint Vinegar
Brandied Peaches
Marinated Mushrooms
Dried Tomatoes in Oil
Peach Chutney
East India Chutney
Boursin Party Spread
Quick Chicken Liver Pâté
Raisin Sauce
Holiday Fruitcake
Gingerbread Puzzles
English Toffee
Tortoni
Mincemeat
Sugared Almonds
Sugared Pecans
Candied Citrus Peel
Sugar Flowers

Raspberry Vinegar

The basic recipe for vinegar with raspberries can be varied to take advantage of other fruits and herbs you might have in abundance.

1 pound fresh raspberries
3 cups malt vinegar
3 cups sugar

1. Rinse raspberries and place them in a sterilized glass jar. Stir in the vinegar and mash the berries a bit with a spoon. Cover and store in a cool, dry place for 3 days.

2. Strain the vinegar from the berries through a cheesecloth or coffee filter and either discard the fruit pulp or use it in **Liquid Fertilizer**, page 298.

3. Place the vinegar in a glass or an enamel pan, add the sugar, and bring to a boil. Boil for 5 minutes, stirring constantly until the sugar is dissolved. Cool.

4. Pour into sterilized bottles or jars and cover or cork tightly. Vinegar will keep in the pantry for up to 4 months.

Herbal Vinegar

1/4 cup marjoram
1/4 cup mint
2 tablespoons basil
2 tablespoons tarragon
1 tablespoon rosemary
1/2 teaspoon dill
1/2 teaspoon allspice
1/2 teaspoon ground cloves
1 quart cider vinegar

1. Place all ingredients in a sterilized glass jar or crock, cover, and let stand in a cool, dry place for 4 weeks. Stir and mash herbs once a day.

2. Strain vinegar through a cheesecloth or coffee filter and

retain herb pulp for **Liquid Fertilizer**, page 298. Pour clear vinegar into sterilized glass jars or bottles, cap or cork, and store in the pantry for up to 4 months.

Mint Vinegar

2 cups mint leaves
1 quart white or cider vinegar

1. Place mint and vinegar in a sterilized glass jar, cover, and store in a cool, dry place for 2 weeks. Crush and stir mixture once every day. Strain and store as for other vinegars.

Variations:

Use other berries in this recipe for different flavors and combinations. Try blueberries mixed with 1/2 cup chopped lemon or strawberries and oranges.

Other herbs to try include summer savory or thyme; 1 cup white wine may be added to the vinegar, and as an added touch, it's always pretty to return a stalk or two of a fresh herb to the clear, bottled vinegar.

To Use:

Try a cooling, snappy summer drink by mixing 1/2 cup Raspberry Vinegar with 1 cup water, pour over ice, add lemon and mint, and serve.

Try mixing the fruit vinegars with mild olive oil, salt, and pepper and drizzle over fresh fruit and avocado wedges for a tangy summer salad.

*Mix **Herbal Vinegar** with 2 tablespoons of **Great Seasonings Salad Dressings Mix**, page 34, for a tasty salad dressing.*

Freeze mint vinegar into cubes in an ice cube tray and add to lemonade and other summer drinks.

Yield: 32 ounces

Cost of Ingredients: $5.60
Comparable Purchased Product: Silver Palate Raspberry Vinegar, 12 ounces, $4.99 ($13.30)
Savings: $7.70

Brandied Peaches

This recipe should be made well in advance of holiday or gift-giving time. Since peaches are plentiful in late summer, you will want to take advantage of their low prices then and make up your jars, but because the flavors must mellow and stew awhile, you will have to wait until Christmas or the New Year to enjoy this treat.

> **2 pounds peaches**
> **2 cups sugar**
> **2 cups water**
> **Brandy**

1. Peel, halve, and pit peaches.

2. Place the sugar and water in a saucepan, bring to a boil, boil for 10 minutes, add the peaches, and simmer for another 10 minutes.

3. Pour off the syrup into a measuring cup and combine with an equal quantity of brandy.

4. Pack peaches in sterilized wide-mouth glass jars without crowding them too tightly. Pour the syrup-brandy mixture over the peaches to cover. Close the jar tightly and put it away on a cool, dark pantry shelf to rest for 6 months.

Ideas:
> *One of the best ways to enjoy your brandied peaches is to pour them over vanilla ice cream, adding a dollop of sweetened whipped cream if you like.*
> *Save every bit of the liquid from your peaches and you can add more fruit throughout the year, indefinitely.*

Yield: 32 ounces

Cost of Ingredients: $2.21
Comparable Purchased Product: Raffetto Brandied Peach Halves, 18 ounces, $5.55 ($9.86)
Savings: $7.65

Marinated Mushrooms

The type of oil you use in this recipe can change the taste of the final marinade as well as change the price. It doesn't hurt to try the recipe with regular vegetable oil because the addition of several spices and the mustard will help to spruce up the flavor.

A high-quality olive oil is the way to make this recipe . special, and costly, but if you're giving it as a gift, it will still save you money over the gourmet brands in specialty stores.

> **2 cups fresh mushrooms**
> **1 cup vegetable oil**
> **1/2 cup red wine vinegar**
> **3 cloves garlic, chopped**
> **2 tablespoons chopped parsley**
> **1 teaspoon Tangy Mustard (page 29)**
> **1/2 teaspoon rosemary**
> **1/4 teaspoon thyme**
> **1/4 teaspoon oregano**

1. Clean the mushrooms by wiping them gently under running water and trimming off the tough stems. Drain and pat dry on paper toweling.

2. Place all the ingredients except the mushrooms in a sterilized glass jar, cover, and shake well to mix. Drop in the mushrooms, making sure they are completely covered with the liquid, and marinate overnight. Mushrooms will keep, refrigerated, for 2 to 4 months.

Variations:

The marinade is good for other vegetables, especially as you use some of the mushrooms up and find yourself with a supply of seasoned marinade on hand. Try dropping in onion slices or green pepper for a different tasting combination.

You can also add the artichoke hearts that are canned in water. Drain them for 10 minutes on paper toweling before dropping them into the marinade. I've dropped blanched green beans into the marinade, as well as cauliflower.

Yield: 16 ounces

Cost of Ingredients: $3.77
Comparable Purchased Product: Cara Mia
    Marinated Mushrooms, 4 ounces, $.99 ($3.96)
Savings: $.19

Dried Tomatoes in Oil

These tomatoes are very expensive in gourmet shops, and once you taste them, you'll want to make your own to use with abandon. They are perfect served with very fresh, creamy mozzarella cheese and garnished with fresh basil. Use the very best olive oil you can afford for this recipe and save the oil for delicious salads.

Since the tomatoes must be slowly and carefully dried, it's a good idea to place a thermometer in your oven so that you can maintain an even temperature of 150 degrees. It is not recommended that you try sun-drying your tomatoes because our summers are neither hot nor long enough to do the job as slowly and thoroughly as necessary.

3 pounds ripe plum tomatoes
2 teaspoons salt
1½ cups olive oil

1. Preheat oven to 150 degrees.

2. Rinse tomatoes in warm water and pat dry. Cut lengthwise and place, cut side up, on a cake rack over a baking sheet. Sprinkle with salt.

3. Place racks of tomatoes in the oven and leave the door ajar about 4 inches. Check temperature every 2 hours and turn the pans to insure even drying. Turn off the oven for 30 minutes if the temperature rises over 150 degrees. Dry for 12 hours or until tomatoes are flexible but not moist. Cool.

4. Pack dried tomatoes in a sterilized glass jar, cover with olive oil, and store in a cool, dry place for 1 month before using.

Yield: 16 ounces

Cost of Ingredients: $3.10
Comparable Purchased Product: Quo Vadis
    Dried Tomatoes in Oil, 16 ounces, $17.50
Savings: $14.40

Peach Chutney

*This recipe makes a nice batch of chutney that you can use
to accompany main courses or to serve as a before-dinner
palate teaser with some crackers or toasted wheat bread.*

> 4 quarts peaches
> 5 cups white vinegar
> 1/2 cup chopped onions
> 1/2 cup sugar
> 1/2 cup raisins
> 1/4 cup mustard seeds
> 2 ounces fresh ginger root, minced, or 1 teaspoon
>   ground ginger
> 2 tablespoons red pepper
> 5 to 6 cloves garlic, chopped

1. Peel, pit, and quarter the peaches. Place peaches in a
saucepan and add 2 cups of the vinegar. Cook over medium
heat for 30 minutes, or until peaches are soft.

2. Add 3 cups of vinegar and the rest of the ingredients. Cook
for 15 minutes more.

3. Pour mixture, while still hot, into sterilized canning jars
and store in the refrigerator. Chutney will keep for 2 to 4
months while refrigerated.

East India Chutney

> 12 apples
> 4 cups brown sugar
> 8 cups apple cider
> 4 cups raisins
> 1 onion, chopped
> 2 red peppers, chopped

1/4 cup dry mustard
1/4 cup ground ginger
1 tablespoon salt

1. Core and chop apples, combine all ingredients, and place mixture in a large saucepan. Bring to a boil, boil 1 for minute, reduce heat and simmer for 1 hour.

2. Pour mixture, while still hot, into sterilized canning jars and store in the refrigerator. Chutney will keep for 2 to 4 months while refrigerated.

Yield: 48 ounces

Cost of Ingredients: $2.88
Comparable Purchased Product: Raffeto Peach Chutney, 10.5 ounces, $3.19 ($14.58)
Savings: $11.70

Boursin Party Spread

Everyone who tastes this cheese loves it. This version is easy to make, inexpensive, and even a little lower in calories than the store brand. Enjoy it with a dry white wine, crackers, slices of pepperoni, and white grapes.

1/2 cup cottage cheese
2 tablespoons butter, softened
2 tablespoons chopped fresh parsley
2 cloves garlic, pressed
1 teaspoon salt
1 teaspoon freshly ground pepper

1. Drain liquid from the cottage cheese by lining a kitchen strainer with cheesecloth or muslin, spooning in the cottage cheese, and letting it sit suspended over a bowl for 1 to 2 hours. Save the liquid, and use it in **Light Skin-bleaching Cream**, page 216.

2. In a food processor, blend the cheese and butter until you have a smooth paste; add herbs, salt, and pepper, blending well.

3. Shape cheese into a ball and flatten the top. Chill for several hours, but remove from refrigerator one hour before serving.

Yield: 6 ounces

Cost of Ingredients: $.69
Comparable Purchased Product:
   Philadelphia Crémerie Cream Cheese with
   Herb & Garlic, 4 ounces, $1.59 ($2.38)
Savings: $1.69

Quick Chicken Liver Pâté

This creamy spread can be served at parties and for holiday buffets as an appetizer. A pretty crock of pâté is an especially welcome addition to any one of the many gift basket ideas that I've described in Chapter 12.

> 1/2 cup butter
> 1/2 cup Homemade Cream Cheese (page 19)
> 1 pound chicken livers
> 1 cup water
> 1 small onion, quartered
> 2 cloves garlic, minced
> 2 ounces chicken bouillon *or* 4 cubes
> 1 teaspoon thyme
> 1 teaspoon paprika
> 1 teaspoon tarragon
> 1/2 teaspoon cayenne
> 1/4 teaspoon allspice
> 1/4 teaspoon ground cloves
> 2 tablespoons brandy

1. Have butter and cream cheese at room temperature.

2. Carefully rinse chicken livers, cut in half and remove any connecting tissue. Place chicken livers in a saucepan with the

water, onion, garlic, and chicken bouillon. Bring to a boil, cover, and simmer for 20 minutes, or until livers and onion are tender.

3. Place livers, onion, garlic, 2 tablespoons of the boiling liquid, and spices in a blender or food processor. Blend for 1 minute, add butter and cream cheese and blend for 1 minute more. Scrape down container, add the brandy, and blend until mixture is smooth.

4. Pour pâté into a small crock or serving dish, cover with plastic wrap, and refrigerate for 2 hours. Let pâté warm for 15 minutes before serving. Pâté will keep in the refrigerator for 2 weeks if you cover it tightly.

Yield: 24 ounces

Cost of Ingredients: $2.66
Comparable Purchased Product:
  Baldingle's Chicken Liver Pâté, 8 ounces,
  $2.29 ($6.87)
Savings: $4.21

Raisin Sauce

Try this sauce brushed on a nice Sunday ham before you place it in the oven. Baste the ham with the juices and add additional sauce as the ham bakes. You can add any sort of fruit as a garnish near the end of the cooking time: peaches, pineapple, or raisins and grapes.

> 1/2 cup brown sugar
> 1 tablespoon flour
> 1 tablespoon Tangy Mustard (page 29)
> 11/2 cups water
> 1/2 cup cider vinegar
> 1/2 cup raisins

1. Mix all ingredients in a saucepan and simmer for 10 minutes. Store sauce in a sterilized glass jar in the refrigerator. Sauce will keep for 2 to 4 months.

To Use:

Brush this sauce as a glaze over ham or poultry. The glaze is best brushed on as you begin to roast, and then refreshed during the roasting process.

You can make a delicious gravy by thickening the juices that are flavored with the Raisin Sauce by adding 2 tablespoons **Instant White Sauce Mix**, page 89.

Yield: 16 ounces

Cost of Ingredients: $1.12
Comparable Purchased Product: Chelten House Raisin Sauce, 10 ounces, $1.59 ($2.54)
Savings: $1.42

Holiday Fruitcake

There are as many types of fruitcakes as there are nationalities of people celebrating the holidays with sweet cake. One of my favorites, and I like all of them, is a white fruitcake which is attributed to Martha Washington. Here is my version of it.

Since this cake has to age and mellow, you should plan to make it well in advance of the holiday rush—it's a nice, rich, cozy way to welcome the first gray day of November.

1 cup golden raisins
1 cup chopped dried apricots
1/2 cup brandy
1/2 pound Candied Orange Peel (page 164)
1/2 pound Candied Lemon Peel (page 164)
1/2 pound candied pineapple, chopped
1/4 pound candied citron
1/4 cup chopped walnuts
4 1/2 cups flour, sifted
1 teaspoon mace
1 teaspoon cinnamon
1 teaspoon allspice
1 teaspoon nutmeg
2 cups butter

2 cups sugar
1 cup brown sugar, lightly packed
8 eggs
2 tablespoons molasses
1/4 cup dry sherry
1 cup brandy for seasoning

1. One day before baking, mix together the raisins, apricots, and 1/2 cup brandy in a medium-size saucepan. Simmer for 5 minutes, remove from heat, and let stand for 30 minutes.

2. Combine raisin-apricot-brandy mixture with the orange and lemon peel, pineapple, citron, and walnuts. Toss to coat all the fruit and let the mixture stand at room temperature overnight.

3. Preheat oven to 325 degrees.

4. Sift together flour and spices. In a separate bowl, cream butter, sugar, and eggs together until the mixture is light and fluffy. Stir in the molasses, sherry, and brandied fruits and nuts.

5. Pour into a greased and paper-lined loaf or bundt cake pan and bake for 2 hours or until a cake tester inserted in the center comes out clean. If necessary, cover cake with aluminum foil during baking to prevent excessive browning. Remove cake from pan and cool.

6. Wrap cake in cheesecloth and place in an airtight tin or on a layer of thick aluminum foil. Sprinkle 2 to 4 tablespoons brandy on the cheesecloth, wrap or cover tightly, and store in a cool, dry place or the refrigerator.

7. Once every 5 days, unwrap cake, brush with brandy, and rewrap and store. Continue this seasoning for 4 to 6 weeks.

Yield: 1 cake

Cost of Ingredients: $5.60
Comparable Purchased Product:
    Entenmann's Fruitcake, 16 ounces, $5.99
Savings: $.39

Gingerbread Puzzles

*This batter can become the basis for a castle or a
gingerbread man or woman, but a holiday puzzle that children
can actually play with before eating is a nice idea if you're
making the gingerbread for a special small person. Follow a
simple puzzle design from a child's set or invent a simple one
to suit the occasion or the interests of the child.*

> 1/2 cup light molasses
> 1/2 cup butter or margarine
> 1/2 cup sugar
> 1 egg lightly beaten
> 1 teaspoon baking soda
> 1 teaspoon cinnamon
> 1 teaspoon ground cloves
> 1 teaspoon ground ginger
> 2 3/4 cups flour

Frosting

> 1/2 cup Vanilla Sugar (page 8)
> 2 tablespoons Homemade Cream Cheese (page 19)
> 1 tablespoon milk
> 1 teaspoon grated orange peel

Decoration

Silly Sparkles (page 11)

1. In a medium-size pan, heat molasses to boiling. Remove
from heat and add butter and sugar. Cool.

2. Stir in egg, baking soda, spices, and flour, 1/2 cup at a time.
Wrap dough in plastic wrap or aluminum foil and refrigerate
overnight or for at least 8 hours.

3. Preheat oven to 350 degrees.

4. Remove dough from refrigerator and let it soften for 15
minutes before rolling it out on a floured surface. Divide dough
in half and roll each half 1/8-inch thick. Cut into two 12-by-9-
inch rectangles and place on two greased baking sheets.

5. Bake for 10 minutes and remove from oven. Leave dough on baking sheets and cut the design out with a sharp paring knife. You can place an outline cut from paper for the main figure in the middle to guide you, or you can cut the design out freehand. Cut remainder of rectangle to resemble puzzle pieces. Do not lift any of the pieces up, but make sure you've cut all the way through the dough. Return the dough to the oven and finish baking for another 5 minutes or until set. Test gingerbread by inserting a toothpick in the thickest part—the toothpick will come out clean when the gingerbread is set.

6. Cool for 5 minutes in the baking pan and then carefully lift onto a cake rack and cool completely.

7. To make frosting, stir milk into cream cheese and add the sugar slowly, stirring briskly to blend. Frosting will be thin. If you would like a thicker frosting, add a bit more sugar.

8. Cut the corner off a clean envelope to make a funnel for the Silly Sparkles. Frost the cookies and before the frosting is completely dry, sprinkle the puzzle pieces with the sugar.

Yield: Two 12-by-9-inch cookies

Cost of Ingredients: $3.35
Comparable Purchased Product: Betty Crocker Gingerbread Mix, 14.5 ounces, $1.35 ($4.05)
Savings: $.70

English Toffee

Melt your chocolate chips over very low heat or in a double boiler, and chop your peanuts up rather fine before you begin the recipe. Then you can assemble this layered toffee all at once, and enjoy.

> 1 pound butter
> 2 cups sugar
> 1 cup chocolate chips, melted slightly or 1 cup Basic Chocolate Sauce (page 45)
> 1/2 cup salted peanuts, chopped coarsly

1. Cut butter into small pieces and place in a heavy skillet with the sugar. Cook slowly over medium-high heat, stirring constantly until butter melts and is completely blended into the sugar.

2. Insert a candy thermometer into the mixture, reduce heat and cook for 30 minutes, stirring constantly, until the mixture is a deep amber in color and thermometer registers 285 degrees.

3. Pour mixture into an ungreased cookie sheet and allow to cool completely. Spread melted chocolate chips over the toffee and press the chopped peanuts on top. When the chocolate has hardened, break the toffee into small pieces and store them in a tightly covered container.

Yield: 18 ounces

Cost of Ingredients: $3.98
Comparable Purchased Product: Callard & Bowser English Toffees, 7.5 ounces, $1.69 ($4.05)
Savings: $.07

Tortoni

You will need fluted paper cups or small dessert cups for this traditional Italian delicacy.

> 1 egg white
> 6 tablespoons Vanilla Sugar (page 8)
> 1 cup heavy cream
> 1/2 cup macaroon or Sweet Crumbs (page 23)
> 2 teaspoons rum
> 1/4 cup chopped unsalted almonds

1. With an electric mixer, beat the egg white until stiff peaks form and continue beating while you gradually fold in 3 tablespoons of the Vanilla Sugar.

2. Beat the heavy cream and 3 tablespoons Vanilla Sugar with an electric mixer until thick but not stiff. Mix the crumbs into the cream, add the rum, and beat until soft peaks form.

3. Fold the cream mixture into the egg whites, spoon into fluted paper cups or dessert cups, top with almonds, and freeze until firm.

Yield: 2 cups

Cost of Ingredients: $1.72
Comparable Purchased Product: Napoli
   Tortoni, 3 ounces, $1.09 ($5.81)
Savings: $4.09

Mincemeat

There are many old-time versions of mincemeat, and most contain various forms of meat as well as beef suet. You can also make a nice fruity mincemeat without the added fats and flavors of the beef, if you prefer. You can vary some of the fruits and spices, below, depending on what fruit you might have a quantity of on hand. However, the traditional apples and raisins should remain.

2 cups beef, boiled and chopped fine (optional)
4 cups chopped apple
2 cups apple cider
3 cups raisins
2 cups sugar
1 cup currants
1/2 cup chopped almonds
1/2 cup Candied Orange Peel (page 164)
1/2 cup Candied Lemon Peel (page 164)
1/2 cup chopped dried figs
2 teaspoons cinnamon
1 teaspoon nutmeg
1 teaspoon allspice
1 teaspoon ground cloves
1 teaspoon salt
2 cups brandy
1 cup dry sherry

1. Combine all ingredients except brandy and sherry in a large saucepan. Stir, and cook over low heat for 2 hours. Remove from heat and cool.

2. Stir in brandy and sherry and spoon mixture into sterilized glass jars. Cover and store mixture in a cool, dark place for 4 weeks.

3. Check mixture periodically and add more brandy if mixture looks too dry. Mincemeat will be ready to use after 6 weeks. Refrigerate if you intend to store the mincemeat for a longer period than 2 months.

Yield: 12 cups

Cost of Ingredients: $8.64
Comparable Purchased Product: Borden Mincemeat with Rum and Brandy, 26 ounces, $3.10 ($11.44)
Savings: $2.80

Sugared Almonds

A jar of these snacking treats can be a welcome gift to someone who can use a little comforting. If you prefer, other nuts, such as filberts or macadamia nuts, can be substituted for the almonds.

> 1 cup sugar
> 1 cup honey
> 1/2 cup water
> 1 pound unblanched whole almonds
> 1 teaspoon cinnamon
> 1 teaspoon allspice

1. Mix sugar, honey, and water in a heavy skillet and boil the mixture for 5 minutes, or until it is thick.

2. Add nuts and cook until the nuts start to crackle. Sprinkle on the cinnamon and allspice, reduce heat, and continue stirring until the mixture is dry.

Sugared Pecans

1/3 cup butter or margarine
1/4 cup sugar
1/2 teaspoon cinnamon
1/4 teaspoon ground ginger
1 pound pecan halves

1. Preheat oven to 275 degrees.

2. Heat butter, sugar, and spices in a small saucepan until butter melts. Pour mixture over the pecans, making sure to coat all the nuts.

3. Bake in a shallow baking pan for 30 minutes, stirring several times during baking. Cool and store in an airtight container. Nuts will keep well for 4 to 6 weeks.

Yield: 32 ounces

Cost of Ingredients: $10.24
Comparable Purchased Product: Fisher Honey Roasted Almonds, 11 ounces, $4.99 ($14.51)
Savings: $4.27

Candied Citrus Peel

You can use any kind of citrus for this recipe, and a nice variety of peel will give you a good range of color and flavor for your dishes. No matter what citrus you use—orange, lemon, lime, tangerine, grapefruit—remember to scrape away every trace of the white pith under the peel because it tastes bitter.

2 cups citrus peel
Water for boiling
1/2 cup water
1 cup sugar

1. Wash and dry fruit carefully before using. Remove peel from fruit with a vegetable peeler or sharp paring knife. Trim all pith away and cut peel into narrow strips about 1 inch long.

2. Place peel in a pan with 2 cups water and simmer for 10 minutes. Drain, add 2 cups water and simmer for another 10 minutes. Repeat until peel has been simmered and drained 4 different times.

3. Combine 1 cup sugar and 1/2 cup water and bring to a boil. Boil for 1 minute and add the drained peel. Simmer gently until peel has absorbed the liquid—about 20 minutes.

4. Spread peel on a rack to dry. Roll the candied peel in sugar and dry on wax paper or plastic. Store in an airtight container. Candied peel will keep for 2 to 4 months on the pantry shelf.

Variation:
*Peels are delicious dipped into **Basic Chocolate Sauce**, page 45, for a special treat.*

Yield: 16 ounces

Cost of Ingredients: $.47
Comparable Purchased Product: J&W
   Candied Citron, 3.5 ounces, $.79 ($3.61)
Savings: $3.14

Sugar Flowers

Try making and carefully storing some of these beautiful blossoms and you will never again wonder how to finish off a special cake or dessert. The flowers are sweet, beautiful, and ready to eat. Violets have always been the traditional flower to sugar, but you can also try tiny rosebuds or just the rose petals.
   It would help to assemble all your supplies and ingredients before beginning this recipe, because you should work quickly and with a delicate touch. You will need a small paintbrush and a paper-covered cake rack for drying.

1/2 cup sugar
1 egg white
Freshly picked blossoms, with stems

1. Place the sugar in a blender or food processor and process

until the sugar is a fine powder. Pour the sugar into a shallow bowl and set aside.

2. Beat the egg white until foamy and pour into a shallow bowl. Paint the egg white carefully on the flower blossom, sprinkle the blossom with the sugar powder, and carefully lay the blossom on the paper to dry. The flowers will dry in the positions you arrange them, so be careful to spread out the petals. Sprinkle with a bit more sugar.

3. Dry the flowers in a sunny spot, or you can prewarm your oven to 200 degrees, turn it off, and place the flowers inside to dry with the door left open.

4. Carefully remove the completely dried flowers and layer them, nestled on tissue paper, in a box. The flowers will keep for 6 to 9 months in a cool, dry place.

To Use:

> Place the flowers on white icing on a wedding or bridal shower cake.
>
> Or make **Violets in the Snow**: whip heavy cream with 1 teaspoon vanilla, 1 teaspoon grated orange rind, and 1 teaspoon sugar until stiff. Dot with the violets and serve.

Yield: 8 ounces of blossoms (about 8 flowers)

Cost of Ingredients: $.18
Comparable Purchased Product: Yellow Brick Toad Sugar Flowers, $1.25 each ($10.00)
Savings: $9.82

Chapter 5

Beverages, Wines, and Liqueurs

Short of serious wine and beer brewing, you can concoct a wide variety of interesting fruit-based drinks at a fraction of their retail cost. In addition, you can control the amount of sugar or alcohol your drinks contain and still have an ample supply on hand for hot summer days, cold windy evenings, and unexpected company.

Fuzzy Fruit Sodas
Tangy Berry Fizz
Orange-y Julius Drink
Frozen Lemonade Capsules
Sipping Yogurt
Rainbow Drink Mix
Creamy Hot Cocoa Mix
Herb Teas
  Good Digestion Tea
  Balmy Lemon Tea
Mulling Mix
Bloody Mary Mix
Rum Coffee
Spiced and Fancy After-dinner Coffee
Thrifty Sangría
Guillermo's Summer Sangría
Champagne Cooler
Sweet Berry Cordial
Grenadine Syrup
Blueberry Cordial
Prune Cordial
Plum Cordial

Pear Cordial
Spicy Orange Cordial
Cranberry Liqueur
Dandelion Wine
Coffee Liqueur
Irish Cream Liqueur
Homemade Galiano
Homemade Drambuie
Homemade Crème de Menthe
Pippins and Port
Holiday Eggnog
Christmas Wassail

Fuzzy Fruit Sodas

*Here is the healthiest alternative possible if you or
members of your family enjoy the fizz and pop of soda. If you
are watching calories, make the soda up without using sugar or
Sweet Berry Syrup, which is made with sugar. The natural
sweetness of the fruit is often enough for most tastes.*

> **1 tablespoon frozen juice concentrate or Sweet Berry
>   Syrup (page 44)
> 8 ounces club soda**

1. Pour club soda into glass and swirl in a tablespoon of fruit
juice concentrate or syrup. Taste and add a bit more
concentrate, if necessary.

Yield: 8 ounces

Cost of Ingredients: $.33
Comparable Purchased Product: Sunkist
    Light Berry, 2.4 ounces, $2.99 ($9.96)
Savings: $9.63

Tangy Berry Fizz

*This is an old-fashioned way to refresh a hot, tired palate
on a summer's day. Try it with strawberries, blueberries,
raspberries, or a combination of berries.*

> **4 cups strawberries
> 1 cups white vinegar
> 2 cups sugar**

1. Place 2 cups of the strawberries in a sterilized glass jar and
pour the vinegar over them. Stir to moisten, cover the jar, and
place in a cool, dark place for 2 days.

2. Strain the liquid from the strawberries through a cheesecloth
or coffee filter. Discard the strawberries and pour the liquid
into a sterilized glass jar. Add the remaining 2 cups of
strawberries, cover, and place in a cool, dark, place for 2 days.

3. Strain the liquid from the second batch of strawberries, discard the fruit and place the liquid in a saucepan. Add the sugar, heat the juice and sugar slowly, bring it to a boil, and boil for 20 minutes. Skim off any foam that comes to the surface as it is boiling. Cool the liquid and store it in a clean glass jar in the refrigerator.

To Use:
       Use 2 tablespoons of Berry Fizz to 8 ounces of water or club soda. Add ice and a slice of lemon.

Yield: 16 ounces; makes 8 sodas

Cost of Ingredients: $1.82
Comparable Purchased Product: Manhattan
       Special Beverages, 28 ounces, $1.09 ($8.72)
Savings: $6.90

Orange-y Julius Drink

       There is a myth that the original Orange Julius contained ground eggshells because they can be whipped to a foamy mass. This version is tasty and light, sweet and foamy, but—no eggshells.

       3 oranges, peeled and sliced
       1 egg
       1/4 cup sugar
       1 teaspoon Vanilla Bean Extract (page 12)
       6 ice cubes

1. Combine all ingredients in a blender, whirl at high speed for a minute or two or until frothy. Drink immediately.

Variations:
       *Even though it doesn't have a famous name, a Lemon Julius, made with 3 lemons or 3 **Frozen Lemonade Capsules**, page 171, is delicious, too.*

Yield: 24 ounces

Cost of Ingredients: $.64
Comparable Purchased Product: Orange
Julius, 12 ounces, $1.75 ($3.50)
Savings: $2.86

Frozen Lemonade Capsules

Nothing says summer as much as lemonade, yet it's a real pain in the neck to mix it up fresh each time you want some.

Since the mixes are expensive and don't last nearly long enough, try this idea for instant lemonade—it's delicious, convenient, and thrifty.

> **6 lemons**
> **1 1/2 cups sugar**

1. Preheat oven to 250 degrees.

2. Warm lemons in the oven for 30 minutes. Slice them into very thin slices, place in a saucepan, and stir in the sugar. Warm the slices for 30 minutes over very low heat, stirring constantly.

3. Strain the juice by pressing the lemon pulp through a cheesecloth-lined strainer or through a coffee filter. Discard the pulp.

4. Pour juice into a segmented ice cube tray and freeze. Transfer cubes to a plastic bag for storage once they are frozen solid.

To Use:

There are several nice ways to reconstitute your Lemonade Capsules:

You can place a cube in a glass, microwave it for a minute, add plain ice cubes, and enjoy.

Or, you can whirl a few Lemonade Capsules in a blender with plain ice cubes and enjoy a lemony slush.

Or, you could drop a few Lemonade Capsules into a glass of iced tea or hot tea and let them melt and flavor the tea.

Variations:
>	Add oranges to the lemon slices for a different tasting drink.
>	Try some strawberries or a few drops of red food coloring for pink lemonade.
>	For limonade, add some lime slices to the mixture, and a sprig or two of mint.

Yield: 12 ice cubes; 10 ounces

Cost of Ingredients: $.39
Comparable Purchased Product: Minute Maid Lemonade Concentrate, 6 ounces, $.49 ($.81)
Savings: $.42

Sipping Yogurt

This is a nutritious, quick drink that can constitute a fast breakfast on the run or a substitute lunch.

>	**1 cup Homemade Yogurt (page 121)**
>	**1/2 cup fresh or frozen berries**
>	**1 tablespoon instant nonfat dry milk**
>	**1/2 teaspoon lemon juice**
>	**Cinnamon and sugar to taste**

1.	Combine all ingredients in the blender; blend and drink at once.

Yield: 10 ounces

Cost of Ingredients: $.38
Comparable Purchased Product: Tuscan Strawberry Lowfat Yogurt Drink, 32 ounces, $1.29 ($.40)
Savings: $.02

Rainbow Drink Mix

*Drop a tablespoon or two of this mix into your child's milk and watch the milk turn a pretty shade of pink, yellow, blue, or green. Your child thinks the drink is fun, but you will have added a nice nutritional boost as well. You can also use this mix to make **Silly Saturday Cereal** (page 118) as an alternative to the coated cereals that young children like so well.*

> **2 cups instant nonfat dry milk**
> **1/4 cup Silly Sparkles (page 11)**
> **2 tablespoons protein powder**
> **1 teaspoon Vanilla Sugar (page 8)**

1. Combine the ingredients and store in an airtight canister or a tightly covered jar for up to 4 months. Stir well before using.

To Use:

    For fortified milk, add 1 to 2 tablespoons to a glass of cold milk, place in a jar, cover and shake vigorously. Or place milk and mix in a blender and whirl on high speed 1 minute.

Variations:

    For yellow or orange milk, add 1 tablespoon grated orange peel or 1 teaspoon grated lemon peel to the mix.
    For green milk, add 1 teaspoon dried mint leaves, ground fine between two spoons, to the mix.
    For pink milk and sophisticated children, add 1 teaspoon dried rose petals, ground fine, to the mix.

Idea:

    Add a teaspoon or two to hot cereal, add a splash of cold milk, and swirl to make a marble pattern with a spoon.

Yield: 19 ounces

Cost of Ingredients: $.73
Comparable Purchased Product: Nestlé Quik, Strawberry Flavor, 1 pound, $1.79 ($2.12)
Savings: $1.38

Creamy Hot Cocoa Mix

Make up quantities of this mix in the nippy days of October and November and you will always have a warm, nourishing drink on hand.

> **2 cups instant nonfat dry milk**
> **3/4 cup sugar**
> **1/2 cup unsweetened cocoa**
> **1 teaspoon salt**
> **1 cup miniature marshmallows**

1.   Stir all ingredients together and store in a tightly closed jar or container for up to 2 months.

To Use:

> *Put 2 to 3 heaping tablespoons of the mix into a mug and fill with boiling water or, for an extra rich drink, hot milk. Top with whipped cream and cinnamon for a special treat.*

Yield: 20 ounces

Cost of Ingredients: $1.67
Comparable Purchased Product: Carnation Mini-Marshmallow Cocoa Mix, 12 ounces, $1.19 ($1.98)
Savings: $.31

Herb Teas

Try making some of your very own seasoned and herb teas, and if you find a blend that particularly suits you, remember that it would make a nice gift for someone else to sample. A word of caution: never try to brew a tea from an herb you can't identify. Even though a certain herb may look small and harmless, it could be dangerous and even lethal.

*You can buy all the herbs listed in the following blends at the health food store or through one of the mail order firms listed in the **Resources** section, page 389. Or, if you are patient, you can plan ahead and begin to grow some of the herbs in your annual or perennial flower beds.*

Good Digestion Tea

2 tablespoons dried peppermint leaves
1 tablespoon rosemary
1 tablespoon dried comfrey leaves

1. Blend, store in an airtight container, and steep 1 tablespoon of the tea in 1 cup of water for 5 minutes.

Balmy Lemon Tea

9 tablespoons lemon thyme
3 tablespoons lemon basil
2 tablespoons chamomile
1 tablespoon lemon balm

1. Blend, store, and steep as above. Lemon balm is said to reduce fevers, so you might sip this tea if you feel a fever coming on.

Variations:
The following herbs will make a nice tea, alone or in combination. Test and find the flavors you like best.

__Anise__ will give you a sweet licorice flavor that is supposed to be good for coughs and as an aid to sleep.
__Chamomile__ is mild, apple-flavored, very soothing, and is said to prevent nightmares.
__Catnip__ has a very strong flavor and is said to have been an old-fashioned cough remedy. It is probably best to leave it to your cats.
__Dill__ and __fennel__ are familiar and strongly flavored. Boil the seeds for tea.
__Lavender__ imparts a delicate and unusual fragrance and flavor when mixed with other herbs in tea.
__Rose hips__ are an excellent source of vitamin C and add a fruity, spicy flavor.
__Rosemary__ and __sage__, both kitchen favorites, are spicy and soothing to sore throats.
__Strawberry__ leaves and fruit make a sweet and fragrant tea.

Yield: 2 ounces

Cost of Ingredients: $.98
Comparable Purchased Product: Celestial
Seasonings Herb Teas, 2 ounces, $1.99
Savings: $1.51

Mulling Mix

Sprinkle a few tablespoons of this mix over fresh cider before you warm it, or combine it with a quart of hearty burgundy wine for a different-tasting drink. A batch of this mix makes a great winter house-warming gift.

> 1/4 **cup orange peel**
> 1/4 **cup lemon peel**
> 2 **tablespoons Grenadine Syrup (page 183)**
> 3 **sticks cinnamon**
> 2 **whole nutmegs, crushed, or 2 tablespoons ground**
> 6 **whole cloves**
> 1/2 **teaspoon cardamom**
> 3 **tablespoons brown sugar**

1. Mix all ingredients together and store in an airtight tin or a tightly covered glass jar.

To Use:
        Measure 2 tablespoons of mix for every cup of apple cider or wine. Place mix and liquid in a pan and simmer gently for 10 minutes. Strain and serve.

Idea:
        Try adding a tablespoon or more of one of your homemade fruit brandies for a different flavor.

Yield: 4 ounces

Cost of Ingredients: $.61
Comparable Purchased Product: J. Crow
Mulling Mix, 6 ounces, $1.29 ($.86)
Savings: $.25

Bloody Mary Mix

This "mix" is also terrific as it stands—it's a delicious, strong tomato juice drink that will really open your eyes in the morning, without the addition of liquor. If you do choose to add vodka, this brew will hold up, even over ice.

4 cups tomato or vegetable juice
2 tablespoons lime juice
2 tablespoons Worcestershire sauce
2 teaspoons horseradish
1 teaspoon salt
1 teaspoon Tabasco sauce

1. Mix all ingredients and store in a sterilized glass jar or covered pitcher in the refrigerator. Use within 4 days for the freshest taste.

To Use:
        If you want to spike your mix and make a traditional Bloody Mary, fill an 8-ounce glass with ice and pour a jigger, or 2 ounces, of vodka over the ice. Fill to the brim with the mix, add a wedge of lime and a hearty stalk of celery as a stirrer, and serve.

Yield: 34 ounces

Cost of Ingredients: $1.89
Comparable Purchased Product: Harvest Moon Fireworks Cheer, 25.4 ounces, $4.99 ($6.67)
Savings: $4.78

Rum Coffee

*This is an alternative to **Spiced and Fancy After-dinner Coffee**, page 178, and is tasty on those bitter cold nights when the wind is howling about and you want to feel warm all over.*

3 tablespoons honey, warmed slightly
1 cup heavy whipping cream
3 cups freshly brewed coffee

> 1 pint vanilla ice cream
> 1/2 cup rum

1. Assemble all ingredients beforehand so that you can perform the steps in quick succession. Begin by stirring the honey into the whipping cream and setting the mixture aside.

2. Pour the hot coffee over the ice cream and stir the honey-cream mixture into the coffee-ice cream mixture. Add the rum and stir well. Serve immediately.

Yield: 32 ounces

Cost of Ingredients: $4.70
Comparable Purchased Product: Yellow Brick Toad After-dinner Rum Coffee, 9 ounces, $3.50 ($14.44)
Savings: $7.74

Spiced and Fancy After-dinner Coffee

If dinner was special, why not make the coffee that ends the meal special, too? Or, if you're dieting and want to forgo fattening desserts, try one of the following fancy coffees to quell your sweet tooth.

> **4 cups freshly brewed black coffee**
> **4 whole cloves**
> **1 stick cinnamon**

1. As soon as the coffee is finished brewing and still piping hot, place the spices in a decanter or Thermos, pour in the coffee, and let it sit for about 10 minutes.

To Use:
*Pour the spiced coffee without removing the spices and serve with a dollop of whipped cream dusted with more cinnamon, or try adding a spoonful of **Spicy Orange Cordial** (page 187) or **Coffee Liqueur** (page 190).*

Variations:

To freshly brewed coffee, add 1 tablespoon grated
orange peel or **Vanilla Bean Extract**, page 12.
Try adding 1 teaspoon **Basic Chocolate Sauce**, page 45,
and topping with crushed mint.

Yield: 4 servings

Cost of Ingredients: $.44
Comparable Purchased Product: Bigelow
Cafe Orange Delight, 1.75 ounces, $2.39 ($.68)
Savings: $.24

Thrifty Sangría

*This is the sangría to make to compete with the store brand,
both for price and flavor. If you want a special-occasion
sangría, see **Guillermo's Summer Sangría**, page 180.*

1 quart California burgundy wine
5 teaspoons sugar
1 ounce brandy
1 orange, sliced
1 lemon, sliced
1 lime, sliced
2 cups club soda.

1. Pour wine and sugar into a large jug and stir until the sugar
is dissolved. Add brandy and stir well.

2. Add fruit slices and chill for at least 2 hours. Just before
serving, stir in chilled club soda.

Yield: 48 ounces

Cost of Ingredients: $3.90
Comparable Purchased Product: Yago
Sangría, 1 liter, $2.50 ($4.14)
Savings: $.24

Guillermo's Summer Sangría

There's really nothing like this drink to make a party happy—it is a big hit all during the party and again with the clean-up crew the following day because the fruit that remains is very tasty and very potent.

*This is **not** a low-cost version of sangría. The only relevant price comparison would be a very high priced custom-made party punch, but for special occasions, this is a special brew.*

> 1 large watermelon
> 1 cantaloupe
> 1 honeydew melon
> 12 to 24 oranges
> 12 limes
> 12 peaches
> 6 to 8 bottles Spanish Rioja wine
> 2 cups brandy
> 3 cups vodka

1. First, prepare fruit. Cut watermelon, cantaloupe, and honeydew meat into medium-size chunks, wash and slice the oranges and limes, leaving the skins on; peel and slice the peaches.

2. Place all the fruit in a very large bowl, pot, vat, or container roomy enough to hold all the fruit and liquid. Pour in the wine, brandy, and vodka; cover the container with cheesecloth, and let it stand so the flavors can mellow for 24 hours.

3. Serve the wine punch right from the big container by dipping in a soup ladle, or transfer it in smaller batches, along with the fruit, to a big punch bowl.

Yield: 1 1/2 gallons

Cost of Ingredients: $46.82
Comparable Purchased Product: Yellow Brick Toad Custom Party Sangria, 1 gallon, $50.00 ($75.00)
Savings: $28.18

Champagne Cooler

Here is an elegant solution to the problem of what to serve on an elegant occasion—it's simple to make, tastes light and delicious, and looks very light and pretty. Serve it in a clear punch bowl, and float slices of fruit in the punch as a finishing touch.

3 cups fresh whole strawberries
3 liters German dry white wine
1 liter domestic champagne

1. Place the strawberries in a pitcher or a large bowl and pour 1 liter of the white wine over them. Cover and refrigerate for 4 hours.

2. Two hours before you intend to serve the punch, place the champagne and the remaining white wine in the freezer to chill.

3. Assemble the punch at serving time by pouring the wine and strawberries into a punch bowl and adding the rest of the wine and champagne. Add flavored or decorated ice, if desired, and serve immediately.

Yield: 64 ounces

Cost of Ingredients: $21.49
Comparable Purchased Product: Silver's
   Champagne Cooler, 4.5 ounces, $4.75 ($67.55)
Savings: $46.06

Sweet Berry Cordial

This brew is a cheery cherry color and looks fantastic in a cut-glass cruet, if you're lucky enough to have one. Look in antiques shops for pretty containers for all your cordials and liqueurs, and at holiday time, you can arrange them like liquid jewels on the sideboard or nestled in evergreen branches on top of the liquor cabinet.

2 cups sweet black cherries
1 cup pie cherries
1 cup raspberries
3 cups vodka
4 cups sugar
1/4 cup lemon juice
2 cups water

1. Gently mash cherries and raspberries together. If you don't have pie cherries, use 3 cups of sweet cherries instead, and reduce the sugar by 1/2 cup. Don't worry about removing the pits or seeds. Put fruit mash into a clean, half-gallon-size jar.

2. Pour vodka over the fruit, cover, and let the mixture sit in a dark place for at least 4 weeks. Shake fruit every other day or so without opening the jar.

3. Boil sugar, lemon juice, and water together for 1 minute; let cool.

4. Strain fruit-vodka mixture through a cheesecloth or coffee filter. Press out all the juice and discard the pulp. You should have at least 4 cups of juice.

5. Stir in the sugar-water syrup and pour into clean glass bottles. Cap or cork with new corks and let the brew sit for another 2 weeks before serving. Liqueur will keep indefinitely in a cool, dark place.

Yield: 48 ounces

Cost of Ingredients: $13.54
Comparable Purchased Product:
  Schladerer's Fruit Cordials, 24.6 ounces,
  $13.99 ($26.88)
Savings: $13.34

Cheap Trick . . . . ✂ . . . .

A little bit of fruit cordial poured over vanilla ice cream is one of the easiest ways to end a fancy dinner. Add some Candied Citrus Peel (see page 164) for extra flair.

Grenadine Syrup

You can buy pomegranates on the East Coast from late October until the end of December, so check their availability in your area if you want to try this recipe. If you've never opened a dull-red, heavy pomegranate, the amout of juice will be a surprise. Open the fruit over a bowl to catch all the juice, because these are messy fruits. Use only the tiny, pulpy seeds only and not any of the bitter white pith surrounding the seeds.

1 pomegranate
1 cup sugar
1/4 cup water

1. Remove all the seeds from the pomegranate and combine them with the sugar and water in a glass or an enamel bowl. Use a fork to mash the seeds a bit, cover the bowl, and let it sit in the refrigerator for 5 days, stirring the mixture once each day.

2. Strain the mixture and discard the pulp or use it for **Liquid Fertilizer**, page 298. Place the juice in a glass or an enamel pan and slowly heat until it just barely simmers. Cook, stirring, at low heat for 2 minutes. Cool before pouring into a sterilized glass bottle or jar, cap, and store in the refrigerator for up to 6 months.

Variations:
Although it is not traditional, I like to reduce the extreme sweetness of this drink by adding the juice and pulp of one lime along with the sugar and water in Step 1.

To Use:
Fresh grenadine syrup is delicious poured over ice cubes and combined with club soda for a fizzy summer drink. Or, try serving a spoonful over vanilla ice cream, with sliced peaches, or its usual fate: as a red coloring in mixed drinks.

Yield: 8 ounces

Cost of Ingredients: $.63
Comparable Purchased Product: Rose's
Grenadine, 12 ounces, $1.69 ($1.12)
Savings: $.49

Blueberry Cordial

*If you're lucky enough to have more blueberries than you know what to do with, this cordial is a good place to start. Another idea is to make a **Blueberry Syrup**, page 44, for your **Quick Pancakes**, page 71.*

This is one of the prettiest-looking cordials that you can make, so celebrate its lovely hue by finding a wonderful decanter or cruet to show it off in. The secret to a clear cordial is in the straining, so be sure to follow the directions exactly.

> 4 cups blueberries
> 3 cups vodka or gin
> 1/4 cup lemon juice
> 1 1/2 cups water
> 4 whole cloves
> 1/2 teaspoon coriander seeds
> 3 cups sugar

1. Wash and drain the blueberries. Crush them in a bowl, blender, or food processor and scrape the mash into a sterilized 2-quart jar.

2. Add the vodka or gin, lemon juice, water, cloves, and coriander. Cover and store in a dark place for 10 days. Stir the mix every other day.

3. Strain the mixture through a cheesecloth or coffee filter, discarding the pulp. Strain a second time, using a fresh filter or a clean cheesecloth. Add the sugar to the juice, stir, and pour the mixture into a sterilized glass bottle. Store in a dark place for 4 weeks. Use within 1 year.

Yield: 36 ounces

Cost of Ingredients: $12.11
Comparable Purchased Product:
   Schladerer's Fruit Cordial, 24.6 ounces, $13.99
   ($20.16)
Savings: $8.05

Prune Cordial

Of all the cordial recipes, this one is possibly the easiest to make, and certainly the ingredients are available all year long.

1/2 pound dried prunes
Water to cover prunes
1 pint whiskey
2 teaspoons sugar

1. Simmer prunes in water for 5 minutes and drain. Discard water.

2. Place prunes in a sterilized quart-size glass jar with whiskey and sugar. Stir to mix. Cover and let mixture sit for 2 weeks.

3. Strain mixture through cheesecloth or a coffee filter and discard fruit. Store the juice in a sterilized glass jar, corked or capped tightly, for up to 1 year on the pantry shelf.

Yield: 32 ounces

Cost of Ingredients: $5.97
Comparable Purchased Product:
  Schladerer's Fruit Cordial, 24.6 ounces, $13.99
  ($17.92)
Savings: $11.95

Plum Cordial

This brew has a very long storage time, so plan on serving or giving it as a gift one whole season after making it. The longer it is stored, the richer the flavor, so don't rush this one. After six months, it's at its best for drinking, and it will keep well for another 6 months after that.

3 pounds ripe plums
2 cups sugar
1 quart vodka

1. Pit plums and slice them. Place plums into a sterilized glass quart-size jar, cover with sugar and stir to further bruise them, add vodka and cover. Let mixture sit for 2 weeks.

2. Strain through a cheesecloth or coffee filter and discard plums. Pour juice into a sterilized container, cover tightly, and store for 2 to 4 more months, or until mixture is clear.

Yield: 32 ounces

Cost of Ingredients: $13.75
Comparable Purchased Product:
   Schladerer's Fruit Cordial, 24.6 ounces, $13.99
   ($17.92)
Savings: $4.17

Pear Cordial

This is a very sweet, somewhat unusual cordial, and it is a delicious accompaniment to fresh apples in the fall. If you start this cordial just when the first pears of the summer are in, you will have a delightful treat to enjoy in October.

> **1/2 cup water**
> **1 cup sugar**
> **4 ripe, firm pears**
> **4 whole cloves**
> **1 teaspoon allspice**
> **1 teaspoon nutmeg**
> **4 cups vodka**

1. Mix water and sugar in a small pan and bring to a boil. Boil for 5 minutes, stirring constantly. Remove from heat, and cool.

2. Do not peel the pears, but slice them into large pieces and place them in a sterilized 2-quart-size glass jar. Sprinkle on the cloves and spices and stir in the sugar-water and vodka. Cover and store in a dark place for 10 weeks. Turn the jar upside down to mix the contents once a week.

3. Strain the mixture through a cheesecloth or coffee filter and discard the fruit. Pour the liquid into a sterilized glass bottle, cap securely, and store for another 2 weeks in a cool, dark place.

Yield: 48 ounces

Cost of Ingredients: $10.65
Comparable Purchased Product:
Schladerer's Fruit Cordial, 24.6 ounces, $13.99
($27.29)
Savings: $16.64

Spicy Orange Cordial

Try a teaspoon of this delicious liquid mixed into your **Basic Chocolate Sauce,** *page 45, before you spoon it over ice cream, or swirl a spoonful into hot coffee and top with whipped cream, or add some to a cup of hot tea and make it something special.*

6 oranges, peeled and chopped
2 cups vodka
1 cup brandy
1 teaspoon cinnamon
1/2 teaspoon allspice
1/2 teaspoon nutmeg
2 whole cloves
2 cups sugar
2 cups water

1. Wash and rinse oranges well and carefully peel them, avoiding the white pith under the peel. Chop the peel and place it in a sterilized quart-size glass jar.

2. Add the vodka, brandy, and spices, cover the jar, and place in a cool, dark place for 2 weeks. Shake the bottle twice a week to mix contents.

3. Strain the mixture through a cheesecloth or coffee filter and discard the orange peel or use it to make **Candied Citrus Peel,** page 164.

4. Combine the sugar and water in a pan and bring to a boil. Boil for 5 minutes and remove from heat. Cool.

5. Stir the sugar-water mixture into the strained orange-liqueur mixture, pour the liquid into a sterilized glass bottle and cap securely. Store in a cool, dark place for 2 to 4 weeks.

Yield: 32 ounces

Cost of Ingredients: $8.90
Comparable Purchased Product: Cointreau, 24.6 ounces, $21.49 ($27.95)
Savings: $19.55

Cranberry Liqueur

This is one of the finest, prettiest drinks you can serve with your holiday dinner. You can show off the pretty color best by storing the liqueur in a glass cruet right out on the holiday sideboard nestled in a bed of evergreens.

> 2 cups sugar
> 1 cup water
> 2 cups cranberries, chopped
> 1 teaspoon grated orange rind
> 1 teaspoon grated lemon rind
> 3 cups vodka

1. In a medium-size saucepan, combine sugar and water and bring to a boil. Lower heat and simmer for 5 minutes, or until all sugar is dissolved. Stir in cranberries, orange and lemon rinds, and immediately remove from the heat. Cool.

2. Pour cranberry mixture into a sterilized glass jar with a tight-fitting lid. Pour vodka over cranberries and stir. Cover and store in a cool dark place for 4 weeks. Shake container every 4 days or so.

3. Strain cranberry mixture through a cheesecloth or coffee filter and discard pulp. Strain juice two more times or until liquid is clear. Pour into a sterilized quart-size bottle to store.

Cover tightly and put back into a cool dark place for another 4 weeks.

Yield: 32 ounces

Cost of Ingredients: $8.85
Comparable Purchased Product:
   Schladerer's Fruit Cordial, 24.6 ounces, $13.99
   ($18.19)
Savings: $9.34

Dandelion Wine

This wine is a close companion to **Spicy Orange Cordial,** *page 187, but with the sunny addition of dandelion flowers. Be certain that the dandelion flowers you are using have not been sprayed with herbicide.*
The art of making real wine requires special equipment and an understanding of fermentation and bottling procedures. This wine can be made without specialized equipment as long as you remember to cap the jar **loosely,** *as described in Steps 4 and 5. This will allow any carbon dioxide gas that results from the fermentation to escape safely. The wine is ready to drink when it is no longer cloudy but clear.*

> 1 quart dandelion flowers
> 1 quart boiling water
> 1/2 pound raisins
> 2 oranges
> 2 lemons
> 1 pound sugar
> 1/2 yeast cake

1. Pick over the dandelion flowers and make sure that there are no green seed pods, stems, or leaves remaining. Place flowers in a large sterilized glass jar and pour the boiling water over them. Cover and let the flowers stand undisturbed in a dark place for 3 days.

2. Strain the flower-water mixture through cheesecloth or a coffee filter and discard the flowers or add them to **Liquid Fertilizer,** page 298.

3. Wash and peel oranges and lemons, slice and chop the peel, and add peel and juice to the flower water. Add the raisins and boil the liquid for 20 to 30 minutes. Remove from heat and cool.

4. Add sugar and yeast to the cooled mixture. Place mixture in a clean glass jar and cover loosely by placing clean cheesecloth over the mouth of the jar and then resting, not securing, the lid on top. Let the mixture sit undisturbed for 3 days in a dark place.

5. Strain the mixture and return it to a sterilized glass jar. Cover loosely and allow the mixture to stand for 3 weeks. By this time, any bubbling from the fermentation should have stopped. If not, let the mixture rest for another week or until fermentation stops.

6. Rebottle the wine in sterilized glass containers, cork with new corks, and let the wine age a few more months before drinking.

Yield: 32 ounces

Cost of Ingredients: $1.37
Comparable Purchased Product: Yellow Brick Toad Dandelion Wine, 22.5 ounces, $4.00 ($5.68)
Savings: $4.31

Coffee Liqueur

This drink is welcome with coffee and dinner mints.

> 4 cups sugar
> 6 cups freshly brewed very strong coffee
> 1/2 vanilla bean
> 1 fifth vodka
> 1 tablespoon Basic Chocolate Sauce (page 45)

1. Mix sugar into the coffee and bring to a rolling boil; immediately turn off heat. Let cool.

2. Chop vanilla bean into small pieces, being very careful to keep the little seeds. Place the pieces in the bottom of a large sterilized glass jar and pour in the vodka.

3. Add cooled sugar-coffee mixture and Chocolate Sauce. Stir and cover container; let mixture rest for 30 days. Strain twice through cheesecloth or a coffee filter. Liqueur will keep well for several months on the pantry shelf.

Yield: 80 ounces

Cost of Ingredients: $9.27
Comparable Purchased Product: Kahlúa, 25. 4 ounces, $12.69 ($39.96)
Savings: $30.69

Irish Cream Liqueur

This is a rich drink that can be savored for special occasions.

> 2 eggs
> 2 cups Sweetened Condensed Milk (page 17)
> 1 teaspoon chocolate syrup or Basic Chocolate Sauce (page 45)
> 1 teaspoon instant coffee
> 2 cups vodka
> 2 cups heavy cream

1. Beat eggs until thick and lemon colored. Slowly add the rest of the ingredients one at a time beating well after each addition.

2. Pour mixture into sterilized dark glass bottles and let it rest for one week before drinking. Mixture will keep for up to 3 months in the refrigerator or 1 month on the pantry shelf.

Yield: 46 ounces

Cost of Ingredients: $9.21
Comparable Purchased Product: Bailey's Irish Cream, 25.4 ounces, $14.49 ($26.24)
Savings: $17.03

Homemade Galiano

This liqueur is known by its bright yellow color, but it can also be made without adding the food coloring, if you prefer.

 2 cups sugar
 1 cup water
 1/4 cup anise extract
 1 teaspoon vanilla extract or Vanilla Bean Extract
   (page 12)
 3 drops yellow food coloring
 1 fifth vodka

1. Combine sugar and water in a pan and bring to a boil. Boil for 1 minute and immediately reduce heat. Simmer for 1 hour or until thickened. Remove from heat and cool.

2. Pour sugar-water syrup into a sterilized quart-size bottle. Add anise extract, vanilla, and food coloring. Stir gently and add the vodka.

3. Cover and let the mixture sit for 10 days to 2 weeks before serving.

Yield: 32 ounces

 Cost of Ingredients: $9.28
Comparable Purchased Product: Galiano,
  25.4 ounces, $17.18 ($21.64)
Savings: $12.36

Homemade Drambuie

This mixture is smooth and as inexpensive as the type of Scotch you use. The anise extract is something of a specialty item, but you should be able to find it in a gourmet store or a large, well-stocked grocery store.

 2 cups sugar

1 cup water
1 teaspoon anise extract
1 pint Scotch

1. Combine sugar and water in a pan and bring to a boil. Boil for1 minute, then simmer for 30 minutes, stirring occasionally. Cool.

2. Pour sugar syrup into a sterilized quart-size bottle. Add anise and Scotch. Shake gently and cover.

3. Let mixture age in a dark place for 1 to 2 weeks before serving.

Yield: 32 ounces

Cost of Ingredients: $6.43
Comparable Purchased Product: Drambuie, 25.4 ounces, $20.01 ($25.20)
Savings: $18.77

Homemade Crème de Menthe

This favorite after-dinner drink is a good addition to chocolate sauces and desserts. It's refreshing in the summer poured over ice and topped with a few sprigs of fresh mint.

2 ounces fresh mint leaves
1 fifth vodka
4 cups sugar
2 cups water
10 drops peppermint oil
2 to 3 drops green food coloring

1. Crush mint leaves in a mortar and pestle or place them between a tablespoon and a teaspoon and macerate. Place crushed leaves in a sterilized glass jar and pour vodka over them. Cover and let sit for 10 days.

2. Strain vodka through cheesecloth or a coffee filter and discard mint.

3. Make a syrup of the sugar and water by bringing the mixture to a boil, boiling for 30 minutes, and then letting it cool. Add syrup to the mint-flavored vodka, add peppermint and coloring, and stir.

4. If liqueur is not clear, you may want to filter it a second time. You may also want to omit the green food coloring. Liqueur will keep for a year on the pantry shelf.

Yield: 48 ounces

Cost of Ingredients: $10.42
Comparable Purchased Product: Crème de Menthe, 25.4 ounces, $7.43 ($14.04)
Savings: $3.62

Pippins and Port

The pippin in this recipe is the apple, and the best apple to use is the Granny Smith.

> **4 cups sugar**
> **4 cups water**
> **2 cinnamon sticks**
> **2 tablespoons ground ginger**
> **2 tablespoons lemon rind**
> **4 pounds apples, peeled and sliced**
> **2 cups port wine**

1. Combine the sugar, water, cinnamon, ginger, and lemon rind in a pan and bring to a boil. Boil for 10 minutes, strain the syrup, and discard the spices. Cool the syrup.

2. Place the apples in a large bowl and cover with the syrup. Cover the bowl with plastic wrap and refrigerate overnight or for at least 8 hours.

3. Transfer the apples and syrup to a saucepan, cover, and simmer for 20 minutes or until the apples are tender. Remove from heat and cool the apples to room temperature. Stir in the port wine.

Idea:
> Serve **Pippins and Port** by spooning some of the apples into a serving dish, covering them with the syrup, and topping with sweetened whipped cream.

Yield: 40 ounces

Cost of Ingredients: $4.85
Comparable Purchased Product: Yellow Brick Toad Pippins and Port, 1 gallon, $65.00 ($20.31)
Savings: $15.46

Holiday Eggnog

Although the recipe for this festive eggnog contains liquor, it will taste delicious without brandy or whiskey. It's a good idea to make up the basic eggnog first without any liquor, taste it, and then only add the liquor at the last minute, if preferred, and if there is any eggnog left.

> **6 eggs, separated**
> **1/3 cup sugar**
> **1 quart whole milk**
> **1 cup heavy cream**
> **1 teaspoon Vanilla Bean Extract (page 12)**
> **1 1/4 cups brandy or Kentucky bourbon (optional)**
> **Ground nutmeg**

1. Beat the egg yolks and sugar with an electric mixer or in a food processor until the mixture is pale and light.

2. Gradually add the milk, cream, and vanilla to the mixture, beating well after each addition.

3. In a separate bowl, beat the egg whites until stiff and then gently fold them into the egg yolk mixture until well combined. Chill until ready to serve.

4. Pour eggnog into a punch bowl, stir in the brandy if desired, and dust the top of the drink with nutmeg.

Yield: 54 ounces

Cost of Ingredients: $6.78
Comparable Purchased Product: Heublein's
   Egg Nog, 32 ounces, $5.59 ($9.18)
Savings: $2.40

Christmas Wassail

This very festive holiday drink is always served from a fancy punch bowl, and the man of the house should be prepared to give a hearty toast before serving the drink to his guests.

> 12 apples, sliced
> 1 cup water
> 4 cups sugar
> 2 tablespoons nutmeg
> 2 tablespoons ginger
> 2 tablespoons allspice
> 6 whole cloves
> 1/2 teaspoon mace
> 2 sticks cinnamon
> 12 eggs, separated
> 4 cups dry sherry
> 2 cups brandy

1. Combine the apples, water, and spices in a pan and bring to a boil. Reduce heat and simmer for 20 minutes. Cool.

2. Whip the egg yolks and whites separately until the yolks are blended and lemony colored and the whites are stiff. Fold the whites into the yolks.

3. Strain the apple mixture and discard the apples and spices. Blend the juice into the egg mixture.

4. Combine the sherry and brandy in a pan and bring to a boil. Boil for 1 minute, remove from heat, let cool for 5 minutes and stir a tablespoon of the warm liquid into the egg mixture. Gradually stir in a few more tablespoons before combining the two mixtures completely.

Idea:

    Surround the wassail bowl with holly and candles and float some baked apples stuffed with brown sugar directly in the brew.

Yield: 11 cups

Cost of Ingredients: $11.62
Comparable Purchased Product: Yellow
   Brick Toad Wassail, 1 gallon, $65.00 ($44.68)
Savings: $33.06

Chapter 6

Health and Personal Care Aids

All the items in this chapter are safe, very effective, and fun to make. They save you hundreds of dollars over the same items from department and drugstores because not one extra penny is spent on packaging or advertising. There is everything here you need to pamper yourself, your baby, your best friend, and your wallet.

Skin Clarifier
Light-skin Bleaching Cream
Simple Skin-lightening Masks
Lemon Lightening Pack
Skin Bleaching Tonic
Avocado Scalp Pack
Super-body Hair Treat
Egg Shampoo
Herbal Secret Shampoo
Hair Rinses and Toners
Herbal Rinse for Normal Hair
Lemon Rinse for Light Hair
Sage Rinse for Dark Hair
Sea Rinse for Damaged Hair
Dandruff Control Rinse
Lemon Hair Spray
Soothing Bath Salts
Ultra Bubble Bath
Perfumed Bath Powder
Home Remedies for Coughs
Sweet Solution Cough Syrup
Expectorant Cough Syrup
Sunflower Cough Syrup for Grown-ups
Nighttime Cold Remedy
Vegetable Juice Laxative
Iodine Antiseptic Wash
Rose Beads

Gritty Scrub Hand Cleaner

This is one of the best ideas in the book, as far as I'm concerned, because it cleverly solves the problem of what to do with all those infernal slices of leftover soap that no one, not even James Michener, can ever bear to throw away. I once read an article about the fabulously successful writer of those world-sized sagas, and the interviewer reported that there, in the great man's bathroom, was a plastic margarine container filled with soap slivers, just waiting to be reborn.

**1 cup Soft Soap (page 278) or several small bits and
    pieces of soap, thoroughly dried
1 cup cornmeal
1/4 cup blanched almonds
4 tablespoons corn oil**

1.   Break up soap into chunks and feed into a food processor or blender and whirl until the soap is granulated. Add the cornmeal and almonds and continue to process until you have a fine meal.

2. Blend meal with the corn oil until you have a paste smooth enough for the container of your choice. If you want to store the paste in a plastic margarine tub with a lid, the paste should be semisolid. If you want to pour the hand cleaner into a pump-type dispenser, add more oil until the right consistency is reached.

Yield: 18 ounces

Cost of Ingredients: $1.02
Comparable Purchased Product:
    Workman's Scrub Hand Cleaner, 14 ounces,
    $3.49 ($4.48)
Savings: $3.46

Cheap Trick ....✂....

Substitute dried, ground-up citrus peel for the cornmeal in this recipe for an even more effective hand cleaner. See page 26 for how to dry the peels.

Superwhite Tooth Powder

The basic tooth powder recipe given here works very, very well to keep your teeth bright and clean. It is as old as all of our grandmothers, of course, and there are numerous variations, some of which are listed. Do not add salt to the basic recipe if you even suspect you have an allergy to salt.

2 tablespoons lemon or orange rind, dried (page 26)
1/4 cup baking soda
2 teaspoons salt

1.   Place the orange or lemon rind in a blender or food processor and grind until the peel is a fine powder. Add baking soda and salt and process for a few seconds more, or until you have a fine powder. You can also use a mortar and pestle to grind the rind and salts together.

To Use:
       Store the powder in a large salt shaker and shake directly onto your wet toothbrush, or keep the powder in an airtight tin and dip your moistened toothbrush into the mix. Brush thoroughly and rinse well.

Superwhite Toothpaste

1 teaspoon Superwhite Tooth Powder
1/4 teaspoon hydrogen peroxide

1. Brush your teeth with the mixture, but be careful to rinse and spit out rather than swallow any of the peroxide because it could make you sick if you drank a lot of it. It will taste crummy enough, so you won't be tempted. This solution is very healing to gums and teeth, and my sister's dentist says that it keeps plaque from forming.

Instant Sweet Toothpaste

This is a dandy homemade recipe to try if you have small children who are reluctant to brush.

1 teaspoon Superwhite Tooth Powder
1 tablespoon crushed ripe strawberries

1. Mix strawberries and powder into a paste and brush as usual. This is a much sweeter tasting toothpaste than the other mixture, and it also whitens teeth over time.

Yield: 4 ounces

Cost of Ingredients: $.09
Comparable Purchased Product: Crest
Toothpaste, 8 ounces, $1.69 (.84)
Savings: $.75

Chapped-lip Stick

To avoid having wind-roughened lips, try smoothing this mixture on before, during, and after exposure to the elements. It's an extremely soothing and protective cover, so you might spread some on other parts of the body exposed to cold or wind—cheeks, nose, even your hands, before you put on your gloves.

1/4 cup paraffin
1/4 cup petroleum jelly
Few drops oil of lemon or other scent (optional)

1. In a glass or an enamel double boiler, melt the paraffin slowly, stirring constantly until completely melted. Add the petroleum jelly, stirring until completely combined. Remove from heat and add the scent, if desired. You can also melt the paraffin in a small glass bowl that you've placed in a pan of water or in the top of the double boiler.

2. Pour while salve is still liquid into a container with a snug-fitting lid. For carrying convenience, you can pour a small amount of the salve into a tiny pillbox or fancy tin.

Yield: 4 ounces

Cost of Ingredients: $.85
Comparable Purchased Product:
Chapstick, 1 ounce, $.89 ($3.56)
Savings: $2.71

Deep Tanning Oil

This preparation is for those who tan easily—it should not be used on children or on people with fair skin. However, if you like to sit in the sun and roast, in spite of all the health warnings to the contrary, at least slather this soothing oil all over. It is guaranteed to hasten the tan along if you behave sensibly: start out slowly, add a little more time each day, and reapply the oil often.

To save money on this product, I always use a leaf from my aloe plant for the gel. Break off the leaf near the spine of the plant and place the leaf between two sheets of plastic wrap. Roll toward the cut end with a rolling pin and scoop the gel into the mixture. One large leaf equals about 2 tablespoons of gel. Another money-saving hint is to buy your wheat germ oil from a store that sells farm or horse-grooming supplies—it's much cheaper and it's fine for topical use.

> **1/2 cup very strong tea (4 tea bags, 1/2 cup water)**
> **1 cup wheat germ oil**
> **1/4 cup sesame oil**
> **1/4 cup apple cider vinegar**
> **2 tablespoons aloe gel**
> **1 teaspoon iodine**

1.   Brew the tea by using 4 tea bags to 1/2 cup water. Allow the tea to sit for a few minutes before combining it with the rest of the ingredients.

2. Stir the oils and vinegar together, and then gently beat in the aloe gel, using a wire whisk or wooden spoon. Add the tea and iodine and pour into a tightly capped plastic container.

3. Mixture will keep for up to 3 months in the refrigerator.

Yield: 16 ounces

Cost of Ingredients: $2.86
Comparable Purchased Product:
   Coppertone Oil, 8 ounces, $5.79 ($11.58)
Savings: $8.72

Quick Sunburn Soother

If you have a mild case of sunburn, here's a quick rinse that will relieve the pain and soreness. Refrigerate this solution for even greater benefit.

> 1 cup white wine vinegar
> 5 tablespoons salt
> 5 tablespoons Homemade Yogurt, plain (page 121)
> 2 tablespoons aloe gel

1. Combine the ingredients and stir briskly until smooth and creamy. Pour into a pump-type container and store in the refrigerator. Shake vigorously before using.

To Use:

Smooth on affected areas every hour or so until the burning sensation is gone. Or, you can saturate a clean washcloth with the solution and gently lay it on the affected area.

Yield: 8 ounces

Cost of Ingredients: $.35
Comparable Purchased Product: Solarcaine
   Aloe Vera Gel, 4 ounces, $3.89 ($7.78)
Savings: $7.43

Cheap Tricks ....

If you have a hard time convincing young children to stand still long enough to apply sunscreen, try this trick: squeeze out several blobs of zinc oxide into a few paper cups. Color each cupful a different color with food coloring or a few drops of Nature's Colors, page 367. Mix thoroughly and apply to your child's nose, cheeks, tops of shoulders, and ears. Yes, your child will look like an Indian, but you will be able to tell when the sun protection has worn off.

If you have only a slight case of sunburn or general skin itchiness, try adding 2 tablespoons of cornstarch to your bath.

Fun and Fruity Complexion Masks

There are probably as many ways to layer fruit and other goodies upon your face as there are days in the year. In fact, you should try every one you can until you find your personal favorites. The following are some of mine.

Whenever I'm creating a mask or any preparation for my face or hair, I try to avoid using anything I don't personally like to eat, on the theory that I'm not going to enjoy the scent if I don't enjoy the food. Enjoyment, after all, is what all these beauty rituals are about—so put your feet up, relax, and don't be afraid to try something new.

Peach Tightening Mask

**1 fresh, ripe peach, peeled and pitted
1 egg white**

1. Whip peach and egg white together in a blender until smooth.

2. Gently pat the mixture all over your face, relax for 30 minutes, and then rinse off with cool water.

Strawberry Drawing Mask

**1/2 cup very ripe strawberries
1/4 cup cornstarch**

1. Mix strawberries and cornstarch together to make a paste and apply it to your face, avoiding the delicate area around your eyes.

2. Leave on for 30 minutes and rinse off with cool water.

Apple Mask for Normal Skin

**1 apple, cored and quartered
2 tablespoons honey
1/2 teaspoon sage**

1. Drop the apple into a blender or food processor and chop. Add the honey and sage and refrigerate for 10 minutes.

2. Pat the mixture onto your face with a light tapping motion, tapping until the honey feels tacky. Leave mask on for 30 minutes; rinse.

Cucumber Mask for Oily Skin

**1/2 cucumber
1 egg white
1 tablespoon lemon juice
1 teaspoon mint**

1. Puree ingredients in a blender and refrigerate for 10 minutes.

2. Apply the mixture to your face and leave on for 15 minutes. Rinse with hot, then cool water.

Blemished Skin Mask

**1 ripe tomato, chopped
1 teaspoon lemon juice
1 tablespoon instant-style oatmeal *or*
    old fashioned rolled oats**

1. Place ingredients in a blender and blend until just combined.

2. Apply to skin, making sure the mixture is thick enough to stay on blemished areas: cheeks, forehead, or chin. Add a bit more oatmeal to thicken the mask, if necessary. Leave mask on for 10 minutes, then scrub off with a clean washcloth dipped in warm water.

Toning and Soothing Masks

The following masks should get you started on the lifetime adventure of taking care of your skin. Try these, of course, because each one is a classic, and then go on to make up your own, using combinations of ingredients that work best for you.

*If you have the time, it's always a good idea to steam your face by pouring some boiling water into a large metal bowl or pan, making a tent over your head with a towel, and letting your skin absorb the steam. Before applying any of the following masks determine if your skin is oily, dry, or a combination of both and choose herbs and soothers especially formulated for your skin type. After using a mask, it's also a good idea to follow up with either one of the **Facial Rinsing Lotions**, page 212, or a **Fresh Facial Cream**, page 210.*

Then branch out and create sensual skin treats for those you love—children, spouse, parents, friends—these remedies are safe and sure.

Yogurt Mud Pack

3 tablespoons fuller's earth
3 tablespoons plain yogurt

1. Mix fuller's earth and yogurt to make a paste and pat onto your face with gentle, upward strokes. Let dry on your skin for 15 to 20 minutes and rinse off with warm water.

Avocado Honey Mask

1 large, ripe avocado
1 tablespoon honey

1. Peel and slice avocado and puree it in a blender with the honey. Apply the whip to your face by patting it gently and then continuing to pat until the mask feels extremely tacky to the touch. Relax and leave the mask on for 20 to 30 minutes and then rinse off with warm water.

Yield: 1 application each

Cost of Ingredients: $.24
Comparable Purchased Product: Aapri Apricot Facial Scrub, 2 ounces, $3.19
Savings: $2.95

Skin Scrubbing Grains and Creams

*Scrubs are different from masks in that you are expected to take an active part and gently agitate the materials on your skin to create a sloughing action. Only use these scrubs on skin that can take it—firm, young, oily, or resilient skin. If you or your skin feels especially fragile, use one of the gentle fruit masks, such as the **Apple Mask for Normal Skin** or the **Strawberry Fruit Mask**, instead.*

Oatmeal Citrus Scrubbing Grains

1 cup dried orange and lemon peel (page 26)
1 cup cooked oatmeal
1 cup blanched almonds

1.   Place peels, oats, and almonds in a blender or food processor and whirl until the mixture is a fine powder. Store powder in an attractive container near the bathroom sink and use a tiny portion as needed.

To Use:
*Place a bit of the scrub in the palm of your hand and moisten with a few drops of warm tap water. Rub the paste onto your face with a gentle circular and upward motion. Rinse off with tepid water and pat dry. You can finish your cleansing by rinsing your face with one of the **Facial Rinsing Lotions**, page 212, or smoothing on some **Fresh Facial Cream**, page 218.*

Idea:
Consider storing this scrub in one of the big shakers meant for the kitchen and keep it handy at the bathroom sink.

Oatmeal Honey Scrubbing Cream

1/2 cup uncooked oatmeal
1 tablespoon honey
1 tablespoon cider vinegar
1 teaspoon ground almonds

1. Combine all ingredients in a glass or an enamel bowl.

To Use:

　　If at all possible, first steam your face with one of the **Herbal Vinegars,** *page 148. Or, wet a clean washcloth with very warm water and lay it on your face for a minute.*

　　Apply the oatmeal mixture to your face, being careful to avoid the sensitive area around your eyes. Let mixture dry on your skin completely.

　　If your skin is young and firm, you can gently rub the dried mixture off with a clean terry washcloth or towel. Lean over the sink and rub your face in brisk but gentle circles with the cloth. Rinse with warm water, pat dry, and apply one of the **Fresh Facial Creams,** *following.*

Yield: 24 ounces

Cost of Ingredients: $3.41
Comparable Purchased Product: Mill Creek Wild Oats Facial Scrub, 5 ounces, $5.49 ($26.35)
Savings: $22.94

Fresh Facial Creams

　`This cream is soothing for simple cases of windburn, sunburn, insect bites, or poison ivy, and it even calms the ravages of air pollution if you apply it right after cleansing. As with the creation of any creams, remember the lessons learned from making simple mayonnaise—slowly, very slowly, add the oil, drop by drop, to the wax.

Antiaging Cream

　If you smooth a bit of this antiwrinkle preparation every night around the tender skin of your face and neck, and remember to smile every time you think about aging, I promise you will never have to worry about lines and wrinkles. It's not that you won't have them—it's just that you won't worry about them so much.

　　1 ounce glycerin
　　1 ounce witch hazel

1/2 ounce rose water
3 tablespoons honey
3 tablespoons wheat germ oil

1. Combine the ingredients in a glass or ceramic bowl and gently whisk until they are thoroughly combined.

2. Store the emulsion in a tightly sealed container at room temperature. It should last for at least 1 month, which is about when you will want to make up a new batch.

To Use:
Massage the solution into the skin around your eyes and mouth, using a circular and upward motion. This motion will counteract the natural droop of gravity. If you have the time, it's a good idea to hang your head over the edge of the bed and massage the cream in while you're partially upside down. This seems to bring a nice blush to the skin as well.

Soothing Cucumber Cream

1 whole cucumber, unpeeled
1/2 ounce white paraffin
2 ounces sweet almond oil

1. Cut the cucumber into chunks and puree it in the food processor or blender. Strain the pulp through a strainer lined with cheesecloth. Retain the peel and seeds in the cheesecloth to use in **Liquid Fertilizer** (page 298).

2. Melt the wax in a small bowl in the top of a glass or an enamel double boiler over medium heat. As soon as the wax is melted, slowly add the oil, stirring gently. Add strained cucumber and blend thoroughly.

3. Remove the pot from the heat and cover with a clean kitchen towel. Let the mixture cool very slowly to prevent crystals from forming in the wax. Stir mixture once or twice until cool.

4. When the mixture is completely cool and smooth, store it in a labeled, tightly capped glass container in the refrigerator. Cream will keep for 60 days.

Yield: 4 ounces

Cost of Ingredients: $1.57
Comparable Purchased Product: Oil of
    Olay, 4 ounces, $4.69
Savings: $3.11

Facial Rinsing Lotions

These facial lotions soothe and seem to revitalize oily skin. Because they are so refreshing, either one is ideal after a sauna or long session in the sun. If you cannot find chamomile blossoms at your health food store or pharmacy, try substituting fresh lilac, wisteria, heather, or magnolia blossoms instead.

Rosemary Chamomile Rinse

1 tablespoon dried or 2 tablespoons fresh rosemary
2 tablespoons dried or 1/4 cup fresh chamomile flowers
4 cups water

1.   Boil all ingredients in a glass or an enamel pan for 15 minutes. Strain, and retain the liquid. Cool before using. The herbs and flowers are useful when added to **Liquid Fertilizer**, page 298.

To Use:
   Wipe the liquid over your face with a fresh cotton square or pour it into a pump-type plastic or glass container and spritz it on your face. Let the solution remain for 30 minutes, rinse with cool water, and then pat dry.

Hint:
   It's never a bad idea to apply the facial, close the curtains, and relax with your feet elevated higher than your head for 20 or 30 minutes.
   Try brewing a big mug of tea with 2 teabags, squeeze out the teabags as usual, let them cool slightly, and then apply them to your closed eyes while you rest. The tannin in the tea is said to reduce the puffiness around your eyes.

Cider Stabilizing Rinse

1/4 cup cider vinegar
1/4 cup water

1. Combine vinegar and water and gently wipe your face with the mixture. Let this rinse dry on your skin.

Yield: 32 ounces

Cost of Ingredients: $4.35 for rinse made with dried ingredients
Comparable Purchased Product: White Lily Pore Reducing Solution, 8 ounces, $5.99 ($23.96)
Savings: $19.61

Bracing Aftershave

This preparation will restore the skin's acid balance to a proper level after washing away the shaving suds. Splash it on with abandon, and it will also heal tiny nicks and razor chinks, giving your skin a healthy glow in the bargain. I've included a few different scents for different moods and different formulas for different types of skin—try each and see which one your skin likes best.

Young Man's Citrus Splash

This recipe is fine for oily or problem skin, but it may be too drying for an older face. If you like the mixture but would like it to be less drying, reduce the isopropyl alcohol to 1 tablespoon.

1 large cucumber
1 teaspoon dried mint or 2 sprigs fresh mint
1 cup witch hazel
1/4 cup isopropyl alcohol
1/4 cup lemon juice
1/4 cup lime juice

1. Chop one large cucumber and place it, peel and all, in the blender. Blend on high for 1 to 2 minutes. Strain the pulp through a cheesecloth-lined sieve or through a coffee filter, retaining the pulp for **Cucumber Mask for Oily Skin**, page 207.

2. Crush the mint between two spoons to bruise it and combine it with the other liquids. Let the mixture sit for 30 minutes, strain, and store in a tightly capped bottle or plastic pump-type atomizer. Keep the aftershave in the refrigerator in the hottest months for an extra refreshing splash.

Variations:

> *Try replacing the isopropyl alcohol with an equal quantity of vodka for a different blend.*
> *One tablespoon of glycerin will further soften the drying effect of this aftershave.*

Savory Herb Splash

> *The spices listed here are one version of this splash to try, and then check under **Variations** for others that might suit your nose or your fancy. Or, each time you mix up a batch of aftershave, you might try a different combination.*

> **2 cups white vinegar**
> **1/4 cup honey**
> **1 teaspoon sage**
> **1 teaspoon thyme**
> **1 teaspoon savory**
> **1 teaspoon ground cloves**
> **1 teaspoon crushed bay leaves**

1. Combine all ingredients and store in a sterilized glass jar for 1 week. Shake occasionally to mix contents. Strain and pour into a tightly capped bottle.

Variations:

> *Another time, try a teaspoon of coriander seeds or rosemary, and use apple cider vinegar.*

Yield: 16 ounces

Cost of Ingredients: $1.51
Comparable Purchased Product: Mennen
  Skin Bracer, 8 ounces, $3.99 ($7.98)
Savings: $6.47

Skin Clarifier

Here is one of those mystery products that people with oily skin swear by—it takes the shine off, seems to tighten the pores, and generally makes your skin seem to wake up. These products can also become wildly expensive if you use them as generously as you should, so here's a low-cost alternative.

If you want to change the smell, try one of the alternatives listed, but remember, this preparation is very drying, so use it with care and only on the oily portions of your face.

2/3 cup witch hazel
1/3 cup rubbing alcohol

1. Mix the ingredients and store in a tightly capped, sterilized glass bottle.

To Use:
  Moisten a clean cotton ball and clean your face with this solution after washing and before applying moisturizer. Your skin should feel tingly when using. If your skin feels too tingly, change the formula to:

3/4 cup witch hazel
1/4 cup rubbing alcohol

Yield: 8 ounces

Cost of Ingredients: $.98
Comparable Purchased Product: Sea
  Breeze, 10 ounces, $3.39 ($2.71)
Savings: $1.73

Light-skin Bleaching Cream

Scarlett O'Hara might have used this simple cream to tone down her freckles and to give her skin a pale, translucent quality. If you can't or won't tan in the summer, try making your skin as white as possible with this preparation.

You will need a double boiler to gently warm the oils and waters and to melt the waxes for your cream. Stir vigorously when mixing the oils, waxes, and liquids—your cream will thicken as it cools.

Even if you haven't saved any whey from the recipes for cream cheese, you can always find whey at the top of your yogurt—it's the thin watery substance. Just pour it off and use it in this recipe.

> 1/4 cup mineral oil
> 1 tablespoon beeswax or paraffin
> 1/4 cup lemon juice
> 1/2 cup whey (see Homemade Cream Cheese, page 19, or Boursin Party Spread, page 154)

1. Use a double boiler large enough to hold three small glass bowls with the separate ingredients, or use two double boilers. First place the mineral oil and paraffin in bowls and then in the top of the double boiler. Watch until the wax is nearly melted and then add a bowl with the lemon juice and whey.

2. Pour the melted wax into a glass bowl and stir in the warm oil, mixing vigorously. Keep mixing and add the warm lemon juice and whey. Cover and refrigerate for 2 hours or until cream is set.

3. Remove the mixture from the refrigerator and whip with an electric hand mixer or with a wire whisk until light and creamy. You may add a drop of your favorite perfume at this step, if desired.

4. Store cream in the refrigerator during the summer months and use up within 4 to 6 weeks.

Simple Skin-lightening Masks

In the event that you have neither the time nor the courage to

*make your own cream, and especially if you find yourself
suddenly out of whey, here are two masks that will lighten and
tighten your skin.*

2 tablespoons fuller's earth
1 tablespoon witch hazel
1 teaspoon honey
1 teaspoon ground cloves

Lemon Lightening Pack

2 tablespoon fuller's earth
1 teaspoon lemon juice
1 teaspoon buttermilk

1. Mix all ingredients into a paste and apply to the skin in
light upward strokes. Sit back with your feet up for 20 minutes;
rinse with the **Skin Bleaching Tonic**, following.

Skin Bleaching Tonic

1 lemon, sliced
1 cup white wine
1 tablespoon sugar

1. Place lemon slices and wine in an enamel or a glass pot
and bring to a boil over medium heat. Boil for one minute.
Remove from the heat, stir in the sugar, and let cool.

2. Strain the mixture and store in a tightly capped bottle. Use as
a skin refresher and after using one of the Skin Lightening
Masks.

Yield: 8 ounces

Cost of Ingredients: $1.21
Comparable Purchased Product: Porcelana
    Cream, 2 ounces, $5.99 ($23.96)
Savings: $22.75

Avocado Scalp Pack

Try this treatment as a simple antidote to too much sun or chlorine for your hair and scalp. It is soothing, especially if you have a sunburn on your scalp.

1 egg
1/2 avocado, peeled and mashed
2 tablespoons wheat germ oil

1.   Beat egg until frothy, either in a blender or by hand. Then add the avocado and the oil, beating until smooth. Use immediately.

To Use:

If you have long hair, divide your hair into several sections and apply the paste first to the scalp and then work outward, massaging the paste along the hair shaft. Cover your head with a plastic cap and leave on for 30 minutes.
Warming your towel in a 200-degree oven for 10 minutes or the microwave oven for 2 minutes is a nice touch and helps your scalp and hair to absorb the solution a bit better.
To cleanse your hair, rinse first in lukewarm water for 5 minutes and then use any of the mild shampoo formulas in this chapter.

Yield: 1 application

Cost of Ingredients: $.27
Comparable Purchased Product: Alberto VO 5 Hot Oil Treatment, 1 ounce, $3.29
Savings: $3.02

Cheap Trick . . . .

Here's another treat for your hair that you can try for conditioning and feeding dry, brittle hair:
Mix a half cup of mayonnaise with a few drops of your shampoo, add enough lukewarm water to mix. Apply to hair after a regular shampoo, leave on for 10 minutes, and then shampoo out.

Super-body Hair Treat

Treat your hair to this plumping rinse when it feels brittle and fragile. It adds incredible body and fullness to the hair and leaves it soft and shiny, too.

> **2 tablespoons molasses**
> **2 tablespoons unflavored gelatin**
> **1 tablespoon Sweetened Condensed Milk (page 17)**
> **1 tablespoon stale beer**

1. Combine ingredients in a small bowl.

To Use:
Comb or brush into your hair. Cover your hair with a plastic shower cap or wrap a sheet of plastic wrap around your hair and cover with a thick terry-cloth towel. Leave the treatment on for 30 minutes, rinse in warm water, and shampoo.

Ideas:
*Complete the body-building routine for your hair by shampooing with **Egg Shampoo**, page 220, and rinsing with **Sea Rinse for Damaged Hair**, page 223.*

Yield: 3 ounces

Cost of Ingredients: $.85
Comparable Purchased Product: Rave Masque Conditioner, Extra Body, 8 ounces, $2.79 ($1.04)
Savings: $.19

Cheap Trick . . . .

Although summer is especially tough on your hair, it is also the best time to find the ingredients for a super hair soother. Try tossing 1 banana, 1 tablespoon yogurt, 1 tablespoon wheat germ oil, 1/4 ripe avocado, and 1/4 ripe cantaloupe into the blender for 1 minute. Apply the mixture at once to freshly shampooed hair, leave on for 10 minutes; shampoo again.

Egg Shampoo

*Use this shampoo after the **Avocado Scalp Pack** or the **Super Body Hair Treat** to complete the job of repairing sun or swimming damage to your hair. Remember to wash and rinse this shampoo out with warm, not hot, water or you will have the interesting scent of fried egg about you for days.*

> 1 egg
> 1 teaspoon olive oil
> 1 teaspoon lemon juice
> 1 tablespoon castile soap or mild, unscented shampoo
> 1/2 cup water

1.   Combine all ingredients in a blender and whip until smooth. Use shampoo immediately, and follow up with one of the hair rinses described in this chapter. Save any remaining shampoo in the refrigerator and use the next day.

Yield: 5 ounces

Cost of Ingredients: $.21
Comparable Purchased Product: Pathmark
   Shampoo with Egg, 32 ounces, $1.69 ($.25)
Savings: $.04

Herbal Secret Shampoo

The real secret of herbs may never be unlocked, but this shampoo is gentle, infinitely variable, and will leave your hair soft and smelling wonderful. Don't expect mountains of soapy lather from this shampoo, however—its cleaning action is gentle rather than supersudsy.

Try to use fresh herbs whenever possible because dried, purchased herbs are very expensive. Remember that 2 tablespoons of dried herbs equal about 6 to 8 leaves fresh. Don't worry if you don't have one or more of the herbs listed here. The shampoo works just as well with a wide variety of

different herbs and spices, and you can vary it season by
season, or customize it for your own hair color.

>1 tablespoon sage
>1 tablespoon rosemary
>1 tablespoon nettle
>1 tablespoon peppermint
>2 tablespoons red clover
>2 tablespoons chamomile
>1/4 cup orange peel
>1/4 cup marigold flowers
>1/4 cup birch buds and leaves
>1 tablespoon orrisroot
>5 cups water
>2 tablespoons aloe gel
>3/4 cup castile soap
>Few drops of your favorite perfume or essential oil

1.   Stir the spices and herbs together in an enamel or a glass
pot and simmer them in the water for 15 minutes. Cover and let
steep for 30 minutes. Strain the liquid and reserve the herbs
separately for **Liquid Fertilizer**, page 298.

2. In a blender, combine 1 cup of the herb liquid with the aloe
gel and blend on low speed until smooth.

3. In a glass or an enamel bowl, blend the soap and the
remaining liquid, and then whip with a wire whisk until
smooth and frothy. Add the blender liquid.

4. Pour the mixture into the containers of your choice and add
the scent last, a few drops to each container. Shake to disperse
the scent. Shampoo will keep for 1 to 2 months.

Variations:
>For **blond hair**, *double the chamomile and omit the*
sage.
>For **brunet hair**, *double the sage and omit the*
chamomile.
>For **oily hair**, *add 1/2 cup lemon peel.*
>For **dry** *hair, increase the marigold to 1/2 cup.*
>*If the castile soap isn't bubbling enough for your taste,*
try mixing 1/2 cup of an inexpensive brand of unscented
shampoo to 1/4 cup castile soap. Vary the proportions of the two

detergents until you get the sudsing action you like.

*Try these more unusual spices and herbs in addition to the others (see **Resources** for where to purchase them). Keep the proportions of 3/4 cup castile soap to 5 quarts liquid:*

> *2 teaspoons fresh birch juice*
> *1/2 cup comfrey root*

Yield: 40 ounces

Cost of Ingredients: $8.70
Comparable Purchased Product: Clairol
    Herbal Essence, 7 ounces, $1.59 ($9.08)
Savings: $.38

Hair Rinses and Toners

These rinses will make your hair sparkle and they will also completely rinse out any soap residue from shampoo or conditioners. You can customize the rinse for either light or dark hair.

Chamomile can be purchased from the pharmacy or the health food store, sometimes in the form of tea. It is most expensive at the pharmacy, so whenever possible, learn to identify the flower, which grows wild all over the country in the late spring and summer, and pick and dry your own blossoms.

Herbal Rinse for Normal Hair

*Use this rinse as a natural finish to the **Herbal Secrets Shampoo**. Just like the shampoo, this rinse can be customized to suit light, dark, dry, or oily hair. The important ingredient is the vinegar, which restores the natural acid balance to the hair and takes out any trace of soap.*

> **1/2 cup white vinegar**
> **1/2 cup water**
> **2 tablespoons rosemary**
> **2 tablespoons red clover**
> **2 tablespoons nettle**

1.   Combine all ingredients and bring to a rolling boil in a glass or an enamel pot. Simmer, uncovered, for 15 minutes and then cover and let steep for 30 minutes.

2. Strain and pour into a glass or plastic container. Rinse will keep for 1 to 2 months.

Lemon Rinse for Light Hair

2 cups white vinegar
2 cups water
1/4 cup lemon juice
1/4 cup chamomile flowers

1.   Combine ingredients in a glass or an enamel pan and boil for 15 minutes. Strain, retaining flowers for **Liquid Fertilizer**, page 298. Cool and store in a tightly capped bottle.

To Use:
      After shampooing, pour 1/2 cup over hair; rinse.

Sage Rinse for Dark Hair

2 cups malt or red wine vinegar
2 cups water
1/4 cup sage

1.   Combine ingredients in a glass or an enamel pan and boil for 15 minutes. Strain, cool, and store in a tightly capped bottle.

To Use:
      After shampooing, pour 1/2 cup over hair; rinse.

Sea Rinse for Damaged Hair

1/4 cup sea kelp
1 cup either Lemon or Sage Rinse

1. Combine kelp and rinse in a pint- or quart-size jar, cap tightly, and shake well. Apply generously to freshly shampooed hair, leave on for 20 minutes, and then rinse thoroughly.

Dandruff Control Rinse

1 cup apple cider vinegar
6 aspirins, crushed
1/4 cup witch hazel

1. Combine all ingredients and store in a tightly capped jar or bottle. After shampooing, gently massage rinse into your hair, leave it on for 10 minutes, and then rinse again with warm water.

Yield: 32 ounces

Cost of Ingredients: $1.92 for Light Hair Rinse
Comparable Purchased Product: Vidal Sassoon Finishing Rinse, 8 ounces, $3.09 ($12.36)
Savings: $10.44

Lemon Hair Spray

This hair spray is so simple, it seems incredible, but it really works. It also adds a bit of body to fine, limp hair, and it gives light hair added shine.

2 lemons, sliced
2 cups hot water

1. Place lemon slices and water in a glass or an enamel pan and bring to a boil. Immediately reduce heat and simmer, uncovered, until the water is reduced to 1 cup—about 30 minutes. Remove from heat and cool.

2. Line a strainer with cheesecloth and strain the mixture. Squeeze out the cloth thoroughly to get all the juice, and retain the lemon pulp for **Liquid Fertilizer**, page 298.

3. Pour the strained mixture into a pump-type container. Mixture will keep for 1 to 2 months in the refrigerator.

Idea:
>   *If you use hair spray very rarely, try adding a few
> drops of your favorite cologne to the mixture to help it last a bit
> longer.*

Yield: 18 ounces

Cost of Ingredients: $.30
Comparable Purchased Product: Final Net
   Pump, unscented, 8 ounces, $2.25 ($5.06)
Savings: $4.76

Soothing Bath Salts

*Soak in this deliciously scented and soothing concoction
whenever the world seems to be too much with you, and just as
in a commercial, your cares will wash away down the drain.
At least you can lean back and relax about your grocery
budget—this bath soak costs only pennies to enjoy.*

   1 cup instant nonfat dry milk
   1 cup baking soda
   2 tablespoons cornstarch
   1 tablespoon cream of tartar
   1 tablespoon cinnamon
   1 tablespoon powdered orrisroot
   Perfume or essential oils, if desired

1.   Combine all ingredients and store in a pretty container in
the bathroom. Add a few sprinkles of the mixture to your bath as
the water is running.

Yield: 19 ounces

Cost of Ingredients: $1.31
Comparable Purchased Product: Ponds
   Cream and Cocoa Butter Bath Beads, 15
   ounces, $2.59 ($3.28)
Savings: $1.97

Ultra Bubble Bath

*Try this bath when you want to feel glamorous—these
bubbles have staying power, so you can let the glamour soak in
for a long time.*

*Because the kind of bubbles you see in the movies are
rather hard to come by in a homemade preparation, you will
need shampoo or dishwashing liquid to achieve mountains of
suds, but save money by using the very cheapest brands you can
find.*

> 1 cup Soft Soap (page 278)
> 1/2 cup purchased shampoo or dishwashing liquid
> 2 tablespoons glycerin
> Few drops essential oil or your favorite perfume

1. Combine the ingredients and store the liquid in a pretty
container near the tub.

To Use:

> *Pour a tablespoon or two under rapidly running water to
release bubbles.*

Yield: 12 ounces

Cost of Ingredients: $1.10
Comparable Purchased Product: Bare
   Elegance Body Shampoo, 8 ounces, $3.29
   ($4.93)
Savings: $3.83

Cheap Trick ....

*A nifty present to yourself or to a loved one: sew up a few bath
bags from plain muslin or cheesecloth. Simply make a pouch
from the fabric and fill the pouch with uncooked oatmeal. At
bath time, tie the bag over the faucet, turn the water on, and let
the water bounce over the bag. You will have a soothing
bathwater concoction. You can also add some cloves, lavender,
cornstarch, or cinnamon to the bag to vary the scent, if you
wish.*

Perfumed Bath Powder

*Here is a simple and inexpensive way to surround
yourself with clouds of fragrance—you can be as lavish as you
like with this powder because it is easy and inexpensive to
make and store. The rice powder is available from the health
food store and the orrisroot powder from a pharmacy.*

*If you are making your own bath powder because you are
sensitive to talc, or if you are making baby powder, you can
remove or reduce the orrisroot powder, as well as the perfume,
if you fear an allergic reaction.*

*Try a little of this mixture before altering the recipe,
however, because the orrisroot is very mild and it is used to
extend the fragrance in the mixture.*

> **2 cups cornstarch**
> **1 cup rice flour**
> **1 teaspoon orrisroot powder**
> **Several drops of your favorite perfume or essential oil**

1.   Mix all the ingredients together and store the powder in a
tightly closed tin for 1 week so that the orrisroot powder will
absorb the scent. Transfer powder to other containers of your
choice, if desired.

Ideas:

> *This powder can be sprinkled from the kind of big
shaker that is normally used in the kitchen, or from a used
talcum powder tin. For a special gift, cover a box with an
antique style of paper, add a pretty puff topped with a fancy bow,
and enjoy.*

Variations:

> *An especially nice powder can be made by omitting
any fragrance from the recipe, and adding 1/2 teaspoon vanilla
to the powder and 1 or 2 vanilla beans. Store the powder in a
tightly closed tin.*

> *Another pretty idea is simple but elegant: sprinkle a
cup of rose petals into the mixture, cover, and let the roses scent
the powder.*

Yield: 24 ounces

Cost of Ingredients: $1.92
Comparable Purchased Product: Johnson &
    Johnson Baby Powder, 14 ounces, $1.99 ($3.41)
Savings: $1.49

Home Remedies for Coughs

Here is a soothing throat remedy that works for roughness brought on by too much exertion, be it from singing, shouting, or running in the coldest weather.

Sweet Solution Cough Syrup

1 lemon
1 tablespoon glycerin
1/2 cup honey

1.   In a small saucepan, cover the entire lemon with water and boil for 1 minute. Remove, and while still hot, slice the lemon in half and squeeze all the juice into a bowl. Remove the seeds.

2. Stir in the glycerin and honey and store the syrup in a sterilized glass jar, tightly capped, in the pantry or bathroom. If the syrup becomes too cold, warm it slowly by sitting the jar in a pan of warm water. The syrup will keep for 1 to 2 months.

Expectorant Cough Syrup

Here's a cough syrup remedy that is as old as the common cold—and it helps clear up some of the congestion associated with coughs and colds. The honey is also quite soothing to the throat. Remember, however, what they say on the bottles of cough syrup that you buy in the store: if a cough persists or gets worse, see your doctor.

2 tablespoons diced onion
1/2 cup honey

1.   Mix the ingredients in the top of a double boiler and cook

very slowly over very low heat for 2 hours. Strain the mixture through a coffee filter or a cheesecloth and discard the onion pulp or use it in **Liquid Fertilizer**, page 298.

2. Allow the syrup to come to room temperature before using, and store at room temperature for 1 to 2 months.

To Use:
>   *Adults should take 1 to 2 tablespoons every 4 hours. If cough persists, or there is a fever, call the doctor.*
>   *For a child between the ages of 8 and 15, take 1 teaspoon every 4 hours. For a child younger than 8 who seems ill with a cough, you should probably call a doctor rather than try home remedies.*

Variation:
>   *If you have an annoying cough that occasionally keeps you up at night, simply keep a jar of honey and a spoon at your bedside and slowly suck on a spoonful of honey when the urge to cough comes upon you. The cough will magically go away.*

Sunflower Cough Syrup for Grown-ups

>   *Since this preparation contains a generous amount of gin, take it only if you can handle this ingredient. Do not take this solution when you might be called upon to drive or to operate a machine. Instead, relax and let the syrup do its job.*

>   **1/2 cup sunflower seeds**
>   **5 cups water**
>   **3/4 cup gin**
>   **1/2 cup sugar**

1.   In a glass or an enamel pan, boil the sunflower seeds in the water until the water is reduced to approximately 2 cups. This should take 45 minutes to an hour. Strain the juice, discarding the seeds.

2. Stir in the gin and sugar and store in a tightly capped container.

To Use:
>   *For those coughs and colds that you want to treat*

yourself, take 1 to 2 teaspoons four times a day until you feel better. If you have a severe cough, fever, or if your symptoms worsen, discontinue all remedies and make sure you see your doctor.

Yield: 5 ounces

Cost of Ingredients: $1.51 for Sweet Solution Cough Syrup
Comparable Purchased Product: Triaminic Cold Syrup, 8 ounces, $4.29 ($2.68)
Savings: $1.17

Nighttime Cold Remedy

This remedy is guaranteed to let you sleep just as soundly as the store-bought kind, and it tastes better, too. It has no real medicinal claims, unless you believe that a good night's sleep is all you need to cure your common cold.

> **1 lemon**
> **1/4 cup maple syrup or Quick Maple Syrup (page 43)**
> **1/4 cup hot water**
> **2 tablespoons brandy**

1.   Squeeze all the juice from the lemon and stir it into the maple syrup. Add the hot water and brandy. Use entire recipe.

To Use:
> *Bundle yourself up in your warmest pajamas, turn on the electric blankets and heating pad, slowly sip the **Nighttime Cold Remedy** while it's good and hot, and go to sleep for 8 hours. Repeat after 24 hours, if necessary.*

Yield: 6 ounces

Cost of Ingredients: $.69
Comparable Purchased Product: NyQuil, 6 ounces, $2.00
Savings: $1.31

Vegetable Juice Laxative

A glass of this good-tasting laxative as a breakfast drink will relieve mild constipation, usually by lunchtime.

> 1 cup tomato or vegetable juice
> 1/2 cup sauerkraut juice
> 1/4 cup carrot juice

1. Mix in a tall juice glass and drink all at once. On hot days, you can pour this concoction over ice, or add Tabasco for spice.

Yield: 14 ounces

Cost of Ingredients: $.44
Comparable Purchased Product: Ex-LAX, 30 ounces, $3.19 ($1.48)
Savings: $1.04

Iodine Antiseptic Wash

Keep this solution in a pump-type spray container and use it to spritz small cuts and abrasions. It always seems to feel better to spray gently than to dab with the little glass applicator that comes in the iodine bottle.

> 1 teaspoon iodine
> 3 tablespoons isopropyl alcohol

1. Combine the two ingredients and store in a pump-type spray container and keep handy for minor cuts, scratches, and abrasions.

Yield: 2 ounces

Cost of Ingredients: $.52
Comparable Purchased Product: Bactine Spray, 3 ounces, $4.29 ($2.86)
Savings: $2.34

Rose Beads

These beads are meant to be worn against the skin so that the warmth of the body will release their fragrance gently and magically. It's one of the most wonderful, romantic ideas I've seen in a long time—make a batch of these for yourself, or as a very special bon voyage gift for a woman traveling to a warm, sunny climate where they will feel wonderful against tanned skin.

> **4 cups rose petals**
> **Essential oil or perfume (optional)**
> **Toothpicks**
> **Nylon fishing filament or baby ribbon**

1. Place the rose petals in an enamel or a glass saucepan and cover with warm water. Heat gently, and simmer for 1 hour. Do not allow the liquid to boil. Cover and cool overnight.

2. Repeat the cooking process three more times. Add oil or perfume, if desired, just before cooking for the last time. You should have a smooth, soft paste by now; if not, continue cooking until all the liquid is absorbed. Let paste cool completely.

3. Moisten your fingers with a few drops of essential oil or perfume and pinch off a bit of the paste. Roll it into a ball, pierce the ball all the way through with a toothpick, and place the bead and toothpick on a piece of plastic wrap to dry. Continue until all the paste is used and allow the beads to dry on the toothpicks for 3 hours.

4. Carefully remove the toothpicks and allow the beads to dry overnight. Thread a needle with the nylon fishing filament or baby ribbon and string the beads into a necklace long enough to fit over the head. Knot the ends securely and cut off any excess ribbon or filament.

Variations:
*If you don't have enough rose petals, try mixing other fragrant flower petals in with the roses. Try tinting the mixture with a few drops of **Nature's Colors**, page 367, if you*

want vividly colored beads, but remember that the color may rub off along with the fragrance.

Hint:

When setting aside your rose petals to boil, keep them in an open container like a basket or an open tin in a sunny location. Toss the petals once or twice a day as you gather enough for your recipes. A closed container or a dark storage place will encourage mold to form and the fragrance will be lost.

Yield: One 12-inch necklace

Cost of Ingredients: $1.29
Comparable Purchased Product: Gazebo
   Galley Summer Necklace, $30.00
Savings: $28.71

Chapter 7

Household Cleaning Supplies

The cleaning and maintenance of the house is a job most people would rather not have—let alone pay dearly for. You usually pay more for the package and the promise than for the product itself. The recipes in this chapter will still get the job done, even though the ingredients for most of the items are common, readily available, and extremely cheap.

Pine Furniture Cleaner
Lemon-oil Furniture Polish
  Furniture Refinishing Polish
Dust-control Spray
Polishing Cloth
Dry Carpet Cleaner
Air Refresher
Disinfectant Spray
All-purpose Cleaner
Pine Cleaner
Easy Scrub
Scouring Cleanser
Ceramic Tile and Grout Cleaner
Toilet Bowl Cleaner
Wall Cleaner
Glass Cleaner
  Greasy-glass Cleaner
  Paint-removing Glass Cleaner
Refrigerator Deodorant Pretties
Oven Cleaner
Dishwasher Spot Stopper
Drain Cleaner
Garbage Disposal Cleaner
Coffeepot Cleaner
Aluminum Pan Cleaner
  Calcium-deposit Remover
Stainless Steel Cleaner

Copper Cleaner
Brass Polish
Marble Cleaner
Pewter Cleaner
   Formula 1
   Formula 2
   Formula 3
Silver Polish

Pine Furniture Cleaner

*Unlike a simple polish which just shines your fine wood, this cleaner will remove some dust residue while returning a shine to the finish. For heavily soiled furniture or wood, wash first with **All-purpose Cleaner**, page 244, and then follow up with this solution to bring back the shine.*

> **1 cup mineral oil**
> **1 tablespoon pine oil**
> **1/4 cup Soft Soap (page 278)**
> **1 cup warm water**

1. Mix mineral and pine oils in a glass or an enamel bowl. Stir in the Soft Soap and warm water, continuing to stir until all ingredients are thoroughly combined.

2. Pour into a clean quart-size jar or bottle; cap and label. Keep out of the reach of children.

To Use:
Pour about 1 tablespoon of the solution onto a soft cloth and then polish. Turn the cloth frequently, adding more solution if necessary, to clean the wood. Finish by buffing with a clean, dry cloth. Repeat the process if the wood is especially soiled, but do not allow the wood to become soaked.
If you're working with fine furniture, use a minimum of cleaning solution and clean with gentle strokes.

Note:
Never use any cleaning solution made with ammonia to wash your furniture because the ammonia will dissolve whatever kind of finish is on the wood.

Yield: 16 ounces

Cost of Ingredients: $1.64
Comparable Purchased Product: Wood Scent Pledge Furniture Polish, 14 ounces, $2.49 ($2.84)
Savings: $1.20

Lemon-oil Furniture Polish

This polish is every bit as effective as the purchased product, and it should be used sparingly to best effect. Too much polish, wax, or oil on your furniture will only trap more dust, so work harder to buff this solution off than to pour it on.

> **1 cup mineral oil**
> **1 teaspoon lemon oil**

1. Pour both oils into the clean container of your choice. Close tightly, label, and keep out of the reach of children.

To Use:
If you like to spray-and-polish, store this solution in a pump-type container. If you like to rub your furniture quietly, store the solution in a squeeze-type container and apply it to an old sock that you've slipped over your hand, and then rub away. In either case, use only a little bit of the polish at a time and then buff the surface dry with a clean cloth or sock.

Furniture Refinishing Polish

Use this solution very sparingly and test it first on a part of the furniture that won't show: rub a bit in gently, wait a minute, and then buff. This polish is a good solution if you have a piece of furniture that seems a bit shabby or dull, but not yet ready for a complete stripping.

> **1/4 cup boiled linseed oil**
> **1 tablespoon turpentine**

1. Combine the two ingredients and store them in a tightly capped jar. Label and keep out of the reach of children.

To Use:
Moisten a disposable cloth or paper towel with a tiny bit of the mixture, wipe over your furniture, and then wipe off any excess solution with a clean cloth. Buff to a shine with a soft cloth.

Yield: 8 ounces

Cost of Ingredients: $1.59
Comparable Purchased Product: Endust
Dusting Spray with Lemon, 10 ounces, $2.59
($2.07)
Savings: $.48

Dust-control Spray

This solution is meant to keep heavy floor dust in cabins, garages, sheds, and outbuildings from climbing up onto the furniture and walls as you sweep. It is not recommended for kitchens or other rooms in the house.

> **1 cup mineral oil**
> **1 tablespoon isopropyl alcohol**
> **2 tablespoons Soft Soap (page 278)**
> **1 cup water**

1. Combine all ingredients in a clean pint-size pump-type container. Shake well to combine.

2. Label and keep container out of the reach of children.

To Use:
> *Spray solution liberally onto the dirty surface or directly onto the broom, cloth, or mop.*

Yield: 16 ounces

Cost of Ingredients: $1.62
Comparable Purchased Product: Endust, 10
ounces, $2.59 ($4.14)
Savings: $2.52

Cheap Trick............................

To clean up large, messy spills, particularly in the garage or near the oil burner, cover the spill with kitty litter to absorb the mess for a few hours and then sweep up the litter and discard.

Polishing Cloth

Here is a real timesaving convenience when you suddenly have to have your furniture all shiny. These times do come up, usually when the doorbell rings before you're ready, so keep these handy cloths available to grab as you run, and your furniture will look as though you've spent the day polishing.

> **1 yard soft flannel, cotton, or terry cloth cut into 4-inch squares**
> **1/4 cup water**
> **Large jar or plastic container with tight-fitting lid**
> **1 cup Lemon-oil Furniture Polish (page 238) or 1 cup Pine Furniture Cleaner (page 237)**

1. Cut fabric into handy-size squares or pieces. Scraps are fine, as are old T-shirts, old pajamas, or cloth diapers. Moisten fabric with water and place in the container for 30 minutes.

2. Pour furniture polish into the container, making sure all the cloth is thoroughly saturated. Keep covered, turning the container frequently until all the pieces are coated. Label and keep the container away from children.

To Use:

> *Remove one of the polishing squares and simply wipe over your furniture. Buff with a clean cloth if there is time. Return the polishing cloth to the container if it is still clean; discard or wash when the cloth becomes soiled.*

Hint:

> *Cover one of your polishing cloths with a tube cut from old pantyhose. Use this cloth to wipe down dark upholstered furniture that is covered with lint or pet hairs.*

Yield: 10 to 15 polishing cloths

 Cost of Ingredients: $2.89
Comparable Purchased Product: Stretch'n Dust Dusting Cloth, $1.39 ($13.90)
Savings: $11.01

Dry Carpet Cleaner

This cleaner looks like it's making a bigger mess than you started with because to use it, you must sprinkle it with abandon all over the rug and then close the door and leave it there for a while.

But the results are worthwhile: a very clean, fresh-smelling carpet and a bonus: a vacuum cleaner that smells extra nice the next time you turn it on, too.

> **2 cups baking soda**
> **1/2 cup cornstarch**
> **4 to 5 bay leaves, crumbled**
> **1 tablespoon ground cloves**

1. Mix ingredients together and store them in a container with a tight-fitting lid. Label and keep out of the reach of children.

To Use:

Plan on leaving the mixture on your carpet overnight if possible. Shake the cleaner and then sprinkle liberally all over the carpet to be cleaned. Close the doors to the room so that pets or children don't get at the carpet, and then vacuum thoroughly the next day.

Yield: 20 ounces

Cost of Ingredients: $1.72
Comparable Purchased Product: Love My Carpet, 14 ounces, $2.39 ($3.41)
Savings: $1.69

Cheap Trick . . . .✂. . . .

If you have deep indentations in your carpet from furniture, you might try this trick to lift the carpet's nap: dip a clean dishtowel in water, wring it out, and lay it down, doubled, over the spot. Set your iron to its woolen, or medium-high setting and carefully lay the iron on the wet towel. Lift the edge and check—a few moments of steaming should do the trick. Be careful not to let the hot iron rest directly on the carpet or you could burn or even melt the fibers.

Air Refresher

After you've mastered the year-round art of making **Sweet Potpourri***, page 282, or and some of the other treats for your home in Chapters 8 and 12, you will probably have solved every room deodorant problem.*

For a quick fix for a stubborn odor, here's a traditional solution that you can customize to your taste.

> **1 cup baking soda**
> **1/4 cup ammonia**
> **1 tablespoon scent of your choice: perfume, lemon extract or juice, Vanilla Bean Extract (page 12), or pine oil**
> **16 cups warm water**

1. Into a clean gallon-size plastic jug pour the baking soda, ammonia, and the scent of your choice. Slowly fill with warm water. Label and cap jug; keep out of the reach of children.

2. Pour small quantities of the solution into pretty containers with spray tops—old perfume containers or atomizers are ideal. Then you can leave the refresher on the counter in rooms where you need it frequently.

To Use:

Simply mist the air where unpleasant odors abound. Try to avoid spraying on or near furniture or pets. Wipe up any residue if you overdo, but the mist will not harm anything if you don't soak an item with the mist.

Especially avoid spraying directly on fine wood furniture—the ammonia, scent, or water could harm the finish.

Yield: 1 gallon

Cost of Ingredients: $.45
Comparable Purchased Product: Glade
   Sunny Lemon Room Deodorizer, 7 ounces, $1.29
   ($23.58)
Savings: $23.13

Disinfectant Spray

Although this spray will not sterilize the surface you spray it on, it will significantly reduce the surface colony of germs that thrive and multiply there. This spray is ideal for disinfecting and refreshing garbage and diaper pails and for spraying under the sink if you keep your garbage can there.

1 cup chlorine bleach
8 cups water

1. Combine bleach and water in a clean quart-size jug. Label and cap tightly; keep out of the reach of children.

2. Pour a small amount into a pump-type spray bottle and spray on surface.

Note:
Avoid spraying this solution on or near wood surfaces or around food. Since this product contains bleach, avoid using anywhere you are using ammonia, since the combination of the two chemicals will produce dangerous fumes.

Yield: 9 cups

Cost of Ingredients: $.08
Comparable Purchased Product: Lysol
  Aerosol Spray, 24 ounces, $1.69 ($9.01)
Savings: $8.93

Cheap Trick . . . .

Another approach to cleaning a smelly item is milder than the one given here: try a cup of borax to 2 gallons of water and use this solution to soak diaper pails or garbage cans.

The mildest solutions of all are lemon juice or white vinegar and water. Rinse and let the item dry in full sunlight.

Remember to let the item dry thoroughly before you press it into service again; a sprinkle of baking soda will keep it fresh.

All-purpose Cleaner

*This is the type of cleaner that is supposed to do everything around the house, and it does—it cleans countertops, painted woodwork, tile, appliances, vinyl floors, and even some painted walls (see page 250 for another **Wall Cleaner**).*

*This **All-purpose Cleaner** is good for vinyl wallpaper, but do not use it on delicate wallpaper. This is not a wimpy cleaner, so if you're timid, try a bit of the solution on an out-of-the-way place just to be sure that it won't harm the surface you want to clean.*

1 cup ammonia (sudsing or nonsudsing)
1 cup washing soda
14 cups warm water

1. Pour ammonia and washing soda into a clean gallon-size plastic jug.

2. Add 2 cups warm water, close jug, and shake to mix ingredients. Fill the jug with the rest of the warm water. Close and label container and keep out of the reach of children.

To Use:

For large jobs, pour 1/2 cup of solution into a bucket, fill bucket with warm water and scrub wall surfaces or floors. To avoid streaks, wash walls from the bottom up, work in small sections, and change water frequently. No rinsing is necessary if you make sure your water stays clean. A good rule of thumb is to make the water as hot as you can comfortably stand and then change the water when it has cooled off.

For small jobs, fill a spray container with the solution and use full-strength on appliances, tile, and for spots on any washable surface.

Yield: 1 gallon

Cost of Ingredients: $.40
Comparable Purchased Product: Ajax with
    Ammonia, 28 ounces, $1.79 ($8.18)
Savings: $7.78

Pine Cleaner

This concentrated cleaning solution is very gentle and can be further diluted to clean the less soiled portions of the nursery, bathrooms, or sickrooms. Full strength will clean floors, pet areas, and kitchens.

2 cups Soft Soap (page 278) or soap flakes
1 cup pine oil
8 cups very warm water

1. Mix the soap and pine oil together and pour into a clean gallon-size plastic jug. Pour in the warm water and agitate to mix thoroughly.

2. Label, cap tightly, and keep out of the reach of children.

To Use:
Dilute 2 cups to a pailful of warm water and use to wash down walls, furniture, and lightly soiled floors.
Dilute 4 cups to 1 cup of warm water for floors.
Solution can also be used full-strength by pouring onto a sponge and wiping. No rinsing is necessary.

Yield: 10 cups

Cost of Ingredients: $1.23
Comparable Purchased Product: Pine Sol
  Liquid Cleaner, 28 ounces, $2.39 ($6.82)
Savings: $5.59

Cheap Trick . . . . ✂ . . . .

For tough jobs when a simple pine cleaner isn't strong enough, I use chlorine bleach to do the trick. Bleach is a very effective, strong cleaner and you must respect its power to harm delicate items as well as clean sturdier things. Bleach will remove the mold from plastic shower curtains if you fill your laundry tub with cold water, 2 cups bleach, and 1 cup laundry detergent. Wash on the gentle cycle, rinse, and then hang up in the shower to dry.

Cheap Trick . . . . ✂ . . . .

Another aid to a shiny clean house is hydrogen peroxide. Like bleach, peroxide is a very powerful cleaner and you should exercise care when you use it. If possible, it is wise to test a small, hidden portion of the object you are trying to clean. For very dirty ivory, a mixture of half peroxide and half water is an excellent cleaner. Sponge it on, let it sit for 10 minutes, and then rinse. Try this same mixture on a burn or scorch stain on fabric and you might save an otherwise ruined article.

Easy Scrub

*Use this solution when you fear that the **All-purpose Cleaner,** page 244, will be too strong—on your Fiberglas tub or the inside of the refrigerator, for example. In fact, it's always a good idea to try the gentle approach first, and if the surface you are working on doesn't come clean, then move up to the **All-purpose Cleaner.***

> **4 tablespoons baking soda**
> **1 tablespoon Soft Soap (page 278)**
> **4 cups warm water**

1. Combine baking soda and water and pour into a clean plastic pump-type spray bottle. Label bottle.

To Use:

Spray directly on the surface to be cleaned and wipe off with a damp sponge.

*If the surface is heavily soiled, make a paste of 2 tablespoons baking soda and 1 tablespoon **Easy Scrub,** leave on the stain for 30 minutes, and then scrub off with warm water.*

Yield: 32 ounces

Cost of Ingredients: $.30
Comparable Purchased Product: Soft Scrub
  Cleanser, 13 ounces, $1.19 ($2.92)
Savings: $2.62

Scouring Cleanser

Here is a custom-designed cleanser to take care of your most delicate new Fiberglas fixtures in the bathroom or spa. Rather than clean with the kind of harsh, sandy abrasives found in powdery cleansers, this softer version depends on chalk dust for its abrasive action, and you can control the amount of abrasion by reducing the amount of whiting you use.

*If your fixtures are brand-new, I'd recommend starting with the mildest version of this mixture. If you're afraid even the mildest version will scratch, use the **All-purpose Cleaner**, page, 244, instead. If your appliances are old, white, scarred and pitted, use the full amount of whiting.*

> **1/2 cup soap flakes or Soft Soap (page 278)**
> **2 teaspoons borax**
> **1 1/2 cups hot water**
> **2 to 5 teaspoons whiting**

1. In a large plastic bowl, mix soap flakes and borax into water until dissolved. Add 2 to 5 teaspoons whiting, checking the consistency and degree of abrasiveness after each teaspoon.

2. Pour desired mixture into a squeeze-top plastic container, label, and keep out of the reach of children.

To Use:
Squeeze some of the cleanser onto a sponge and then wipe down your appliance. Rinse and dry.
For heavily soiled areas, squeeze the cleanser directly onto the spot or stain and let it remain for 30 minutes. Then scrub off, rinse, and repeat if necessary.

Yield: 14 ounces

 Cost of Ingredients: $.40
Comparable Purchased Product: Comet Cleanser, 14 ounces, $.47
Savings: $.07

Ceramic Tile and Grout Cleaner

*This recipe safely removes the soap film that frequently forms on tile surfaces and between the tiles. A more concentrated paste of the cleaner can be made (see **Hint**) and left to clean stubborn stains on the grout.*

> **1 cup baking soda**
> **1 cup ammonia (sudsing or nonsudsing)**
> **1/2 cup vinegar**
> **14 cups warm water**

1. Pour baking soda into a clean gallon-size plastic jug. Add ammonia, vinegar, and warm water to fill. Swish the jug to mix ingredients before it is completely full.

2. Cover jug tightly, label, and keep out of the reach of children. Smaller pump-type containers can be filled from the jug for small jobs—make sure these containers are labeled and kept safely away from children as well.

To Use:

Spray solution directly onto tile and wipe with a damp sponge or the kind of scrubbing pad made for Teflon pans.

Hint:

If grout or tiles are especially soiled, make a paste of:
> *2 tablespoons baking soda*
> *1 tablespoon **Ceramic Tile and Grout Cleaner***

and brush it onto the stains with an old toothbrush. Let the paste remain for 5 minutes, then scrub off and rinse.

Note:

This solution contains ammonia: do not mix with anything in the bathroom containing bleach, or dangerous fumes could result.

Yield: 1 gallon

Cost of Ingredients: $.56
Comparable Purchased Product: Tilex Instant Mildew Stain Remover, 24 ounces, $2.99 ($15.94)
Savings: $15.38

Toilet Bowl Cleaner

This formula is not a formal recipe at all since it has only one ingredient: bleach. However, bleach right from the bottle can be too strong for newer toilets, so you should mix your own concentration to keep in the bathroom.

If you have an old, stained ceramic sink, you can put in the stopper and pour this solution into the sink to whiten or brighten it as well. You can add coffee- and tea-stained ceramic mugs to the solution in the sink and soak them clean as well.

1 cup bleach
1 to 10 cups water

1. Pour bleach and water into a clean gallon-size plastic jug. Label, cap, and keep out of the reach of children.

To Use:
Choose the solution that's best for your appliances, and pour 1 cup into the toilet. Let sit for 30 minutes with the lid closed and then swirl around and under the rim with a toilet bowl brush. Flush.

Note:
Since this product is pure bleach, be careful not to let it splash up on yourself or out onto fabrics or floor surfaces as you clean.

Also, do not let it come into contact with any cleaning solution containing ammonia, since dangerous fumes can be the result.

Do not add this solution to your toilet bowl and then leave it untended if you have small children or thirsty pets wandering about the house.

Yield: 16 to 80 ounces

Cost of Ingredients: $.20
Comparable Purchased Product: Vanish
   Super Toilet Bowl Cleaner, 1.10 ounces, $1.39
Savings: $1.19

Wall Cleaner

When that awful time comes and you have to wash a wall, you certainly want a cleaner that will hold up to the job. This cleaner will, and because it is so cheap, you can wash and scrub away, use more cleaner, and change your water over and over again.

Changing your water is one of the quicker ways to do this job effectively—and if you really want to be efficient, when you change your washing solution because it's too dirty for the walls, go ahead and use it to wipe up any nearby floors with a spare cloth before you change your water and continue with the walls.

Then, to be even more efficient, and only if you have sewers and not a septic system, pour the solution down the toilet and swish it around with a toilet bowl brush before flushing. This way, you clean three progressively more disgusting things with the same bucket of water.

Finally, you start all over again with clean water and fresh solution and go back to where you left off on the wall. By keeping your water clean, you should not have to bother with rinsing.

> **1/2 cup borax**
> **2 teaspoons dishwashing liquid or Soft Soap (page 278)**
> **1 tablespoon ammonia**
> **1 gallon warm water**

1. Mix all ingredients by pouring them into a clean gallon-size jug and shaking well. Add enough warm water to fill, label jug, keep tightly capped, and keep out of the reach of children.

To Use:

Pour into a spray bottle and use full-strength for spots, or add 2 cups of solution to a pail of warm water for larger jobs.

When scrubbing walls, use a soft sponge and work from the bottom up to avoid streaking. Work in small sections at a time.

Yield: 1 gallon

Cost of Ingredients: $.23
Comparable Purchased Product: Spic and
Span All Purpose Cleaner, 16 ounces, $1.09
($8.72)
Savings: $8.49

Glass Cleaner

*When I was first married the first time, we moved around
so much with the Army that I used to believe I would never have
to live in a place long enough to have to wash the windows.
Eventually, I did, and I discovered what everyone else already
knew: this is a hard job because it seems that as you rub, you
only make it dirtier.*

*The solution that follows will work on most general types
of window dirt, and the trick of using a sheet of newspaper as
your cleaning cloth will keep streaking to a minimum.*

*If you've got a real mess on your windows, particularly
outside, then try one of the variations listed here and bring
along a straight-edge razor for scraping.*

*It's worth all the hard work you put into your windows, by
the way—clean windows make everything else in the house
look brighter and shinier. One of the prettiest sights in the
world is to look up from a steaming mug of coffee and watch
one of your own children's faces through clean glass as he or
she cleans the other side of the window.*

> **1 cup ammonia**
> **1 tablespoon mild detergent or Soft Soap (page 278)**
> **13 cups warm water**

1. In a clean gallon-size plastic jug, mix the ammonia
and detergent together. Fill with warm water. Label
jug, keep tightly capped, and keep out of the reach of children.

To Use:

*Pour solution into a clean spray-type bottle. Spray
window with the solution, wait 30 seconds, then wipe window
thoroughly with newspapers, turning paper often. Discard*

*paper when it is very wet. Although you will get your hands
nice and dirty if you are not wearing plastic gloves, the ink on
the paper seems to really shine up the windows without leaving
any streaks at all. If you do notice streaking, it only means
that the windows are still dirty—spray on more cleaner, and go
at them again.*

*For special problems such as dried-on paint or any
other disgusting airborne stuff, wet the offending mess down
with the solution and then scrape with a razor blade. Take
some care not to jam the blade down into the putty that is around
the windows on the outside because you can loosen the glass.*

Greasy-glass Cleaner

For heavily soiled kitchen windows:

**1/2 cup ammonia
4 tablespoons liquid detergent or Soft Soap (page 278)
1 cup warm water**

1. Mix this solution, pour into a small pump-type spray
container, and label.

To Use:
*Have handy a bucket of warm water and clean the
kitchen windows with the concentrated solution, discarding
used newspaper frequently. Finish by rinsing with the clean
water and then buff, if there's time, with a clean, soft cloth or
clean pieces of newspaper.*

Paint-removing Glass Cleaner

**1 cup ammonia
1/2 cup water**

1. Mix the solution, pour into a pump-type spray container, and
label.

To Use:
*Spray directly onto the paint to be removed, being
extremely careful not to get the solution on paint you **don't** want
to disturb. Wait 1 minute and then scrape with a straight-edge
razor. Finish the windows, if necessary, with one of the
cleaning solutions described earlier.*

Hint:

　　　To clean the glass over framed art, always spray the glass cleaner onto your rag or piece of newspaper and then wipe the glass. Never spray directly onto the glass or the solution could drip down between the glass and stain the mat or artwork.

Yield: 1 gallon

Cost of Ingredients: $.38
Comparable Purchased Product: Windex, 22 ounces, 1.69 ($9.83)
Savings: $9.95

Refrigerator Deodorant Pretties

　　　These packets are simply a more elaborate version of the old standby of putting an open box of baking soda in the refrigerator and then replacing it with a new one every 8 weeks or so. This recipe is more concentrated and seems to work harder and faster, so it's a comfort to put one of these in the used refrigerator of a new apartment—it strips out the old odors immediately.

　　　1 cup charcoal
　　　1 cup baking soda
　　　1 tablespoon dried orange or lemon peel
　　　1 teaspoon ground cloves or cinnamon
　　　1 teaspoon Vanilla Bean Extract (page 12)
　　　Old, clean nylon stockings cut into 2-inch squares
　　　1 yard porous fabric—terry cloth, loose-weave cotton,
　　　　　muslin or toweling—cut into 2-inch squares
　　　String or ribbon, in 8-inch lengths for tying and
　　　　　hanging

1. Mash charcoal into small chunks and dust by placing the briquets in a plastic bag and then pounding with a hammer, brick, or other suitable heavy object.

2. In a glass or enamel bowl, mix baking soda, charcoal, citrus peel, and spices. Sprinkle with vanilla and let mixture rest for 1 hour.

3. Place 2 tablespoons of mixture in the center of a square of nylon stocking and then place this packet in the center of a square of colorful fabric. Bring up 4 corners and tie securely with string or ribbon.

To Use:
   Tie packet in an out-of-the way spot in the refrigerator or freezer. You can also tie the packet onto one of the shelves on the inside of the door.
   After 10 to 12 weeks, you can refresh the packet by untying, sprinkling with a few drops of vanilla, and adding 1 teaspoon of fresh baking soda.

Yield: 10 to 15 packets

Cost of Ingredients: $2.10
Comparable Purchased Product: Airwick Stick-ups, $1.29 ($12.90)
Savings: $10.80

Oven Cleaner

This job is traditionally the one most neglected by anyone with a brain—who wants to clean the inside of an appliance, especially one that has a door you can keep closed?
   If you're unlucky enough to have an oven that does not have an automatic- or self-cleaning feature, this solution will take care of the messy job. And you might as well resign yourself to the task if your oven is coated with gunk—you could have a fire if it's grimy enough inside.

   1 cup ammonia
   2 cups boiling water
   1/2 cup baking soda
   1 cup white vinegar

1. Preheat oven to 200 degrees. Leave oven on for 15 minutes; turn off and leave the door closed.

2. Fill a shallow baking pan with ammonia and place on the top shelf of your oven. Fill another pan with 2 cups boiling water and place on the bottom shelf. Close oven and leave pans in for at least 2 hours or overnight.

3. Remove ammonia and make a paste of ammonia, baking soda and vinegar. Spread paste on oven surfaces, leave on for 15 minutes, and then scrub off with a sponge or steel wool.

Hint:
          Clean up spills as soon as they happen and you won't have to do this job very often.

Yield: 20 ounces

Cost of Ingredients: $.44
Comparable Purchased Product: Easy Off Oven Cleaner, 14 ounces, $2.29 ($3.27)
Savings: $2.83

Dishwasher Spot Stopper

Make a quantity of this recipe and then either add a teaspoon of it to your dishwasher each time you use it or mix the Spot Stopper directly in with your dishwashing crystals. Repackage the new mixture in a container with a close-fitting lid and use it as you would the regular cleaner.

     1 cup borax
     1/2 cup baking soda

1. Mix ingredients and store in a clean, tightly closed pint-size jar or can. Label and keep out of the reach of children.

To Use:
          Add 1 teaspoon of the mixture to your dishwasher in addition to your cleaning crystals.

*Or mix 1 cup **Dishwasher Spot Stopper** to 2 cups dishwashing crystals and use according to your machine's directions.*

Yield: 12 ounces

Cost of Ingredients: $.28
Comparable Purchased Product: Cascade, 30 ounces, $1.89 ($.75)
Savings: $.47

Drain Cleaner

*If you use this simple **Drain Cleaner** once a week, you should find that your kitchen drain will remain clean and free-flowing. One advantage to using this cleaner instead of the commercial kind is that you keep one of the more dangerous chemicals—lye—out of your kitchen.*

Other hints for clean drains, including one that isn't supposed to work but does, follows the recipe.

2 cups baking soda
2 cups salt: kosher, rock salt, or regular
1/2 cup cream of tartar

1. Mix ingredients and store in a covered container. Label and keep out of the reach of children.

To Use:

Have 2 cups of water boiling on the stove. Pour 1/4 cup of the cleaner down the drain and then follow immediately with half the boiling water. Wait 30 minutes and repeat. Flush with cold water when second application is finished.

Hints:

Keeping your drains clean involves some common sense: make sure your sink has a strainer-cover and keep it in the sink at all times. You can buy nice plastic replacements at the hardware store, so there's no excuse for not having one.

Try to avoid pouring any kind of grease down the

*drain. For centuries, cooks have saved certain fats, such as those from bacon, for use in cooking. If you decide to do this, make sure you pour your fats into a container that is clean and sturdy—it should not tip over when you're pouring in the hot grease—and then store the accumulated fats in the refrigerator. There are even pretty ceramic crocks for this purpose in gourmet cooking catalogs; see **Resources**, page 389.*

For grease you want to get rid of, keep a supply of old coffee containers with plastic lids under your sink, pour in the grease, let it harden a bit, either in the freezer or refrigerator, and then throw it away. Avoid using old jars for this purpose because the glass could break from the hot grease.

*If your drain gets clogged, keep a plunger handy and if you dislodge any clogs this way, use the **Drain Cleaner** when you are finished.*

*As to the **Hint** that isn't supposed to work, but it does: I pour used coffee grounds down the drain at least twice a day, each and every day, and I never, ever have a clogged drain. My mother does the same thing and she doesn't have clogged drains either, but everyone who sees me do this advises against it. It's supposed to mess up the drain, but confidentially, I think the grains act like little grinders and scrub the inside of the drain clean.*

Yield: 20 ounces

Cost of Ingredients: $1.20
Comparable Purchased Product: Draino Drain Cleaner, 18 ounces, $2.39 ($2.65)
Savings: $1.45

Cheap Trick . . . . ✂ . . . .

Nobody can tell me why some of these cleaning procedures work, but they do work, nevertheless:
A cork from a bottle of red wine will shine up metal.
Cold tea will shine mirrors.
Tang breakfast drink will prevent spots in the dishwasher.
Catsup will remove tarnish from copper.
Worcestershire sauce will shine brass.

Garbage-disposal Cleaner

Making this solution and then feeding it to your garbage disposal unit is a very satisfying way to finish cleaning your kitchen—its scent will waft through the air and the loud, raucous grinding will sound like applause for a job well done.

> **1 cup chopped lemon, orange, or grapefruit—rind and all**
> **1 cup baking soda**
> **1 1/2 cups water**

1. Mix ingredients, pour into an ice cube tray, and then freeze until solid.

2. Remove cubes, place in plastic bag if you don't intend to use them immediately, and label them. Make sure they don't fall into the hands of children.

To Use:

> *Turn on disposal unit, dump in 6 to 10 cubes, and let the machine grind them up. Rinse disposal with cold water.*

Yield: 28 ounces

Cost of Ingredients: $.78
Comparable Purchased Product: FX 5 Drainpipe Bacterial Cleaner, 1 pound, 10 ounces, $7.99 ($8.60)
Savings: $7.82

Cheap Tricks . . . . ✂ . . . .

Another school of thought on garbage disposal cleaning suggests that you make your ice cubes from a mixture of water and vinegar to deodorize the air. Try this method when you don't have any citrus fruits around to use—but remember to label the ice cubes.
And while you're busy cleaning up the kitchen, don't forget your kitchen sponge—I put mine in the dishwasher each night and it's cleaner than clean in the morning.

Coffeepot Cleaner

You can use this cleaning solution in your automatic coffee maker to keep it in good running trim. Either follow the manufacturer's instructions for cleaning or see the instructions, here. This solution will also clean a regular coffee pot or the inside of a Thermos bottle.

> **1 cup white vinegar**
> **1 cup water**

1. Mix vinegar and water. Use solution in the following ways:

To Use:

For automatic coffee makers, put in a clean filter and then pour solution directly into the water reservoir of your coffee maker. If you use a coffee maker with a permanent filter, cover the filter with a square of paper toweling cut to fit. When all the solution has bubbled through, discard filter or paper toweling, fill coffee maker with clean water and run it through to rinse. Discard vinegar-water solution or use it to clean your regular pot or Thermos.

For regular cleaning of coffee oils from the surface of your pot or Thermos, simply soak with the solution for 30 minutes and use a steel wool pad for any stubborn stains. Rinse thoroughly.

Yield: 16 ounces

Cost of Ingredients: $.24
Comparable Purchased Product: Dip-It
   Coffee Pot Cleaner, 3 ounces, $1.09
Savings: $.85

Cheap Trick . . . . ✂ . . . .

Since it's necessary to clean the coffee stains from your appliances and cups, it stands to reason that coffee would make a fine dye, and it does. A pint or two of strong coffee or tea can turn dingy linens into beautiful, antique-looking items.

Aluminum Pan Cleaner

The formula for cleaning aluminum is similar to that for copper, but it is a little milder and you can clean the aluminum with a fine grade of steel wool.

1/4 cup cream of tartar
1/4 cup baking soda
1/4 cup vinegar
2 tablespoons soap flakes or Soft Soap (page 278)

1. Mix cream of tartar and baking soda together, add vinegar and stir to make a soft paste. Stir in Soft Soap or soap flakes.

2. Store mixture in a container with a tight-fitting lid. Label and keep out of the reach of children.

To Use:
     Rub a small amount of the cleaner onto the aluminum pan and scour with fine steel wool.

Calcium-deposit Remover

If the inside of your teapot or kettle has developed a layer of calcium flakes on the bottom, try this solution to remove the accumulation.

1 tablespoon white vinegar
1 cup water

1. Simmer the water and vinegar in the pot for 30 minutes. Once the deposits are loosened, scrub them out with steel wool if you can get at them. Otherwise let the vinegar- and water-mixture sit in the pot overnight, rinse, and try again.

Hint:
     If only the inside of an aluminum pan is discolored, an old folk remedy suggests you simmer some apple peelings in 1/2 cup water until the stain is gone. This remedy smells wonderful and works adequately on lightly discolored pans.

Yield: 6 ounces

Cost of Ingredients: $.86
Comparable Purchased Product: Noxon
Metal Polish, 12 ounces, $2.29 ($1.45)
Savings: $.28

Stainless Steel Cleaner

*Usually, regular cleaning is all that is needed for
stainless steel, but you can use this solution for silverware and
pots when they seem a bit dull.*

> **1/4 cup soap flakes or Soft Soap (page 278)**
> **2 tablespoons whiting**
> **1 tablespoon ammonia**
> **1 tablespoon water**

1. Mix all ingredients and store in a container with a tight-
fitting lid. Label and keep out of the reach of children.

To Use:
*Rub the paste onto the stainless steel item with a soft
cloth, rinse, and buff dry.*

Yield: 4 ounces

Cost of Ingredients: $.24
Comparable Purchased Product: Noxon
Metal Cleaner, 12 ounces, $2.29 ($.76)
Savings: $.52

Cheap Trick........................ ....

*If your stainless steel sink has rust stains in it, try rubbing the
rust with a fresh lemon cut in half and dipped in salt. If your
sink is merely dingy, try cleaning it with a solution of 1 cup
chlorine bleach and 1 cup water. If your sink has stains from
either hard water or chemical cleaners, try using flat Coke on
the spots.*

Copper Cleaner

There are several solutions to use for cleaning copper and all of them work on the principle of an acid combined with a gentle abrasive.

I've created what I think is the best combination of these traditional cleaners into one all-purpose recipe that you can make up in quantity if you are lucky enough to have a lot of copper items to clean.

1/2 cup flour
1/2 cup salt
1/2 cup soap flakes or Soft Soap (page 278)
3/4 cup white vinegar
1/4 cup lemon juice
1 tablespoon whiting
1/2 cup very warm water

1. In an enamel or a glass bowl, mix the flour, salt, and soap together until soap is thoroughly dissolved. Then add the rest of the ingredients, stirring well.

2. Pour into a clean quart-size glass jar and cover tightly. Label and keep out of the reach of children.

To Use:
    Shake solution before using, pour some of the paste onto the copper piece, and then scrub gently with a sponge. Rinse, dry, and buff lightly with a soft cloth.

Yield: 16 ounces

Cost of Ingredients: $.92
Comparable Purchased Product: Twinkle
    Copper Cleaner, 4.37 ounces, $1.29 ($4.72)
Savings: $3.80

Brass Polish

If you have very old, very tarnished brass and the pieces are thick enough and small enough to immerse, then the old remedy of using straight ammonia on the pieces works like a charm. I've filled a plastic container with ammonia, dropped in antique hardware from an old oak apothecary bureau, and then, after letting the pieces soak for at least 30 minutes, I've put on rubber gloves and rubbed the ammonia-black gunk off with steel wool. Nothing works easier or faster.

*A word or two of caution, however. First, this ammonia treatment will not work, obviously, on large pieces because the brass must soak in the solution. If the piece you are working on is not solid brass, the solution could erode the thin coating and ruin the piece. And finally—about the black ammonia-gunk mentioned above. This loosened tarnish residue will stain your hands if you do not wear rubber gloves. Try a mild version or two for cleaning brass and lacquered-brass pieces before you try using the strong ammonia and steel-wool process. Check the **Hint** for more ways to clean and restore your brass.*

> **1 cup soap flakes or Soft Soap (page 278)**
> **1/4 cup whiting**
> **2 tablespoons salt**
> **1/4 cup white vinegar**
> **4 cups boiling water**

1. Mix soap, whiting, and salt together in a glass or an enamel pan. Stir in vinegar and slowly add the boiling water until the soap is thoroughly dissolved. Let cool.

2. Pour solution into a clean quart-size glass jar. Label, keep tightly capped, and keep out of the reach of children.

To Use:

Shake well and pour about 1 tablespoonful of the solution onto a soft cloth and then apply to brass. Rub gently, turning the cloth often. Apply more solution until tarnish is gone, and then buff with a clean cloth until brass is dry and shiny.

Note:

     If the brass you are working on has a lacquered finish, it will be necessary to remove it before you can clean the piece. You can use a commercial lacquer-remover for this purpose, or the ammonia bath described earlier will work if you pull the piece from the ammonia and rub with steel wool several times during the time it is soaking.

Hint:

     It is not necessary to reapply a lacquer finish to brass once it is polished. Instead, you can rub on any grade of car wax or fine paste wax, buff to a shine, and your finish will last for months. The brass will be protected, and the finish will not streak or discolor.

Yield: 32 ounces

Cost of Ingredients: $.86
Comparable Purchased Product: Wright's
    Brass Polish, 12 ounces, $1.39 ($3.70)
Savings: $2.84

Marble Cleaner

    Because marble is such a porous material, you may not have much luck in getting every stain out. Sometimes a marble fireplace, for example, will have suffered the indignities of years and years of neglect and would really need to be sandblasted to become pure white again. The solution that follows will work in many cases, however, and it is certainly worth the effort.

    1/2 cup bleach
    1 cup talcum powder

1. In an enamel or a glass bowl, make a paste by stirring the bleach into the talcum powder.

2. Store the paste in a covered container and use within a day or two. If it dries out, add 1 tablespoon bleach to reconstitute it.

Keep tightly capped, labeled, and out of the reach of children.

To Use:

   If you are working on a vertical surface such as a fireplace facade, you must brush the paste on with a paintbrush and then keep it moist long enough for the bleach to work. After the paste is applied, cover the surface with plastic wrap, sealing the edges with masking tape. Leave on for 24 hours.

   *Then place old newspapers under the surface, remove plastic, and brush the dried paste off with a stiff brush. Rinse thoroughly with a solution of 1/2 cup **Soft Soap** (page 278) and 1/2 cup baking soda in 4 cups warm water. Rinse again, if necessary, and dry.*

   Repeat the whole process if necessary.

Yield: 8 ounces

Cost of Ingredients: $2.26
Comparable Purchased Product: Marble
   Magic, 8 ounces, $2.99
Savings: $.73

Pewter Cleaners

   Following are three pewter cleaning formulas. The first one deserves the name—phew—because it is made with rottenstone, a terrible-smelling but soft abrasive that comes from sulfur. Any hardware store will stock this product.

   The second cleaner will give a shinier finish than the first, and the third formula is a folk formula. Try all three, and see which works best for the pewter you have.

   Remember, however, that pewter is a very soft metal, so don't use anything too harsh or abrasive on it, and especially don't use steel wool or a scouring pad.

Formula 1

1 cup ground rottenstone
2 tablespoons olive oil

Formula 2

1/4 cup whiting
1 tablespoon denatured alcohol

Formula 3

1 cup wood ashes
2 tablespoons water

1. For each formula, combine ingredients to make a paste.
Store any unused paste in a covered container that you have
labeled and keep it out of the reach of children.

To Use:
        Rub the paste onto the pewter with a soft cloth. Rinse;
buff dry.

Yield: *Formula 1:* 8 ounces
        Formula 2: 2 ounces
        Formula 3: 8 ounces

Cost of Ingredients: Formula 1: $.82; Formula
    2: $.18; Formula 3: $.00
Comparable Purchased Product: Noxon
    Metal Polish, 12 ounces, $2.29 ($1.52 over
    Formula 1)
Savings: $.52

Cheap Tricks . . . . ✂ . . . .

Here are some additional cleaning tricks for some of the other
fine items around your house:
        For ivory: try lemon juice or plain yogurt before
resorting to the peroxide treatment described on page 246.
        For television and computer screens, save the dryer
sheets from your laundry after they've softened a load of wash.
They will wipe the screen clean and reduce the static as well.
        For wax-covered candlesticks, I've run the hottest tap
water on the wax to loosen it and then polished as usual. Other
people put the candlestick in the freezer and pop the wax off.

Silver Polish

*The job of cleaning silver only involves getting rid of the tarnish that accumulates on it—the metal itself is soft and stays quite shiny if you can find a way to foil the accumulation of the tarnish. Several **Hints** might help. No matter which cleaning method you decide to use on your silver, remember to rub gently with a soft cloth, sponge, or old toothbrush—never use steel wool or a scouring pad because the silver surface will scratch.*

1 cup soap flakes or Soft Soap (page 278)
1 cup whiting
1 tablespoon ammonia (sudsing or nonsudsing)
2 cups boiling water

1. Mix soap, whiting, and ammonia together in a glass or an enamel pan. Pour in the boiling water and stir to dissolve. Let solution cool.

2. Pour into a clean quart-size glass jar. Label, cap tightly, and keep out of the reach of children.

To Use:
*Wash silver in soap and warm water. Do not rinse; shake polish and apply to silver with a soft cloth or sponge. Rub gently, rinse silver pieces in warm water, buff, and dry. See **Hints** for storage techniques.*

Hints:
If your silver is hardly tarnished at all and you want to try a more gentle polish, experiment with the following:
1. Soak tarnished pieces overnight in a bowl of milk. Rinse; buff dry.
2. Make a paste of either:
2 tablespoons baking soda
1 tablespoon cigarette ash
1 tablespoon water
or:
1/4 cup mashed, pureed banana skins
1 tablespoon baking soda

Apply, rub, buff dry.

To Store:
      The secret of keeping silver shiny is to keep it dry and free from humidity during storage. There are silver cloths you can buy to wrap your silver in, or clear plastic wrap will work for short storage periods.
      You can sprinkle powdered alum (from the pharmacy) over the plastic or silver cloth before you wrap the silver. The alum will absorb the excess moisture, but don't sprinkle it directly on the silver. You can also place the packets of silica gel that come packaged with cameras and computers in your silverware drawers to absorb moisture.
      Finally, remember to use your silver often and it will stay naturally clean and polished. More important, it will impart a special pleasure to everyday times while acquiring a subtle patina with use.

Yield: 20 ounces

Cost of Ingredients: $1.28
Comparable Purchased Product: Hagerty
    Silver Polish, 8 ounces, $3.69 ($11.07)
Savings: $9.79

Chapter 8

Clothing Care and Closet Items

With all the money you can save by using the following products to clean and maintain your clothing, you can add a number of fancy items to your closets and drawers. The items in this chapter will maintain clothing against odors, spots, moths, and even regular wear and tear.

> **Soft-Hard Water Test**
> **Laundry Pretreating Spray**
> **Spot Remover**
> > *Ink Remover*
> **Fabric Softener**
> **Delicate-care Bleach**
> **Delicate-care Soap**
> **Diaper Presoak**
> **Automatic Washing Machine Soap**
> > *Basic Washing Mix*
> > *Soft Water Mix*
> > *Hard Water Mix*
> > *Liquid Laundry Detergent*
> **Spray Starch**
> **Soft Soap**
> > *Basic Supersaver Soft Soap*
> > *Scented Soft Soap*
> > *Rich Soft Soap*
> **Classy Closets**
> **Spicy Closet Pomanders**
> **Sweet Potpourri**
> > *Spicy Mixture*
> > *Springtime Mixture*
> > *Moth-be-gone Mixture*
> **Simmering Scents from the Stove**
> **Sweet Air Spray**
> **Jewelry Cleaner**

Soft-Hard Water Test

*Before you make up your own private stock of **Automatic Washing Machine Soap**, page 276, perform this simple test on your water supply to see how hard or soft your water is. If your water tests out somewhere between the two sudsing extremes described here, use the Basic Mix. If your water is hard or soft or your laundry especially dirty, vary the formula according to the directions.*

> **1 teaspoon soap flakes**
> **2 cups warm water**

1. Place the soap flakes and water in a jar, cover, and shake well.

2. If the solution makes a nice quantity of suds that lasts for up to 5 minutes, you have soft water. Follow the instructions for the Soft-water Mix, page 276.

3. If the solution produces very few suds that disappear quickly, follow the instructions for Hard-water Mix, page 276.

Laundry Pretreating Spray

This spray gives you confidence that the extradirty parts of your laundry will be getting special attention in the washing machine. The solution loosens the dirt and concentrates cleaning action where you want it. This recipe makes a big batch to store and use liberally.

> **1/2 cup ammonia**
> **1/2 cup white vinegar**
> **1/4 cup baking soda**
> **2 tablespoons liquid soap or Soft Soap (page 278)**
> **2 quarts water**

1. Mix ingredients and shake well. Pour a portion into a pump-type spray container and store the rest in a clean gallon-size jug. Label and keep out of the reach of children.

To Use:
   Spray the solution on the dirtiest parts of your laundry while you are sorting—let the spray sit on the stain or dirty collar for a minute or two before putting the item in with the rest of the laundry.

Yield: 43 ounces

Cost of Ingredients: $.22
Comparable Purchased Product: Spray 'n Wash, 16 ounces, $2.29 ($6.15)
Savings: $5.93

Spot Remover

   This remover is especially good on delicate fabrics. However, the recipe is for a small amount because you must use it and then discard any that might be remaining. This cleaner will not keep, and worse, it will eat through any container you put it in because the two chemicals generate heat if left together for long.

   3 tablespoons hydrogen peroxide
   1 tablespoon ammonia

1.   Mix ingredients and dab on the stained area. Leave on for up to an hour, rinse off, and reapply if necessary.

Hints:
   Fumes from this cleaner may seem strong, so work in a well-ventilated area.
   It's a good idea to perform a **patch test** if you are unsure about working on a particular fabric. Dab a bit of the cleaner onto an inconspicuous part of the garment—an inside seam is good—wait, and make sure the color doesn't run or the fabric itself doesn't seem badly affected.
   Never combine this cleaner with any cleaner containing chlorine bleach because the combination of ammonia and bleach will give off dangerous fumes. Make this solution up in a small batch in a glass or an enamel bowl and discard any leftovers immediately.

Ink Remover

1 tablespoon white vinegar
1 tablespoon milk
1 teaspoon lemon juice
1 teaspoon borax

1. Place the portion of fabric with the ink stain between several thicknesses of paper toweling. Combine the four ingredients in a small bowl and "paint" the spot. Wait for a few minutes and sponge the area with cool water. Repeat until the stain is gone.

Yield: 2 ounces

Cost of Ingredients: $.05
Comparable Purchased Product: Carbona Spot Remover, 4 ounces, $1.39 ($.69)
Savings: $.62

Fabric Softener

*This softener can be customized by using any of the different **Herbal Vinegars**, page 148. Each of these will impart a slightly different, subtle scent, and you should try each one until you find a scent that smells nice to you.*
If you want your clothes to have no scent at all, simply use plain white vinegar in the recipe.

2 cups baking soda
2 cups Herbal Vinegar or white vinegar
4 cups water

1. Mix ingredients and store in a plastic or glass container in your laundry area. Label the container and it keep out of the reach of children.

To Use:
*Add 1/4 cup to the final rinse water in your washing machine. If your water is particularly hard (see the **Soft-Hard***

Water Test, page 276), you may have to add a bit more, so experiment and see how much is best for your laundry.

Yield: 64 ounces

Cost of Ingredients: $.96
Comparable Purchased Product: Snuggle
Fabric Softener, 33 ounces, $1.29 ($2.50)
Savings: $1.54

Delicate-care Bleach

I use regular household bleach when I'm sure my fabrics can take it, and I use it lavishly. I pour it into the wash water before I put the clothes in, and I use it for cottons and sweat suits, jeans and anything too dirty to worry about.

For delicate colors and synthetic fabrics, here is a safe, gentle bleach that reduces yellowing in silks and delicate woolens.

> **2 cups hydrogen peroxide**
> **14 cups water**

1. Mix ingredients and store in a plastic gallon-size jug. Label container and keep out of the reach of children.

To Use:

> Soak items to be cleaned in this solution for 10 to 30 minutes. Rinse and wash with **Delicate-care Soap**, page 274.

Hint:

> To avoid adding new spots to your clothing during the washing process, it's better to use one of the powdered bleaches on the market, rather than a liquid bleach if your water has a high iron content. Check for iron in your water this way: pour 1 teaspoon liquid chlorine bleach into 1/2 cup water. If the water turns yellow, there is iron in your water and you should use powdered bleach.

Yield: 1 gallon

Cost of Ingredients: $.39
Comparable Purchased Product: Vivid
Color Safe Fabric Bleach, 32 ounces, $1.39
Savings: $1.00

Delicate-care Soap

This soap is for hand washing delicate items. However, before you wash any item, be sure it can withstand being submerged in water—check the manufacturer's care label for water temperature and how to dry the item.

1 cup soap flakes
1/2 cup borax
4 cups boiling water

1.   Combine soap flakes and borax in a large pan or bowl and pour the boiling water over the mixture, stirring until soap is dissolved. Cool.

2.   Store in a plastic squeeze or pump-type container and keep in the laundry room. Label the container and keep it out of the reach of children.

To Use:
Measure out approximately 1/4 cup of Delicate-care Soap to each quart of water. Add items to be washed and squish them around a bit. Mixture should produce gentle suds. If it doesn't, add another squirt or two.
For heavily soiled items, it's a good idea to let them soak for an hour or two in the cleaning solution before laundering them, as above.

Yield: 32 ounces

Cost of Ingredients: $.67
Comparable Purchased Product: Woolite, 8
ounces, $1.29 ($5.16)
Savings: $4.49

Diaper Presoak

If you still use cloth diapers, you will want to make up a batch of this solution. The presoak can also be used for heavily soiled laundry—it's what I have a lot of now that my baby no longer wears diapers but instead crawls around under a car.

> 1/2 cup baking soda
> 1/4 cup ammonia
> 1 gallon warm water

1.   Combine ingredients in a clean gallon-size plastic jug and shake to mix thoroughly. Label jug and store solution away from children.

To Use:

Pour as much of the solution as you need into a pail or laundry tub and soak the dirty items in question for several hours before washing.

You can also put the clothing to be soaked right into the washing machine, pour the presoak over them and allow them to soak overnight. In the morning, fill the machine with cold water, agitate and rinse, and then wash as usual.

Yield: 1 gallon

Cost of Ingredients: $.13
Comparable Purchased Product: Lysol
   Laundry Sanitizer, 14 ounces, $.99 ($9.05)
Savings: $8.92

Cheap Trick . . . . ✂ . . . .

If you've ever used, laundered, used, and laundered again a batch of cloth diapers, I hope you've saved them carefully—they are worth their weight in gold as the best rags you'll ever own. I would advise a new mother to suffer through the year or so of diaper laundry just to possess these valuable rags all the rest of her life. The repeated launderings and, I suppose, the close contact with baby's skin, create a soft, lint-free cloth that is perfect for craft clean-ups, windows, and for buffing and shining graphic, automotive, and fine works of art.

Automatic Washing Machine Soap

*The proportions in this mix are infinitely variable—you should customize the solution to your own type of water depending on its relative hardness or softness (see the **Soft-Hard Water Test**, page 270, for details), and according to how soiled or how delicate your laundry items are.*

The Basic Mix can be considered a middle solution to all the above problems. Add more washing soda if your water is particularly hard and add more soap flakes if your clothes are particularly soiled.

Basic Mix

1 cup soap flakes
1/2 cup washing soda
1/2 cup borax

Soft Water Mix

1 cup soap flakes
1/4 cup washing soda
1/4 cup borax

Hard Water Mix

1 cup soap flakes
1 cup washing soda
1 cup borax

Liquid Laundry Detergent

1 cup of any of the above mixes
2 tablespoons glycerin
2 cups warm water

1. Mix ingredients and store in a lidded, labeled canister in the laundry room. Keep out of the reach of children.

To Use:

Measure out 1/2 cup to 3/4 cup and wash your clothing in warm or cold water. Use cold water for the rinse cycle.

Yield: 12 ounces

Cost of Ingredients: $.80
Comparable Purchased Product: Fresh
    Start Laundry Detergent, 20 ounces, $2.49
    ($1.49)
Savings: $.69

Spray Starch

I may be the last person left on earth who enjoys ironing; worse, I even like to dampen clothes and starch things as I iron. When I was growing up, my mother ironed just about everything—underwear, dish towels, sheets—and the nice clean smell of freshly ironed clothes is right up there with roses and baked bread.

The starch that follows is simple to make and scented slightly, because I love the vapors of fragrance that rise as I iron away.

> **4 teaspoons cornstarch**
> **1/2 teaspoon cologne**
> **2 cups warm water**

1.   Mix ingredients, pour into a plastic spray bottle and shake well. Label, and keep the bottle on or near your ironing board.

To Use:
    Spray evenly on cuffs and collars and on especially wrinkled areas.
    To thoroughly starch a large item or a lot of laundry at once, dampen the items slightly by sprinkling a little warm water on them, spray with the starch, roll tightly, and store them in a plastic bag in the refrigerator for 1 to 12 hours.

Hint:
    Remember to rinse the spray nozzle of your plastic bottle after each use to keep the starch from clogging it.

Yield: 16 ounces

Cost of Ingredients: $.02
Comparable Purchased Product: Spray 'n
Starch Fabric Finish, 16 ounces, $1.19
Savings: $1.17

Soft Soap

Here is the soap that is good for everything, depending on how you vary or customize it. You will find references to Soft Soap throughout **Cheaper & Better**—*use it in the plain, basic formula for simple washing of delicate items and for adding to other recipes. Add scent for personal use—spritz some in the tub as the water is running, and add oils if you would like softer-feeling skin.*

If you don't have enough bits of soap collected to make **Soft Soap,** *you can add soap flakes to make 1 cup, but begin your collection of soap slivers right away—see page 201 for another use for them.*

Basic Supersaver Soft Soap

**Several bits, slivers, and pieces of used soap—enough
   to make 1 cup, dried out, or 1 cup soap flakes
1 cup boiling water**

1. If you are using soap bits, grind them to a fine powder in your food processor or blender. Mix with the soap flakes, if necessary, to make 2 cups.

2. Pour boiling water over the soap and stir until soap is completely dissolved. Cool.

3. Label and store in a pump-type dispenser or a squeeze-top plastic container.

Scented Soft Soap

**Several drops essential oil, or your
      favorite perfume
1 cup Basic Supersaver Soft Soap**

Mix and store as for **Basic Supersaver Soft Soap.**

Rich Soft Soap

2 tablespoons olive, wheat germ, or almond oil
1 cup Basic Supersaver or Scented Soft Soap

*Warm the oil and mix with the soap. Use a blender or an
electric mixer to make sure oil is distributed evenly; mix and
store as for* **Basic Supersaver Soft Soap.**

Yield: 8 ounces

Cost of Ingredients: $.63 if using soap flakes
Comparable Purchased Product: Ivory
Liquid Soap, 18 ounces, $1.69 ($.75)
Savings: $.12

Classy Closets

When the time comes to refresh your plain, boring closets
or bureau drawers and treat yourself or someone you love to a
closet face-lift, here's how to do it from top to bottom.

Plan on doing this project when you have some time on
your hands because the first step in any closet clean-up
campaign is always pretty messy. You should remove
everything from the closet, sort and organize things to keep,
things to give away, and things that should be thrown out.
Then, treat your closet to a thorough scrubbing with **All-purpose
Cleaner**, page 244, before beginning.

1 or 2 rolls of wallpaper or a wallpaper sample book
Wallpaper paste
Newspaper
Small paintbrush
Scissors
White glue
Various-size boxes
Small cup hooks
Spray cologne
Scented Soft Soap (page 278)
Spicy Closet Pomander (page 281)
Sweet Potpourri (page 282)

1. If you're talented enough to wallpaper your own walls, you should empty the closet and go at this job first. If you're timid about your wallpapering skills, consider the closet as a good place to practice because your mistakes will be less visable to visitors. You can use prepasted paper, sticky-back paper, or a combination of odds and ends that you've collected from other jobs. You can patch different paper on each wall if a collage effect looks good to you.

2. Use smaller scraps or the pages from a wallpaper sample book to line your bureau drawers. Make a newspaper pattern for the size and cut out all the linings at once. Use a porous paper rather than vinyl wallpaper for clothing drawers and spray the finished drawers with cologne before filling them again.

3. Cover various-size boxes with wallpaper samples and use them to hold shoes, bags, scarves, sweaters, and, of course, hats.

4. Screw in tiny cup hooks here and there to hold an attractive display of belts, scarves, and jewelry.

5. Give shoes special care: make boot-stiffs from rolled-up magazines covered with pretty paper and sprinkle **Perfumed Bath Powder**, page 227, into shoes you wear often. For shoes worn less often, you might store them in boxes or old socks to keep them dust-free.

6. To finish your pretty closet, hang **Spicy Closet Pomanders**, page 281, place sachets or scented soaps in your drawers, or sprinkle **Sweet Potpourri**, page 282, in a nice bowl or cup and place on the floor or counter.

Yield: 1 scented closet

Cost of Ingredients: $10 (approximately, if using primarily scraps)
Comparable Purchased Product: H. Arthur Ltd., Closet Systems, $100 (minimum)
Savings: $90

Spicy Closet Pomanders

These classic hanging balls are pretty to look at and easy to make. You can make a nice batch while watching television, and you can use a stack of pomanders that you've piled up to "cure" as a pretty centerpiece before they do duty in your closets.

> 1 orange, lemon, or apple
> 1/2 cup whole cloves
> 1 tablespoon cinnamon
> 1 tablespoon allspice, ground cloves, nutmeg, or
>   ginger
> 1 teaspoon orrisroot

1. Working over a bowl, poke small holes into the fruit with the nail or other sharp object. Insert a whole clove into each hole. You can cover the entire surface of the fruit or create a design with the holes, and if you plan to hang the pomander ball, remember to leave some space between the cloves to wrap a ribbon around the fruit.

2. Mix the spices and orrisroot in a shallow bowl. Once the fruit is covered with cloves, roll it in the spices until it's completely covered. It's a good idea to let the pomander ball sit in the spices for a week or two.

3. Turn the pomander once or twice a day as it shrinks and the juices mix with the spices in the bowl. Cure the ball for 1 to 2 weeks and make sure it is thoroughly dried before hanging in your closet.

Hints:
   A centerpiece of balls makes a delightful, wonderfully scented arrangement during the holidays.
   Wrap a ball or two in netting and hang them from your closet rod or give as pretty gifts.
   If the fragrance of the pomander begins to wane, revive it by placing it in the sun or warming it in an oven at 110 degrees for 1 hour. Then moisten it with few drops of oil of orange and oil of clove.

Yield: 1 to 4 balls

Cost of Ingredients: $.87
Comparable Purchased Product: Air Wick
   Stick Ups, 2, $1.29
Savings: $.42

Sweet Potpourri

A potpourri is a mixture of spices, blossoms, herbs, and scented oils that you mix up, let mellow, and then enjoy by mounding the delightful mixture in open bowls, big pearly sea shells, or pretty glass jars. Or, try sewing a bit of the potpourri into small sachets that you tuck into drawers, closets, or suitcases.

Each of the following mixtures imparts a different scent—some spicy, some flowery—all wonderful.

Spicy Mixture

2 tablespoons allspice
2 tablespoons cinnamon
2 tablespoons nutmeg
2 tablespoons whole cloves
2 tablespoons dried citrus: lemon, orange, or lime peel
   (page 26)
2 tablespoons borax
2 teaspoons orrisroot

1. Combine all ingredients and store in a glass jar, tightly covered, and let potpourri sit for 5 to 6 weeks. Turn jar once a day.

Springtime Mixture

2 quarts dried rose petals
1 quart dried geranium petals
1 cup dried peppermint leaves
1/2 cup lavender petals
8 whole cloves
1 tablespoon ground nutmeg
2 teaspoons orrisroot

Moth-be-gone Mixture

1/2 cup lavender petals
1/2 cup cedar shavings
2 tablespoons thyme
2 tablespoons rosemary
2 tablespoons cloves
1 tablespoon caraway seeds
1 tablespoon mace
1 tablespoon cinnamon
1 tablespoon nutmeg
1 tablespoon black pepper
1 teaspoon orrisroot

1. Preheat oven to 110 degrees.

2. To dry flower petals, pick petals in the morning right after the dew has dried. Layer petals on a tray and place in full sunlight or a warm oven for 6 to 8 hours, until brittle. Cool before using.

3. Combine all ingredients and store in a glass jar, tightly covered, and let the potpourri sit for 5 to 6 weeks. Turn the jar once a day.

Ideas:
    Pretty bowls and big seashells are ideal containers for potpourri.
    Make simple little sachets by cutting circles of fabric, adding a teaspoon of potpourri in the middle, and closing with ribbon. Place in drawers or on shelves between linens.
    Fancy lace handkerchiefs make easy sachets, tied and used as above.

Yield: 7 ounces

Cost of Ingredients: $3.74
Comparable Purchased Product: Claire
    Burke Potpourri, 6 ounces, $7.50 ($8.75)
Savings: $5.01

Simmering Scents from the Stove

Mix up a batch of this potpourri and place it on the stove to simmer whenever you want to have a burst of fragrance. It's a most homey mixture and it's especially pleasing in the dead of winter.

> 1/4 **cup pine needles**
> 1 **tablespoon whole cloves**
> 1/2 **cup lemon, orange, or tangerine peel**
> 2 **cinnamon sticks**
> 1 **tablespoon allspice**

1. Combine all ingredients and store in a glass jar or pretty tin, tightly covered.

To Use:

> *Add a tablespoon of the mix to 2 cups water and let mixture simmer gently on your kitchen stove or wood stove.*

Yield: 8 ounces

Cost of Ingredients: $2.21
Comparable Purchased Product:
  Countryside Herb Farm Simmering Potpourri,
  1.5 ounces, $2.50 ($13.33)
Savings: $11.12

Cheap Trick . . . .

Expensive, fragrant soap that you buy should also be pressed into service to scent your drawers, linen closet, and bathroom long before it begins duty as a simple bar of soap. While the soap is brand new and still wrapped, you can tuck it into your drawers and linens. After about a month or two, the soap can be unwrapped and put back. Two months later, move the unwrapped bars to a pretty basket in the bathroom, and then use the bars when needed. Their long air-drying will harden them and they will last longer.

Sweet Air Spray

Use this simple mixture to scent and cleanse the air of smoky or musty odors. Experiment with the herbs and spices that smell the nicest to you—remember that it's your own space that you're improving—so choose a combination that makes you feel good.

You might try scenting your air to produce a special effect: rosemary is supposed to ward off evil spirits, cinnamon smells like a bakery, and pine reminds the nose of Christmas.

You can save money by infusing herbs or teas that you suspect to be buggy or too weak to cook with, or save the peelings from apple or lemons and add them to your brew.

*Plan to keep an open container handy for adding to your collection of items for this potpourri, and for an especially clever way to store your waiting collection, see the **Idea**, that follows.*

> **2 cups white vinegar**
> **Any combination of the following herbs or spices (dried or fresh) to make 1 cup:**
>
> *rosemary, lavender; cloves; rose petals; thyme; cinnamon sticks; pine needles; apple, orange, lemon, or lime peel; honeysuckle or other fragrant blossoms; peppermint, walnut, or Vanilla Bean Extract (page 12)*

1. Place all ingredients in a glass or enamel pan. Heat the mixture to a gentle, simmering boil and simmer for 10 minutes. Cool.

2. Pour liquid and herbs into a large, sturdy jar. Close jar tightly, label, and store it where you will see it for 2 to 4 weeks. Remember to shake the jar once or twice a week.

3. Strain and reserve juice. Use herbs for **Liquid Fertilizer**, page 298. Pour liquid into a pump-type spray container or atomizer. Label container.

Idea:

Take a cup or so of your dried ingredients and pour it into an oven mitt. Sew up the opening with basting stitches and use the scented mitt for a hot plate—fragrance will be released every time you use it and you can recycle the dried materials into Sweet Air Spray when you are ready to wash the mitt.

Yield: 16 ounces

Cost of Ingredients: $.48
Comparable Purchased Product: Glade Air
   Freshener, 7 ounces, $1.29 ($2.94)
Savings: $2.46

Jewelry Cleaner

This recipe is suitable only for fine jewelry. The fittings and glue on costume jewelry are fragile and pieces might come loose if you submerge them in this solution for any length of time.

1 teaspoon dishwashing liquid or Soft Soap (page 278)
1 teaspoon borax
1 teaspoon washing soda
1 teaspoon ammonia
1 cup warm water

1.   Mix ingredients and pour into a glass jar. Label and keep out of the reach of children.

To Use:

Swish items to be cleaned through the solution, or let them sit in it for 1 to 10 minutes. Rinse and dry with a soft, lint-free cloth.

Hints:

An old mascara brush or wand, thoroughly cleaned beforehand in soap and water, will help you get into tiny spaces and crevices to clean.

A soft toothbrush is a good cleaning tool for bigger pieces.

Use a soft chamois cloth to gently rub pearls, rather than wash them.

Remember never to mix this solution with anything containing chlorine bleach, or dangerous fumes will result.

Yield: 8 ounces

Cost of Ingredients: $.22
Comparable Purchased Product: Ritz Gem
   and Jewelry Cleaner, 8 ounces, $1.96
Savings: $1.74

Chapter 9

Garden, Pets, and Pests

The products in this chapter include items for growing a greener garden and keeping it free from pests without harsh chemicals; items for pool maintenance; items for pet care and feeding, and for the elimination of common household and yard pests.

Meaty Doggie and Kitty Biscuits
High-protein Bird Treats
    Soft Peanut Butter Treat
    Canary Paste
Dry Pet Shampoo
Puppy Go Away
Cat-box Deodorizer
House-plant Polish
House-plant Potting Soil
Liquid Fertilizer
Aphid Control
Dormant Oil Spray
Safe Garden Pesticides
    Oily Garden Repellent
    Vegetable-garden Repellent
Fly Repellent
Fly Paper
Roach Balls
Rabbit Repellent
Deer Repellent

Meaty Doggie and Kitty Biscuits

Here is a treat for all those times when your pet deserves a special favor. If the members of your family aren't especially fond of eating things made from that bag of organs found in chickens or turkeys, you can be sure that your pet dog or cat will love these biscuits made from those parts.

When making this recipe for a cat, shape the biscuits into tiny bits for easy chewing, and don't be too disheartened if your cat acts finicky—my cat won't touch "dog" food.

> 1 pound liver, organs, or other meat (enough to make 2
>   cups cooked meat)
> 2 cups bran
> 2 cups old-fashioned oatmeal
> 1/4 cup cooking oil

1. Preheat oven to 250 degrees.

2. Cover meat with cold water and bring to a boil. Immediately lower heat and simmer for 30 minutes. Remove meat from water and let cool; retain water.

3. When meat is completely cool, chop into 1-inch pieces and grind in food processor, chop in blender, or process through a meat grinder until it is finely ground.

4. Mix ground meat, bran, oatmeal, and oil, adding the cooking water from the meat as necessary to make a thick dough. Try to avoid adding any more liquid than you need to make a dough that is coarse and just wet enough to work with.

5. Shape the dough into flattened balls or little bone shapes and arrange on an oiled baking sheet.

6. Bake for 3 hours. Then, rather than remove from the oven immediately, turn off the heat and let the biscuits cool in the oven to make sure they are sufficiently hard and crunchy.

7. Let the biscuits air dry for 24 hours and store in a labeled, closely covered container in the pantry for up to 4 weeks.

Yield: 3 pounds

Cost of Ingredients: $3.76
Comparable Purchased Product: Milkbone
   Dog Treats, 10 ounces, $1.19 ($5.71)
Savings: $1.95

High-protein Bird Treats

One of the most effective ways to control insects on your property is to provide for the care and feeding of those types of birds that like to eat their weight each day in bugs. Once you've become adept at making one of the elementary hanging treats described here, you will be amazed at how quickly the word gets out among the birds that yours is the place to be and be seen.

If you would like to become more sophisticated in your selection process, you can customize your treats to attract a better class of bird. You can also plan a purple martin apartment building to lure that most desirable mosquito-eating type of bird, and be sure to check in the **Resources** for a few publications to get you started if you want to learn more.

Remember as you read this recipe that the amounts and the types of grains and seeds are very approximate—it's the consistency of the final product that's important, as well as a general attempt to use up what's in your kitchen. Remember also if you find yourself with buggy cake, bread, or flour products that a bird would consider your mealybugs a major taste treat.

> **4 cups suet or solid kitchen fat**
> **1 cup cracker or bread crumbs**
> **1/2 cup sunflower seeds**
> **1/4 cup millet**
> **1/4 cup dried fruit: raisins, currants, or dates**
> **1/4 cup peanuts or peanut butter**

1. Melt the suet or solid fat in a large, heavy saucepan until it is liquid. Remove from heat and allow it to cool until slightly thickened.

2. In a separate bowl, combine the rest of the ingredients and pour the cooled suet over the mixture. Stir thoroughly.

292 Garden and Pets

3. While the mixture is still warm and pliable, you can either spread it onto tree trunks or tree limbs for easy feeding; pack it into the spaces in pinecones and hang the pinecones on a nearby tree; or spread it in an inch-deep baking pan or several cake pans and refrigerate overnight. When the suet is completely hardened, cut it into squares to fit your feeder.

Soft Peanut Butter Treat

> 1 cup suet
> 1 cup peanut butter
> 3 cups cornmeal
> 1/2 cup flour
> 1/2 cup bread or cookie crumbs

1. Melt suet in a heavy saucepan and when the fat is liquid, add the peanut butter and cornmeal. Stir and mix completely; remove from heat.

2. Add flour and crumbs and allow to cool and thicken slightly before packing or smearing on tree trunks, as described above.

Canary Paste

If you have a favorite songbird, here is a sweet treat to keep it happy and singing in its cage. You can pack the paste into a purchased feeding tray from the store, or you can granulate the paste by pressing it through a sieve and mounding the paste on the feeding tray.

> 1/4 cup almonds
> 1/4 cup cornmeal
> 2 tablespoons sweet butter, softened
> 2 tablespoons honey

1. Place the almonds in a blender or food processor and process until they are finely ground. Add the cornmeal and process 1 minute more.

2. Cream the butter and honey in a small bowl until thoroughly combined; add the dry ingredients and work into a stiff paste.

Yield: 32 ounces; makes 15 cakes

Cost of Ingredients: $6.42
Comparable Purchased Product: Bird 'n
Hand Suet Cakes, four 2-inch square cakes,
$10.95 ($41.06)
Savings: $34.64

Dry Pet Shampoo

*If your furry animal has fallen into something extremely
gooey, this dry shampoo may be one of the only remedies to try
if you want to get the goop out of the pet's fur. It's a sure and
gentle method, and you must stroke the shampoo into the pet's
fur, all of which will help to comfort a probably upset pet.*

1 cup flour
1 cup cornmeal

1. Mix the ingredients and pour them into a container roomy
enough to hold the pet. A large paper box for a big pet or a deep
roasting dish for a small animal will work.

To Use:

> *Place the container filled with the mixture in the
bathtub and then gently place your pet into the pan or box. Rub
the mixture, by handfuls, in your pet's fur until all the goo or
oil or mess has been absorbed.*
> *Then gently brush the mixture out of the fur. Be careful
to keep the mixture out of your pet's eyes, nose, and ears.
Dispose of the used mixture.*
> *It's a good idea to follow up with a regular mild
shampoo at this point if you can manage it.*

Note:

> *If your pet has had an unfortunate run-in with a skunk
as well as with goo, you will have to bathe him in tomato juice
after the dry shampoo but before his regular shampoo if you
want the smell to go away.*

Yield: 2 cups

Cost of Ingredients: $.35
Comparable Purchased Product: Hartz Pet
   Shampoo, 12 ounces, $3.59 ($4.78)
Savings: $4.43

Cheap Trick . . . . ✂ . . . .

A friend of mine tried a different temporary way to keep her growing dog off the sofa: she placed a large sheet of aluminum foil right on his favorite spot and when he jumped up—caramba! The noise and confusion convinced him the sofa was no longer a peaceful place.

Puppy Go Away

When you have a puppy as rambunctious as ours was, you will do anything you can to save the furniture and rugs. This solution worked for us. The scent isn't distasteful to people, only to ultra-"scent"-sitive puppies.

>   1/4 cup oil of cloves
>   1 tablespoon paprika
>   1 teaspoon black pepper

1. Mix the oil, paprika, and pepper and pour it into a small container with a tight-fitting lid. Label and keep away from children.

To Use:

Since I planned to use all the solution at once, I put it into one of those stamp-moistener tubes from the office supply store so that I could dab it all over the legs of Max's favorite chairs and tables and around the edges of his favorite rugs.

Since the scent will wear off after a while, you may have to reapply it if your puppy isn't completely trained.

Yield: 3 ounces

Cost of Ingredients: $.84
Comparable Purchased Product: Hartz
Indoor NO, 14 ounces, $3.69
Savings: $2.85

Cat-box Deodorizer

*By far the most important thing to remember when trying
to keep your cat box smelling even halfway decent is to clean
out the solid waste every day. If you locate your cat box near a
little-used toilet in your house, cover it with a big hood, and
keep a scooper nearby, you will find it easy enough to keep it
clean.*

*The deodorizer allows you to go a long time between litter-
box changes, as long as you remember to stir up the litter to
aerate it often. If your cat won't tolerate any added scent, leave
out the mint, but no cat should object to the baking soda. And if
you've acquired your cat to keep one of your kids company, by
all means hand over the litter scooper to the young owner.*

One 16-ounce package baking soda
4 teaspoons dried mint

1. Add the baking soda and mint to your kitty litter, stir it up,
and keep it clean.

Hint:
*Since we're talking about some of the more disgusting
aspects of cat care, you might as well try letting your cat lap up
a bit of mineral oil or petroleum jelly once a month if he or she
routinely coughs up hairballs. Try rubbing a bit of the oil on the
back of your hand or directly on the cat's nose and she will lick
it off.*

Yield: 1 cat-box treatment

Cost of Ingredients: $.75
Comparable Purchased Product: Hartz Cat
Litter Deodorant, 7 ounces, $2.19 ($1.09)
Savings: $.34

House-plant Polish

This polish is better for your plants than commercial polishes because it gently cleans the plants while still allowing them to breathe because there are no waxes to interfere with the plant's respiration.

An old-time remedy calls for wiping down your plants with milk, but this is not advisable, according to a gardening friend of mine. He says that the milk may make the leaves look shiny for a short while, but it will clog the plant's pores for a long time afterward.

5 cups warm water
1 tablespoon soap flakes or Soft Soap (page 278)
1 teaspoon wheat germ oil

1. Mix water, soap flakes, and oil very thoroughly; label, and store in a clean bottle .

To Use:

If your plants are especially dusty, it's a good idea to rinse the leaves first with plain water before applying the polish. You can place your plants in the bathtub and turn the shower on to a gentle spray, or you can take them outside and spray them gently with your garden hose. Then saturate a soft cloth with the polish and wipe the leaves gently. For fernlike leaves, pour some polish into a small plastic spray or pump-type container and spritz the leaves.

Variation:

To make this plant wash have a bit of insecticidal power as well as shine, try adding 1/4 cup pureed onions and juice to the mixture. Use as described.

Yield: 5 cups

Cost of Ingredients: $.10
Comparable Purchased Product: New Era
    Leaf Polish, 8 ounces, $2.49 ($12.45)
Savings: $12.35

House-plant Potting Soil

This mixture is a basic one—you can add all sorts of extra goodies to this recipe to further encourage your house plants to thrive. Try adding ground eggshells or used coffee grounds to the basic mix.

Also note the general hints for repotting, and follow the same strict rules for cleanliness around your plants that you use around your food—even though you are working with dirt, you don't want a dirty mixture.

If you are keeping your own compost pile, you will be lucky enough to have very high quality fertilized soil for supplementing your interior and outside plants. If you have no compost, add a feeding with **Liquid Fertilizer***, page 298, once a month.*

4 cups topsoil from your garden
1 cup sand
1 cup vermiculite
2 cups peat moss
4 to 6 cups sifted compost (if available, otherwise see Variations)

1. Preheat oven to 300 degrees.

2. Spread the topsoil onto several cookie sheets and place in the over for 1 hour. Let cool.

3. Spread newspapers over your worktable and lay an old screen or coarse grater over a large container to create a large sifter. Spoon the topsoil onto the sifter and shake it through. Return any debris that won't go through the screen, along with the newspapers, right back into your compost.

4. Stir sand, vermiculite, peat moss, and sifted compost into the clean topsoil.

5. Store the mixture in a large, clean plastic container, small clean garbage can with a tight-fitting lid, or large plastic bag.

To Use:
If you're transplanting plants into a clay pot, make sure the pot is clean by scrubbing first with soap and water and

rubbing the pot briskly with a stiff brush. A discarded vegetable brush works well. Then rinse the pot thoroughly and let it sit in clean water until you are ready to begin. If you're using plastic pots, rinse and let drain—no soaking is needed.

Add about 1 inch of chunky, nonporous material to the bottom of the pot. Broken pieces of clay pots, washed bottle caps, styrofoam packing pellets, or clean gravel and rocks are all good in the bottom of the pot for drainage.

Add about 2 inches of your potting soil mixture, then your plant, and then the rest of the potting soil. Water gently, tamp down, and then add more soil.

Hint:

Always transplant a plant that is growing out of its pot into a pot that is just a little bigger. Too big a change of size seems to stunt the plant's growth, while just the next size seems to encourage the plant to grow. After newly potting, allow the plant to rest quietly for 24 hours before putting it out into full light.

If your potting soil is going to be used for succulent plants, try making the mixture very porous by adding one part sand and one part peat moss to each part of potting soil.

Yield: 1 gallon

Cost of Ingredients: $1.02
Comparable Purchased Product: Channel
Potting Soil, 16 quarts, $4.59 ($1.14)
Savings: $.12

Liquid Fertilizer

The herbs in this mixture will provide a good general-purpose fertilizer that is gentle enough to use each time you water your plants. If you replenish a portion of the herbs once a month, the mixture can be self-generating indefinitely.

All the herbs can be purchased at a large health food store or ordered directly from one of the suppliers listed in the **Resources** *section under Chapter 9. In addition, any of the residue from the herbs used for beauty preparations in Chapter 6 or the nonalcoholic berries left over from drink making in*

Chapter 5 can also be added to the brew. Simply spoon the herbs or berries into the fertilizer liquid after you've strained them for your primary recipe.

1 ounce nettle
1 ounce comfrey root
1 ounce kelp
Additional herb or berry mash (see above)

1. Chop the herbs with a knife or scissors and place them in a gallon-size plastic jug. Fill the jug with warm water, cover, and let the mixture steep for 24 hours.

To Use:
You can use the liquid directly from the jug for watering, but be careful not to pour the herbs on the plant. If you intend to make a lot of fertilizer, you might keep one jug for steeping and strain the liquid before watering. Add fresh herbs to your steeping jug at least once a month.

Yield: 1 gallon (1 to 2 applications)

Cost of Ingredients: $1.09
Comparable Purchased Product: Plantabs, 3 ounces, $1.79 ($3.58)
Savings: $2.49

Aphid Control

Here is a quick, effective remedy for aphids on your flowers—simply spray this on and the bugs are gone. Because this remedy is as strongly scented as your flowers, spray a day before you plan to cut flowers for any arrangements inside the house.

1 cup chopped onions or shallots
1 cup water

1. Puree the chopped onions or shallots in a blender until they are a fine mush. Add the water, a little at a time, and continue blending, scraping down the sides if necessary, so that there are no large chunks.

2. Label and store in a glass jar, tightly lidded, in the refrigerator for up to 6 weeks.

To Use:
Pour into a spray container and spritz the liquid all over the plant, even under the blossoms. It is best to spray in the early morning, after the dew has dried, or in the late afternoon when the sun is not too hot. Make sure there isn't a stiff wind or you will end up covered with the spray instead of your flowers.

Yield: 16 ounces

 Cost of Ingredients: $.50
Comparable Purchased Product: New Era Insect Spray, 8 ounces, $2.29 ($4.58)
Savings: $4.08

Dormant Oil Spray

It seems that there are as many natural repellents for unwanted insects and other garden pests as there are insects and pests—nature has probably planned it that way. Before you reach for any toxic sprays from the store, you should at least try some of the following solutions.

And don't give up too quickly: sometimes it takes more than one application, as noted, to do the job; sometimes you must time your remedy to the season to achieve the desired effect.

Also, don't neglect long-term remedies—look elsewhere in this chapter for ways to attract the kinds of birds to your property that will munch their weight in insects every day. (See page 291.) Or, try planting your garden differently next year, alternating fruits and vegetables with flowers and herbs that repel unwanted bugs and pests.

Finally, practice good housekeeping both inside and outside the home and many of your insect problems will be eliminated. Chapters 7 and 8 contain many ways to keep unwanted pests out of your clothing and closets, as well as solutions for cleaning out garbage pails and other breeding grounds for bugs.

1/2 cup mineral oil
1/4 cup fish oil
1/2 cup liquid detergent or Soft Soap (page 278)
15 cups water

1. In a clean, gallon-size plastic jug, mix oils and detergent and add 1 cup of water. Close the container and shake well. Add the rest of the water to fill.

2. Label the jug and keep tightly capped and out of the reach of children. Pour into a sprayer when needed. This spray will keep for 6 months in a cool, dry place.

To Use:

Apply to fruit trees on a calm, dry, moderately warm day. If there is too much wind, a lot of the spray will blow back on you, and although it is not harmful, you will waste too much.

Yield: 1 gallon

Cost of Ingredients: $1.81
Comparable Purchased Product: Ortho Dormant Oil Spray, 32 ounces, $5.98 ($23.92)
Savings: $22.11

Safe Garden Pesticides

Because you certainly don't want to eat chemical sprays or toxins along with your freshly grown produce, try these sprays to control insects. Each repellent is a good use for any garlic or onion that has begun to turn bad. Just whip it up in the blender with a bit of water, label, and store in the refrigerator until you're ready to wage war on aphids and other unwanted garden pests. Although they smell terrible, these sprays do the job.

Oily Garden Repellent

This spray contains mineral oil, so it remains on the plant longer and does its work longer. Use it on flowers, bushes, and shrubs—but not your edible vegetables and fruits.

1/4 cup chopped garlic
2 cups water
2 teaspoons mineral oil
1 ounce oil-based soap (liquid or chopped-up Palmolive
    is good)

1. Puree the garlic in the blender, peels and all. Add 1/4 cup of the water and scrape down the sides. Continue blending until the mixture is a fine mush. Strain through a cheesecloth or an old nylon stocking.

2. In a large, clean glass jar, mix the mineral oil and soap, add the garlic-water mixture and stir thoroughly; then add the rest of the water.

3. Label the jar and store in a cool, dry place for up to 1 month.

To Use:

Pour into a sprayer and spray on the upper and lower surfaces of the plant's foliage. Spray also around roots. It is best to spray in the morning before the sun is too hot or in the late afternoon. Do not water immediately after spraying.

Vegetable-garden Repellent

1/4 cup chopped garlic
1/4 cup chopped hot pepper
1/4 cup chopped onion
1 1/2 cups water
1/2 cup wood ash
1/4 cup hydrated lime

1. Puree the garlic, pepper, and onion in the blender, peels and all. Add 1/4 cup of water and scrape down the sides. Continue blending until the mixture is a fine mush. Strain through a cheesecloth or an old nylon stocking.

2. In a large, clean glass jar, mix the wood ash and lime, add the garlic-onion mixture, and stir thoroughly; then add the rest of the water.

3. Label the jar and store in a cool, dry place for up to 1 month.

To Use:

>Pour into sprayer and spray on the upper and lower surfaces of the plant's foliage. Spray also around roots. It is best to spray in the morning before the sun is too hot or in the late afternoon. Do not water immediately after spraying.

Yield: 16 ounces

Cost of Ingredients: $.45
Comparable Purchased Product: Ortho
  Tomato Pest Repellent, 15 ounces, $4.99
  ($5.32)
Savings: $4.87

Fly Repellent

*If you have heavily traveled doorways in the summer, making up these little packets of Fly Repellent may be your only hope of peace from flies. For extra protection, you can make **Fly Paper**, page 304, but these packets can be much more attractive for kitchens and porches.*

>**2 tablespoons crushed bay leaves**
>**2 tablespoons pennyroyal**
>**2 tablespoons ground cloves**
>**2 tablespoons clover blossoms**
>**2 tablespoons eucalyptus leaves**
>**1 tablespoon eucalyptus oil**
>**1 yard loosely woven fabric, cut into 4-inch squares**
>**8-inch lengths of string or ribbon**

1. Mix spices and oil in a glass or an enamel bowl.

2. Place 1 tablespoon in the center of a square of fabric, bring up the 4 sides, and tie with string or ribbon to secure.

To Use:

>Hang up and out of the way in the doorway.

Yield: 10 bags

Cost of Ingredients: $1.76
Comparable Purchased Product: Raid
   Flying Insect Aerosol, 12 ounces, $3.69
Savings: $1.93

Cheap Tricks . . . . ✂ . . . .

*Here are some old-time remedies for avoiding and foiling
some of the other insects that bother us:
Rub Vanilla Bean Extract (page 12) on your skin to keep
gnats away.
Rub ammonia on a mosquito bite to stop the itch.
Sprinkle sulfur on your slacks, legs, and socks to keep ticks
off you.*

Fly Paper

*These hairy, speckled items could be the ugliest-looking
things in the world, but if you want to get rid of flies in places
where you don't mind looking at their dead bodies hanging
stuck on long strips of paper, then this is just the ticket. You can
hang them in out-of-the-way places like barns, sheds, and even
in guest bedrooms. For areas closer to home, try the recipe for
Fly Repellent, page 303.*

> **2 cups milk**
> **2 tablespoons black pepper**
> **2 tablespoons white sugar**
> **2 tablespoons brown sugar**
> **Brown paper bags, cut into strips**

1. Boil the milk, pepper, and sugar together for 5 minutes.
Simmer uncovered for 5 minutes more, until thickened, and
then let cool.

2. Wind the brown paper strips into a tight roll and drop them
into the milk mixture. Let them become completely saturated.

3. Rewind the strips gently and let them air dry on a cookie
sheet. They are ready to hang when they are sticky to the touch.

To Use:

     Suspend the strips up and out of the way wherever flies are a problem, but keep the strips away from young children, especially after they are covered with flies.

Hint:

     I am a master at killing flies with a flyswatter, and I feel a righteous territoriality about my kitchen, so the flies must go. If you want to make your own flyswatter, keep these facts in mind: flies can't hear you coming, but they can sense a change in air velocity. Therefore, if you make your own swatter by tacking a square of leather to the end of a stick, you must punch quite a few holes in the leather first. Then, as you whoosh down on the flies, the air rushes through the holes and the fly doesn't feel the end coming.

Yield: 10 strips

 Cost of Ingredients: $.36
Comparable Purchased Product: Flypapers,
    $.25 each ($2.50)
Savings: $2.15

Roach Balls

     This recipe comes from New York City, one of the cockroach capitals of the world. It has been tested in an apartment that is located right next to the incinerator and it works.

      1 cup borax
      1/4 cup sugar
      1/4 cup chopped onion
      1 tablespoon cornstarch
      1 tablespoon water

1. Make a paste of the ingredients and roll the paste into little balls.

To Use:

     Place 2 or 3 balls into a sandwich-size plastic bag and

leave the top open. Place the bag anywhere you have a roach problem. The roaches will eat the balls and carry them away.

The bugs die at home, away from sight. The active ingredient, borax, clogs their breathing passages. The onion scent draws them in.

Note:

Make sure you hide these bag very thoroughly so that children and pets can't get at them.

Yield: 50 balls; about 10 applications

Cost of Ingredients: $.31
Comparable Purchased Product: Raid
Roach Traps, 2 for $1.29 ($12.90)
Savings: $12.59

Rabbit Repellent

This remedy will keep the rabbits away from your tender spring shoots if you spread it about wherever you don't want rabbits to feed. It will not hurt the rabbits—only repel them.

1/2 cup talcum powder
1/4 cup cayenne pepper

1. Mix the ingredients, label, and store in a tightly lidded container. This mixture can be kept indefinitely on the garden shelf.

Variations:

Into the basic mixture, add 1/4 cup bloodmeal and spread it around your plants.

Yield: 8 ounces

Cost of Ingredients: $.32
Comparable Purchased Product: F & B Pest
Repellent, 56 ounces, $4.95 ($ .70)
Savings: $.38

Cheap Trick .... ✂ ....

*A gentle, humane way to keep rabbits and other pests away
from your garden is to place a small transistor radio in a
plastic bag, tie it up tight, turn it on loud, and put it in the
garden right by the food you want to protect. Rabbits, deer,
and other critters will think there are humans about.
However, just to be safe, avoid playing music by the
Animals, the Beatles, or the Beastie Boys.*

Deer Repellent

*Although I think deer are the most beautiful creatures, the
sight of them chewing on my newly planted rhododendron is
one I like to avoid. This method solves the problem and doesn't
hurt the deer. Deer will shy away from the scent of other
animals, so you trick them with the bloodmeal and hair
clippings. If you don't have enough hair from weekly
trimmings, ask your barber for some sweepings.*

> **1 yard old sheeting, cotton, or muslin**
> **1/4 cup bloodmeal**
> **1 cup hair clippings**

1. Cut the fabric into small squares, each about 4 inches by 4
inches.

2. Mix the bloodmeal and hair together and place about a
tablespoon onto the center of each square. Bring up the ends and
secure with string or a rubber band.

To Use:
> *Hang these little packets from the branches of the trees
and shrubs where deer are a problem. You should be able to
notice deer avoiding the spot almost immediately.*

Variation:
> *If your deer problem is especially severe, you might try
a mixture of 1 teaspoon bloodmeal to 1 gallon of water sprayed
on and around the shrubs, trees, and plants the deer like best.*

The bloodmeal solution will not harm the plants, and it will give them a little extra nitrogen.

Yield: About 20 packets

Cost of Ingredients: $.10
Comparable Purchased Product: F & B Pest Repellent, 56 ounces, $4.95 ($1.24)
Savings: $1.14

Chapter 10

High-tech Toys: Auto, Audio, and Computers

This chapter contains a variety of formulas for cleaning and polishing the car, cleaning the leather, and getting extra oomph from your engine; for maintaining your phonograph records and adding to the efficiency and smooth running of your computer.

Safe Car-washing Solution
Tar Remover
Road-salt Cleaner
Leather Upholstery Cleaner
Vinyl Upholstery Cleaner
Windshield Washer Fluid
Automobile Starting Fluid
Gas Line Antifreeze
Rust Preventive
Septic Tank Treatment
Record-cleaning Kit
Disk-drive Head-cleaning Kit
Keyboard Contact Cleaner
Antistatic Spray
Computer Mouse Equipment
Computer Mouse Cover
Computer Mouse Pad
Computer Mouse Trap

Safe Car-washing Solution

I have been told that the biggest danger to your new car's finish is to use any kind of scratchy or abrasive cleaner. This mild soap solution was suggested to me when I first bought my car, and the finish still looks good after three years. It will not remove a wax finish, and if you spray the car with water from your garden hose before you start, you will loosen any sand or grit that might scratch. Then, if you can get your son to wash the car as well as David washes mine, your car will look terrific.

1/3 cup mild soap flakes or Soft Soap (page 278)
1/4 cup baking soda
1 gallon warm water

1. Mix the soap flakes and baking soda together and pour into a clean plastic gallon-size jug. Add warm water to fill.

2. Label and store out of the reach of children.

To Use:

Pour 1 cup of solution into a bucket and fill with warm water. Then thoroughly spray your car to wet it down and loosen any grit. If it's a sunny day, move the car into the shade and work in one small section at a time, scrubbing gently in a circular motion and then rinsing each section as you go.
Do the dirtiest parts, such as wheels and bumpers, last because you don't want to spread the dirt any more than you have to.

Hint:

There are certain tough stains on a car that will not respond to this sort of mild cleaning solution. Remedies for some of the more common problems follow. Remember always to try a mild approach, coupled with elbow grease, first.

Tar Remover

Loosen any glopped-on tar with a rubber spatula or putty knife wrapped in cloth. Then moisten cloth with 1 teaspoon mineral oil and rub into the remaining tar. Wash as above.

Road-salt Cleaner

This winter residue usually consists of a buildup of hardened slush and salts on the bottom of the car, around the wheels, and inside the bumpers. If the weather is warm enough to wash the car, you should be able to direct the water from your hose up and into the spots where the salts are, loosening them with a stick as you spray. To clean the salts splashed onto the sides of the car, make a solution of 1 cup baking soda and 2 cups warm water and scrub the sides with a soft brush. Then wash as usual with the mild solution.

Yield: 1 gallon

Cost of Ingredients: $.27
Comparable Purchased Product: No. 7 Car Wash Concentrate, 8 ounces, $2.19
Savings: $1.92

Leather Upholstery Cleaner

This solution will quickly and efficiently clean your fine leather furniture without harming the skins. It doesn't have to be rinsed off—just buff dry with a soft cloth.

> **1/2 cup isopropyl alcohol**
> **1/2 cup vinegar**
> **1 1/2 cups water**

1. Mix ingredients; store in a clean glass jar. Label jar and keep tightly closed.

To Use:
Apply solution to leather with a soft cloth. Buff dry.

Hints:
To waterproof freshly cleaned leather, apply 1 tablespoon castor oil to a soft cloth and buff vigorously.
Don't use vinyl cleaners on good leather because they can cause the leather to dry out and crack.

If you have a grease spot on leather, try working a bit of butter into the spot, scrape it off, rinse with soap and water, and buff dry.

Another grease remover to try is rubber cement. Apply a small amount to the grease spot, let it dry, then carefully peel it up. The grease should come up with the rubber cement.

You can try removing mud stains from light-colored leather by rubbing the spots with a slice of raw potato.

Yield: 20 ounces

Cost of Ingredients: $.20
Comparable Purchased Product: Tanner Leather/Vinyl Cleaner, 10 ounces, $2.89 ($5.78)
Savings: $5.58

Vinyl Upholstery Cleaner

It's important to avoid using any kind of leather cleaner on your vinyl upholstery because the oils in a commercial leather cleaner will harden the vinyl. Rather, a regular cleaning with a gentle solution like the one listed here will be all you'll need.

> **1/4 cup soap flakes**
> **1/2 cup baking soda**
> **2 cups warm water**

1. Mix soap flakes and baking soda together; add to the water.

To Use:

Rub vinyl with a rough washcloth moistened in the solution; rinse well.

If vinyl is heavily soiled, make a paste of baking soda and water, apply and let sit for 1 hour, and then wash as usual with the solution and rinse.

Yield: 16 ounces

Cost of Ingredients: $.87
Comparable Purchased Product: Turtle
Wax Vinyl-Fabric Upholstery Cleaner, 14
ounces, $2.99
Savings: $2.12

Windshield Washer Fluid

*This solution will not freeze in the winter because it
contains alcohol, and it will clean your windshield every bit as
well as the kind you pay a little more for.*

> **3 cups isopropyl alcohol**
> **1 tablespoon liquid detergent or Soft Soap (page 278)**
> **10 cups water**

1. Pour alcohol and detergent into a clean gallon-size plastic
jug. Add water, cover, and shake well to mix. Label, cap
tightly, and keep out of the reach of children.

To Use:
    *Shake well, then pour into your car's windshield-
washer compartment.*

Other Uses:
    *Pour some of this solution into a smaller spray
container and keep it in your car's glove compartment, along
with some paper towels and an ice scraper.*
    *Then, when you're stuck in line at the bank, you can
clean the inside of the windows, which is where the greatest
accumulation of smoke and grease build up.*
    *Or, if it's an icy day, just spray some washer fluid on
your windows before scraping and the job will be easier. If
you're caught with ice on your windows and you have no
scraper handy, you can use a pocket comb or the side of a credit
card to do the job. The Windshield Washer Fluid that you
spray on will help speed things up.*

Yield: 1 gallon

Cost of Ingredients: $.58
Comparable Purchased Product: Penn-Pride
Windshield Washer Anti-Freeze, 1 gallon,
$1.19
Savings: $.61

Automobile Starting Fluid

*On those really cold mornings when you just can't get
your engine to catch, a quick spritz of this starting fluid should
do the job.*

1 cup ethyl alcohol (grain alcohol)

1. Pour the alcohol into a clean, small bottle with a pump or
spray valve. Label the bottle and keep it in your car in the
winter.

2. To use, spray directly onto the air-intake valve on the
carburetor, one time only. Try to start the car. If the motor
almost seems to "catch," try one more spritz, and you should be
on your way.

Yield: 8 ounces

Cost of Ingredients: $.95
Comparable Purchased Product: Sure-Start
Starting Fluid, 11 ounces, $2.00 ($1.45)
Savings: $.50

Cheap Trick . . . .

*It's a good idea to clean out your car's radiator before you
refill it with antifreeze in the late fall. Drain your radiator,
add 4 cups of washing soda to 3 quarts of warm water and pour
this solution into the radiator, making sure you fill the
radiator completely. Turn your car on and let it run for 30
minutes. Drain the radiator, flush it twice with clean water,
then fill with half water and half antifreeze.*

Gas Line Antifreeze

Water or ice in your gasoline feed lines can literally stop your engine cold in bad weather or when water gets into the cylinders. The alcohol in the following mixture acts as a co-solvent and removes water from the tank and gasoline feeder lines, and it also keeps ice crystals from forming in the gas lines overnight.

3 drops pine oil
4 cups isopropyl alcohol

1. Mix oil add alcohol in a quart-size glass container. Label the container and keep the mixture tightly covered.

2. To use, add 1/2 cup to your fuel tank once a week in the colder months.

Yield: 1 quart

Cost of Ingredients: $.65
Comparable Purchased Product: Channel Gas-Line Antifreeze, 12 ounces, $.39 ($1.04)
Savings: $.39

Rust Preventive

This solution is excellent for painting onto any metal surface before you expose it to the elements, and it is an especially good way to protect your garden tools from rust and corrosion. If you would like to try it on an item that is already rusty, you will first have to get the rust off the item by sanding it with steel wool.
Getting rid of the rust is a hard job, so be prepared to rub and rub, first with a coarse grade of steel wool (2, 1 or 0), and then with a finer grade (00 to 0000). Once you've gotten off all you can, you're ready to paint this solution on. However, this preventive is only for those metal items that you do not intend to paint over.

2 cups raw linseed oil
1/2 cup turpentine

1. Combine oil and turpentine (an old coffee can is a good mixing container—discard after use) and pour into a clean glass jar with a tight-fitting lid. Label the jar.

To Use:

Wear rubber gloves while working with this solution and cover your work area with newspapers. Remove any rust from the item with steel wool (see above), and make sure surface is dry. Paint solution on with a soft brush or dab on with a cloth.

If you are rust-proofing your garden tools, make sure to keep this solution away from the wood. Let dry for 24 hours before using.

Yield: 20 ounces

Cost of Ingredients: $3.23
Comparable Purchased Product:
  Rust-oleum, Clear Sele, 13 ounces, $4.49
  ($6.90)
Savings: $3.67

Septic Tank Treatment

Avoid putting caustic drain cleaners down your septic system—you are risking a costly repair. Instead, use this solution once a month as a preventive measure.

The yeast does the dirty work without wrecking your system.

2 cups brown sugar
1 tablespoon baker's yeast
5 cups warm water

1. Stir sugar and yeast into the warm water until dissolved. Use immediately.

To Use:

    Simple: pour solution into toilet and flush. Wait a half hour before flushing again to let the yeast work.

Yield: 4 cups

Cost of Ingredients: $.92
Comparable Purchased Product: FX 4
    Septic Tank Clogging Preventative, 1 quart,
    $7.99
Savings: $7.07

Record-cleaning Kit

    The real secret to keeping your records clean is to put them back into their jackets each time you finish using them. If, however, you have left them lying about and would like to gently and safely remove any dust that has accumulated on the records, this cleaning kit will do the trick.

    The secret ingredient here is gentleness: this solution contains no alcohol, which will destroy the vinyl, and the cleaning action is accomplished by running the grooves of the velvet in the same direction as the grooves on the record to dislodge stubborn bits of dirt and grit.

    1 tablespoon Soft Soap (page 278)
    1 tablespoon baking soda
    1 cup warm water
    Wooden dowel or wooden block
    Velvet, large enough to cover the dowel or block
    White glue

1. Mix the soap and baking soda together and pour into a clean, small bottle. Add the warm water and shake. Label bottle, keep tightly capped, and out of the reach of children.

2. You will need a dowel or block of wood that is small enough to fit comfortably in your hand. Cover the wood with the velvet as you would wrap a package. Bring all the ends of the velvet to one side and secure with glue.

To Use:

Moisten the velvet with some of the record cleaning solution. Place the dusty record on your turntable and turn the setting to 33 1/3 rpm.

Gently hold the dowel against the surface of the record for one spin. Lift dowel, wipe dust off with a clean paper towel, moisten with cleaner again, and repeat.

If you wipe your records after each use and before you put them back into their jackets, you will find that you have far fewer scratches and skips.

Yield: 1 cup solution; cleaning dowel

Cost of Ingredients: $.20
Comparable Purchased Product:
   DiscWasher, $14.99
Savings: $14.79

Disk-drive Head-cleaning Kit

The commercial disk-drive cleaning kits that you buy at the computer store all have one big problem: you can really only use them one time, even though they never tell you this on the package.

When you use the cleaning disk the first time, you load it up with dirt and grime from the disk drive and you will end up redepositing that grime on your clean drives if you use the cleaning disk again. Therefore, if you value your computer equipment, it's better to make your own disk-drive cleaner fresh each time you need it.

Use lens-cleaning paper that you purchase from the camera store or another type of gauzelike paper that you are certain is lint-free.

1 old, unusable floppy disk to take apart
1 sheet camera-lens-cleaning paper
White glue
Keyboard Contact Cleaner (page 320)

1. Carefully pry open the black cover from the used floppy disk along the seam to expose the Mylar disk inside the jacket.

2. Lift out the thin Mylar disk and gently place it on top of a sheet of lens paper. Using the disk as a guide, mark directly on the lens paper and cut out a circle-size piece of paper. Cut the little index hole and the hub ring out of the center as well.

3. Glue the lens paper to the Mylar disk by placing a few tiny dots here and there on the Mylar and pressing the lens paper in place. Allow the glue to dry completely before reassembling the envelope.

4. Place the covered disk back into the envelope and glue the seam shut again. Make sure the disk can slide around in the envelope, as before.

To Use:

*Carefully place a few drops of **Keyboard Contact Cleaner**, page 320, onto the lens tissue that shows through the large envelope opening. Immediately place the disk into the disk drive, use the command in your operating system to initialize the disk, and let the heads come in contact with the lens paper and cleaning solution. You should hear a gentle swishing sound as the disk spins in the drive.*

Consult your computer manual if you are unsure about the initialization procedure—some computer instructions may indicate that you run a different command for cleaning the heads—just about any command that requires the disk to spin in the drive will work.

When the drives are finished spinning, remove the cleaning disk, open it, and replace the dirty lens tissue. You should clean your drives once every few months.

Yield: 1 head-cleaning kit

Cost of Ingredients: $1.49
Comparable Purchased Product: 3M Scotch
   Head Cleaning Kit, $15.50
Savings: $14.01

Keyboard Contact Cleaner

The first part of the machine that will show its age on a computer is the keyboard, and if you're in the habit of eating or drinking while you work, the problem can be especially bad. Before too long the keys start to stick and little gobs of dirt and icky things get down between them. All the computer needs is a quick shot of cleaner on the contact point of the keys and your keyboard will be as good as new.

3/4 cup isopropyl alcohol
1/4 cup water

1. Combine alcohol and water in a clean bottle. Shake and cap tightly; label bottle and keep it out of the reach of children. Solution will keep indefinitely if it is kept tightly closed.

To Use:
  First, unplug your computer. Then, following the manufacturer's instructions or your own good instincts, remove the mounting screws from your keyboard assembly and gently pry the panels apart. Be very careful not to pull out any wire contacts or break any connections.
  Once you have exposed the circuit board, it is easy to see where the contact points are. Again, check your instruction manual if you have one, or look for small, copper-color metal tabs inside the keyboard assembly. These are the contact points.
  Gently rub the points with a soft pink eraser and then blow gently through the entire assembly to remove loose dust balls. Now you are ready to apply the cleaner. Use a flexible cotton swab to dab your contact cleaner on each contact point, let dry, blow through it again, and reassemble the keyboard.

Yield: 1 cup

Cost of Ingredients: $.12
Comparable Purchased Product: Archer
  Contact Cleaner, 8 ounces, $1.99
Savings: $1.87

Antistatic Spray

If you work with computers, you've already noticed that a simple zap of static electricity can ruin a whole day's worth of data. The problem is made worse in the winter months when the air is hot and overheated; carpets and leather-soled shoes also contribute to the problem. The solution is simple, and cheap—just keep a generous supply of this spray handy.

An added bonus this solution is that the ammonia very effectively dispels any stale smoking or perspiration smells from office air, while the fabric softener imparts a pleasant scent.

> **1/4 cup commercial liquid fabric softener**
> **1/4 cup ammonia**
> **2 cups water**

1. Mix ingredients and store the solution in a spray-type plastic bottle. Label and keep it out of the reach of children, but near your work space.

To Use:

Avoid spraying directly onto your computer terminal, keyboard, or disk drive, but spray liberally everywhere else: on the rug, your shoes, your chair, desktop, or file cabinet—anything metal or nylon that you might rub against in the course of your work.

Variation:

If you're only trying to keep your skirt, slip, or slacks from sticking to your legs on a crisp winter's day, make up a batch of spray without the ammonia and keep it in your desk or dressing space. Spray the offending fabric and it will stop clinging.

Yield: 20 ounces

Cost of Ingredients: $.08
Comparable Purchased Product: Falcon Anti-Static Carpet Spray, 16 ounces, $3.95 ($4.93)
Savings: $4.85

Computer Mouse Equipment

*The little device known as a mouse on many computers is
a small plastic square with a ball underneath that you slide
about with your hand and use in conjunction with your
computer keyboard. The Apple Macintosh, in particular, has a
mouse attached to the main computer with a long wire.*

*The items described here are for the care and easy
maintenance of that mouse: you will make a **Cover** to keep the
dirt out, a **Pad** or surface to allow it to flow across your desktop
more easily, and a **Trap** or holder to contain it when you want
to clear your desk or carry the computer about.*

Computer Mouse Cover

*I wouldn't claim that a cover for your mouse is an absolute
computer necessity, nor would I claim that a cover is going to
keep much dirt out of the mouse's inner workings. However, if
you've got to stare at a piece of plastic on your desktop all day
long, a cover like this one will certainly brighten things up.*

> **One 5-inch-by-6-inch piece of gray felt**
> **One 2-inch-by-4-inch piece of pink felt**
> **Black felt, google eyes (optional)**
> **White glue or rubber cement**
> **3 inches of hook-and-loop tape**

1. Using your own mouse as a guide for size, cut one rectangle
from the gray felt in one piece about an inch larger than the
mouse. Use sharp scissors and leave a hole for the clicker
portion of the mouse. Cut two circles from the gray felt for ears,
two smaller circles from the pink felt for inner ears, and tiny
black circles for the eyes.

2. Glue tiny, 1/4-inch pieces of hook-and-loop tape around the
four sides of the mouse and around the clicker opening. Use
rubber cement if you think you will want to get rid of the mouse
cover at a later date—you still will be able to peel it off. Use
white glue if you intend to make your cover permanent.

3. Place the gray felt over the mouse, mark where the hook-and-
loop tape touches the felt, and glue another piece at
corresponding points on the felt. Replace the felt on the mouse

and trim around the bottom so that the felt doesn't drag when you move the mouse about.

4. Glue on the pink circles for ears; add eyes and nose, if desired.

Computer Mouse Pad

Of all the mouse accessories described here, this one is truly necessary. You will find that you need a special surface on your desktop to allow the mouse to glide freely about without bumping into other objects and without picking up bits and pieces of debris as it glides. In addition, the gliding surface must have a little grip to it or the mouse won't register its messages on the screen as it moves along. Here are two nifty ideas for a mouse surface.

The first Mouse Pad, a framed piece of cork, has a nice soft edge so that the heel of your hand won't begin to ache after a few hours of leaning, pushing, and guiding the mouse.

> **One 12-inch-square piece of cork**
> **Cotton batting cut into inch-wide strips**
> **White glue**
> **Sturdy fabric scraps, cut into 2-by-12-inch strips**
> **Straight pins**

1. Make a soft frame around the cork by gluing the cotton batting along the four edges, wrapping the cotton around and securing it to the back and front with white glue.

2. Fold the fabric strips 1/2-inch in along the long edge and attach to the cork, over the batting, with pins and white glue.

Variation:

Try covering the cork with a piece of synthetic leatherette or vinyl with an embossed surface if you don't like the look of cork in your office. Just make sure that the surface you choose provides enough friction for the mouse as it rolls.

Computer Mouse Trap

Before placing structures or improvements on the side of your computer, you must first decide whether you want your mouse trap to be permanent or removable. If you never travel with your computer or expect to stuff it into a small carrying case, you can go ahead and make the mouse trap a permanent feature. If, however, you foresee a time when you might want to remove it, use the hook-and-loop tape and simply detach the trap if you want to pack your machine up for traveling.

16 inches hook-and-loop tape
1 shrink-wrap plastic bubble cover from a hair brush
White glue (optional)

1. For a detachable holder, cut the hook-and-loop tape into two 3-inch pieces and one 2-inch piece and glue them to the sides of the machine with the white glue. Glue identical pieces of tape to the inside edges of the shrink-wrap cover so that they line up with the tape on the machine. The cover should stick securely in place when you are finished; simply peel off the cover when you wish.

2. For a permanent mouse trap, simply glue the plastic shrink-wrap cover to the side of the computer with white glue.

Hint:
        Since my mouse trap has gotten a lot of use, I use two or three thicknesses of the shrink-wrap bubble, glued together and trimmed with electrical tape, for my trap.

Yield: 1 cover, trap, or pad

Cost of Ingredients: $2.59
Comparable Purchased Product:
   Frontrunner Industries MouseHouse, $5.95
Savings: $3.36

Chapter 11

Children's Play and Rainy-day Items

Toys for children that are created with love and enthusiasm can be as much fun and as full of educational value as the high-priced kind. In addition, many of the items in this chapter are meant to be constructed by little kids themselves, with some adult supervision.

Gooey Glue
Flour-and-Water Paste
Fun Finger Paints
Children's Play Dough
Big Blocks
    Hard-edged Blocks
    Soft Blocks
Castles and Cottages
    Puppet Stage
Sand Sculpture
Sensational Stencil Fun
    Multiple Exposure Shape Book
Silly Stampers
    Rubber-band Stampers
    Potato Stampers
Papier-mâché
    Halloween Masks
    Jack-o'-Lantern Candy Holder
    Mexican Party Piñata
    Model Railroad Scenery
    Relief Maps of Your Neighborhood
    Puppet Stage Background Scenery
Sewing Cards
Decorated Sweat Shirts
    Dribble Painting
    Doily Stencil
    Charm Sweat Shirt

Big Picture Puzzles
   Secret Message Puzzles
Giant Chalkboard Wall
Old-fashioned Computer
Sticky Fingers Catch
Bowling in the Living Room
Bean Bags
Soap Crayons
Rock Candy
Crystal Garden
Birdy Gourds
   Gourd Bird Feeder and Nest
Super Bubbles
Monster-be-gone
Live, Organic Disco Lights
E-Z Ant Farm
Nature's Dolls
   Corn-husk Doll
   Hollyhock Doll
Delicate and Fancy Easter Eggs
   Lacy Eggs
Kids' Gift Wrap
   Crayon Melt
   Paint-blot Paper

Gooey Glue

This is the old standby paste—nice and sticky—that is totally safe for children to make and use.

> **3 tablespoons cornstarch**
> **4 tablespoons cold water**
> **2 cups boiling water**
> **Squeeze-type container**

1. Mix the cornstarch and cold water in a small bowl and then pour the paste into the boiling water, stirring constantly.

2. When liquid is clear and thick, remove from heat and let cool. Pour into a plastic squeeze container and label.

Yield: 14 ounces

Cost of Ingredients: $.05
Comparable Purchased Product: Elmer's
   Sno Drift Paste, 5 ounces, $.89 ($ 2.49)
Savings: $2.44

Flour-and-Water Paste

*Choose this paste when constructing **Papier-mâché** projects, page 339, and for the younger child. This paste is nontoxic and safe, and it will last for months if you keep it, safely labeled, in the refrigerator.*

> **1/2 cup flour**
> **3/4 cup cold water**
> **3 cups boiling water**

1. Slowly pour cold water into flour and stir to make a paste. Pour paste into the boiling water, stirring constantly. Cook for 5 minutes or until the paste is thick and smooth.

2. When cool, pour into a plastic squeeze-top container; label.

Yield: 28 ounces

Cost of Ingredients: $.08
Comparable Purchased Product: Lepage's
    White Paste, 5 ounces, $.48 ($2.68)
Savings: $2.60

Fun Finger Paints

   After you whip up some finger paints for your children's pleasure, why not sit down with them and finger-paint along? I was once at a high-priced therapy session for harried middle management types and one of the "therapies" they insisted on was for all the executives to get their hands wet with these pretty colors and "express" themselves.

   Needless to say, the cost of this homemade therapy is certainly cheaper than the executive version, and if you sit and paint along with your kids, it's the best remedy in the world for stress.

   It's a good idea to store these paints in tightly closed containers if you plan to use them again. Margarine tubs are a good choice.

> **1 envelope unflavored gelatin**
> **1/2 cup cornstarch**
> **3 tablespoons sugar**
> **2 cups cold water**
> **Food coloring, Nature's Colors (page 367), or tempera (powdered or liquid)**
> **Dishwashing liquid detergent or 1 tablespoon Soft Soap (page 278)**
> **White shelf paper**

1. Soak gelatin in 1/4 cup warm water and put aside.

2. In a medium-size saucepan, combine cornstarch and sugar, gradually add water, and cook slowly over low heat, stirring constantly, for 5 minutes or until well blended.

3. Remove from heat and add the softened gelatin. Divide mixture into separate containers for each color.

4. For each color, first add a drop or two of liquid detergent and then the coloring, drop by drop, until you've achieved a shade you like. Food coloring is best for this, but check pages 367 to 370 for other coloring ideas.

5. Store paint in the refrigerator for up to 6 weeks.

To Use:

Allow children (or tense adults) plenty of paper to draw on. The glossy side of freezer wrap is good, as is plain white shelf paper. Spread the paper out onto a hard, durable, waterproof surface. Formica is excellent.

Have clean water and small sponges handy and begin by wetting the paper, running the dampened sponge from the middle of the paper out to the edges a few times until the paper is totally wet. Keep it wet as you work, and only let it dry when you are sure you are finished.

Hint:

If you would like to make sure the paints remain usuable for a long time in storage, add a few drops of glycerin to the mixture when you add the liquid detergent.

Yield: 20 ounces

Cost of Materials: $1.56
Comparable Purchased Product:
   Childcraft Finger Paint and Finger Paint
   Paper, 5 colors, 100 sheets, $12.95
Savings: $11.29

Cheap Trick . . . . ✂ . . . .

If your children love to work with finger paints, you can encourage their creativity by designing a wall mural from their creations. Use a whole roll of white shelf paper for this project and measure along the wall where you intend to hang the mural. Cut the shelf paper into long, equal-size lengths, spread paper and paints out on a newspaper-covered floor, and let your artists plan and execute their work on a grand scale.

Children's Play Dough

There are many different kinds of dough or baker's clay to work with. This version is best for young children because it stays soft and playable, and if you organize the ingredients and measures, even the smallest children can help to mix up and color their own batches.

> **2 cups flour**
> **1 cup salt**
> **1/2 cup water**
> **1 teaspoon vinegar**
> **Food coloring or Nature's Colors (page 367)**
> **1/4 teaspoon peppermint extract**

1. In a large bowl, mix the flour and salt. There is no need to sift the flour first—just spoon it into a measure.

2. Slowly add the water and vinegar, and stir with a wooden spoon until the mixture is stiff. Then pick it up and knead until pliable. If you have a young helper, break off a small piece and let the child mix and knead until the dough is soft and workable.

3. Divide the dough into separate pieces for each color desired. Poke your finger or the end of the wooden spoon into the center of each section of dough, drop in the food coloring and peppermint extract, and knead until the color is uniform and the dough is smooth.

4. Store, tightly covered and labeled, in a plastic bag or container in the refrigerator. Play dough will keep for months if you return it to the refrigerator after each use.

To Use:

Take out of the refrigerator about 5 minutes before you're ready to play so that the dough will be soft. As long as you don't leave objects out in the air for more than a few hours, the dough can be recombined and used over and over again.

On the other hand, if you like something you or your child has just created, you can leave it to air dry for 24 hours or help it along by placing in a warm oven at 200 degrees for several hours. It should harden enough to paint, shellac, or *spray with art fixative as described in the recipes for **Baker's Dough**, page 370, and **Fine Crafty Dough**, page 373.*

Ideas:
A good way to store this Play Dough is to squeeze it into the skinny cans used for potato chips and then slice out small portions for each playtime.
*See the recipes for **Baker's Dough**, page 370, and **Fine Crafty Clay**, page 373 in Chapter 12 for additional ideas.*

Yield: 22 ounces

Cost of Ingredients: $.86
Comparable Purchased Product: Play Doh, 24 ounces, $3.49 ($3.19)
Savings: $2.33

Big Blocks

*Since this is a sensible, safe toy that has been used by thrifty parents and creative day care centers for years with great success, you can now purchase additional covers for the blocks if you or your children tire of making your own (look for the address in the **Resources**, page 395).*

But be sure to try making your own covers at first, and let the kids have a go at it, too. Since the supply of forms is endless, you really can't make a mistake. But you will have lots of fun making custom-designed cities, towers, railroad buildings, castles, and furniture. For tiny children, try Soft Blocks in bright, washable colors. Plan on chewable blocks—don't add any buttons or snaps that could be swallowed.

Supply of gallon, half-gallon, quart, pint, and half-pint plastic-coated cartons
Materials for covers:
    Hard-edged blocks: **Wallpaper samples, shelf paper, construction paper, paper bags, old greeting cards, wrapping paper**
    Soft Blocks: **Cotton batting, fabric**
White craft glue or Gooey Glue (page 327)
Masking and cellophane tape

1. Carefully wash and dry the cartons, being careful not to leave them in the water too long.

2. While the carton is still damp, fold down the flap and tape securely to make a box. If you are going to make houses with peaked roofs, leave the flaps as they are on a few of the cartons.

Hard-edged Blocks

1. Cover with the paper of your choice, as you would wrap a package. Brush on white glue to the sides of the carton or secure the flaps with cellophane or masking tape. Choose plain paper if you are adding your own designs with magic markers, paint or crayons.

Soft Blocks

1. Cover each block first with cotton batting, wrapping as you would wrap a package. Secure ends by basting or taping with masking tape.

2. Cut fabric a little larger than the block to include the batting and then wrap the block and batting, as above. The fabric can be glued in place and the flaps basted or glued. Place a few paperback books on the blocks to hold down the fabric as it dries.

3. You can finish off the edges of the Soft Blocks by adding odds and ends from your sewing basket such as trim, rickrack, and ribbons. Just be careful not to add small pieces that can be chewed off by little children.

Ideas:

Cover quart-size boxes with black paper and white dots for a giant set of dominoes.

Use a roll of fake Christmas bricks to make giant building blocks.

To make a ranch house roof, use a carton the same size as the one for the house and cut it diagonally lengthwise. Tape onto the first block before covering and decorating.

Use **Silly Stampers** , page 337, for some of the repetitive detail: roof tiles, window panes, shutters, and other building details.

A fine way to finish off the inside of your buildings is to use pictures cut from magazines for appliances, furniture, and people. First open the box by carefully cutting along a top and side seam, then cut the window holes and fold the box closed to get an idea where to place the furniture. Then reopen the box and paste the interiors along the proper walls. Furniture and people can also be pasted to stand-up pieces of cardboard for a three-dimensional effect. Then close the box and cover the outside as above.

Yield: 20 blocks

Cost of Materials: $0.00 if using scraps; otherwise $5.00 for fabric, paper, trim
Comparable Purchased Product: Childcraft Super Building Blocks, 16 blocks, $18.95 ($23.68); Childcraft Cloth Blocks, 4 blocks, $6.95
Savings: $18.68

Castles and Cottages

Save the big cardboard boxes that appliances and computers come in and with a few of these and some of the other craft ideas in this section, you have the beginnings of an entire fantasy world for young people.

Several large cardboard boxes
Poster paint, markers, crayons
Scissors, utility knife
Masking tape
Papier-mâché (page 339)
White glue or Gooey Glue (page 327)
Paper

1. Decide just what kind of structure you would like. Try turning boxes on their side and using them to create connecting tunnels between structures, little garages, walls, and bridges.

2. Cut open some of the boxes for roofs and carports. Tape the

various components together with the masking tape. Once
you're satisfied with the general structure, cut doors and
window openings with the utility knife. Use masking tape to
secure the rough edges.

3. You can make your structures as fanciful or as simple as
you and your child desire. Try painting on details, or covering
portions of the boxes with paper for special effects. Colored
cellophane can be used to make stained glass, flags can be
hung from wrapping paper tubes, real twigs and branches can
be added for shrubbery, and **Papier-mâché**, page 339, can be
used to make a little doggie outside the cottage door.

Puppet Stage

*To make a puppet stage, remove the back and top from a
large packing box and cut a large window in the front. Insert a
curtain rod or wooden dowel into two holes cut on either side of
the window opening and hang the stage curtain here. Use the
leftover cardboard for background scenery and flats.*

Yield: 1 city, village, fortress, or puppet stage

Cost of Ingredients: $2.50
Comparable Purchased Product: Muppet
Babies Play House, $19.97
Savings: $17.47

Sand Sculpture

*Here is a special modeling compound for the older child to
tackle. With it, you can make permanent castles and sand
dunes—but you may find that the mixture is too rough for little
fingers to mold with.*

> 2 cups clean sand
> 1 cup water
> 1 cup cornstarch

1. Slowly heat the mixture in a heavy pot, stirring occasionally,
until thick. It will begin thickening in about 30 minutes.

2. Turn the thickened sand mixture out onto a cookie sheet or shallow cardboard box. Work with it immediately.

3. Allow finished pieces to dry for 24 hours or set them in a cool oven (200 degrees) for 4 hours. Turn off oven, open door, and let pieces finish drying for another 4 hours.

4. Finish by sanding rough edges with an emery board. Add fancy details such as flags, house trim, moss, bushes, etc., with white glue.

Yield: 22 ounces

Cost of Ingredients: $.29
Comparable Purchased Product:
 Mattituck Florist Sand Sculpture, $10.00
Savings: $9.71

Sensational Stencil Fun

Now that stencil designs are all the rage for grown-up decorating, it's a good idea to let your young ones in on the fun of creating repetitious and varied designs from precut stencils.

There are two stencil mediums here—cardboard and plastic—and both provide long hours of play. One plentiful source of thin plastic is the lids from margarine tubs and other plastic take-out containers, and if you have many children who will use the same stencil over again, it's a good idea to cut them out of plastic. Otherwise, cardboard is fine for limited or careful use. You can even cover the cardboard with strips of cellophane tape before cutting out the designs to make it a little sturdier.

> **Shirt cardboard or bristol board**
> **Thin plastic (see above)**
> **Black marker**
> **Sharp scissors, X-Acto knife, or utility knife**
> **Fat paintbrush or sponge**
> **Paints: tempera, acrylic, Fun Finger Paints**
> **(page 328)**
> **Masking or cellophane tape**

1. If you are making your stencils out of cardboard, draw freehand directly onto the cardboard or trace the design you like and, using carbon paper, transfer the design to the cardboard.
2. Carefully cut out the design with scissors or the X-Acto knife. For the younger child, choose designs that are big and simple, with limited details.

3. If you are using plastic, simply position the plastic over the design you wish to use and draw directly onto the plastic with the marker. Cut out the design with scissors, X-Acto, or utility knife, depending on the thickness of the plastic.

To Use:
Provide plenty of colorful paint and encourage your child to plan out the design before beginning. Fasten the stencil securely with tape on the surface to be designed and dab the paint gently into the stencil opening. Always use a little less paint than you think you will need because the paint tends to spread, especially under the stencil.

Multiple Exposure Shape Book

Try creating a whole book of cardboard stencils by using cardboard cut to fit a loose-leaf binder. Punch holes with a hole punch or a nail and the child can keep his whole collection of stencils handy.

Hint:
If you find that too much paint is seeping under the stencil, try adding several strips of masking tape on the underside to raise the stencil off the surface a bit. Also, remember to wipe down the stencil with a paper towel after each use.

Yield: 10 to 12 stencils

Cost of Materials: $2.23
Comparable Purchased Product: Childcraft
    Stencibles, 15 designs, binder; $7.95
Savings: $5.72

Silly Stampers

These simple stamps are a good way to introduce your child to the joys of stamping out designs on just about anything: wrapping paper, greeting cards, paper and cloth tablecloths, and stationery.

Rubber-band Stampers

Several different sizes of rubber bands
String
Double-faced carpet tape
Small square of wood or children's block
Rubber-stamp pad or sponge
Tempera paints or concentrated watercolor paints
Felt-tipped markers

1. First plan your design. Choose a simple design than can be represented by the straight, curvy, and parallel lines of rubber bands. Cut rubber bands in half if necessary, and plan on using string the same thickness as the rubber bands for special effects.

2. Remove one side of the protective covering from the carpet tape and press the sticky side firmly onto the wooden block. Then remove the second sheet of protective covering and arrange the rubber bands on the tape in your design, pressing them firmly into the tape.

Potato Stampers

1 firm baking potato, raw and unpeeled
Paper towels
Felt-tip marker
Sharp paring knife
Rubber stamp pad or sponge
Tempera paints or concentrated watercolor paints

1. Slice potato in half and rest the cut halves on a few thicknesses of paper toweling to absorb excess moisture.

2. Draw a simple design on the cut side with a felt-tip marker and carefully carve around the design with a sharp paring knife. Remove about 1/4 inch of potato around the design.

To Use:

Stamps may be used with preinked rubber-stamp pads or with a sponge and paint. If you are using a sponge, place it on a glass or ceramic plate and then pour about a tablespoon of paint or watercolor into the center. Try a few test stampings until the color is even.

Ideas:

Other items and utensils in the kitchen can make excellent stampers, at least temporarily.

Try using: mushroom caps, broccoli flowerets, tiny cloves for dots and asterisks, corks, bits of sponge.

For the older child who can be trusted with an X-Acto knife, all kinds of designs can be created from simple erasers. First draw the design you want to carve on the eraser with a pencil. Choose a chunky, solid design with minimal detail. Run the blade of the X-Acto knife around the design to a depth of one-quarter-inch. Cut away the excess eraser, being very careful to keep your fingers away from the blade.

Hints:

Make sure you use rubber bands of the same thickness on each stamp or your designs will be uneven and some parts may not print.

For variation in color, ink your stamp directly with the felt-tip markers and quickly stamp onto your surface before the ink dries.

To make a good impression when you print, first lay down several thicknesses of newspaper onto the surface and then the item or paper on which you will be printing.

If edges of the stamp pick up too much ink, whittle them down with an emery board and wipe the stamp after printing with a paper towel moistened with a little soap.

Store rubber stamps out of the sun for a longer life and keep potato stamps in the refrigerator in a plastic bag.

Yield: 4 to 10 stamps

Cost of Materials: $1.24
Comparable Purchased Product: Bizzaro
   Rubber Stamps, $2.50 to $10.00
Savings: $1.26

Papier-mâché

Here is a recipe for a paper-mash sculpture material that is cheap and durable, yet easy for an older child to mix up and work with. If you use shredded newspaper in this recipe, make sure that the newspaper ink won't be a problem—wear rubber gloves if you want to keep your hands clean and plan on painting the finished product if you don't want a gray-colored creation.

This recipe creates a heavy mush that must soak for 24 hours before using, so plan ahead if you would like to use the mixture for masks, holiday favors, or special gifts.

See the ideas given after the main recipe for suggestions of additional things to make with the basic mâché, or with a version that uses long strips of paper dipped into paste, or with a finer mixture.

> **6 cups shredded newspaper, paper towels, or other soft, absorbent paper**
> **Large pot**
> **Boiling water to cover**
> **Cheesecloth or porous fabric (optional)**
>
> *Paste*
> **1 cup flour**
> **3/4 cup water**
>
> **Gallon-size, sturdy plastic bags**

1. Make sure the newspaper is ripped into very small pieces—1-inch squares are not too small. Put the shredded paper into a large pot and pour boiling water over it to cover. Stir the paper around with a big wooden spoon or stick to make sure that all the paper is completely saturated with the water. Let this mixture steep for 24 hours.

2. Scoop out the paper mush and place a few handfuls of it onto the cheesecloth. Squeeze, press, and wring as much water as possible out of it. You can also squeeze the water out by placing a small amount of the mush in the palm of your hand and squeezing, but the cloth method is more efficient.

3. Make a quantity of paste to mix in with the shredded paper by slowly adding the water to the flour, stirring constantly.

4. Measure out 1 cup of the squeezed-out mush and place it in a sturdy plastic bag with 1/3 cup of the flour paste. Knead and squeeze the materials in the bag until they are thoroughly mixed. If there is room in the bag, add another cup of mush and 1/3 cup of paste. Repeat the process with extra plastic bags until all the paper mush is combined with paste. Knead until smooth; label and keep the mixture stored in the bag in the refrigerator for up to one month.

To Use:

There are many creative, inexpensive ways to use papier-mâché. One of the most basic procedures begins with making a form or an armature out of chicken wire, bent wire coat hangers, hollow paper tubes, masking tape, and just about any kind of rigid form that you can spare—it will disappear forever under layers and layers of the mush. Once you've constructed the skeleton of your intended figure, you will carefully layer the papier-mâché on top of the form, little by little, building up features, rounding out limbs, making lumps and mounds. Let dry completely and then paint.

Halloween Masks

Use another version of the basic papier-mâché to form very interesting masks at Halloween. This procedure will require an extra batch of the flour and water paste, as well as a supply of newspaper strips that are 1 inch wide.

Begin by blowing up a sturdy balloon. Tape on a wad of crumpled newspaper for the nose, and then use the basic mixture to build up the special features for an interesting face. Two noses might make a creature from another world, but always remember to make eye holes to peer through and a breathing hole somewhere in the front.

Then dip the strips into the paste and carefully lay them on top of the bumps and criss-cross them all over the balloon until the balloon is completely covered. Once your Halloween face has dried, you merely pop the balloon and you can place the big mask over your head.

Or, you could try oiling a big beach ball with petroleum jelly or salad oil and then build the face. In the beach-ball method, remember to work only halfway around the ball and when the mask is completely dry, carefully peel it away from the ball and try it on.

Jack-o'-Lantern Candy Holder

While your child is busy making a mask for Halloween, you can follow the same procedure and make a permanent Jack-o'-Lantern to hold candy and treats at the front door. Use the balloon method with either the papier-mâché mush or strips, and remember to carve out the vertical pumpkin ridges along the sides and back.

Mexican Party Piñata

Another good idea for papier-mâché is to make a piñata for a child's party. Again, form your basic shape around a balloon, but this time, leave an opening in the top large enough to drop in the candies and favors. Then, once your treasures are inside, seal it up with more papier-mâché and paint or decorate with crepe paper.

Model Railroad Scenery

If your child is interested in model railroads, you can make tunnels and all sorts of elevated landscape scenes from papier-mâché. Make a tunnel by stapling chicken wire to a sturdy board and then adding the papier-mâché. Finish your miniature landscapes with coffee grounds for dirt, ground herbs and moss for grass and bushes, and sawdust for sand.

Relief Maps of Your Neighborhood

Using the same principles, you can make relief maps of your neighborhood for a geography project by first studying a contour map of the area and then building up hills and elevations where indicated.

Puppet Stage Background Scenery

You can make very interesting background scenery for a puppet show theater or stage play by first creating flats from sturdy cardboard or plywood and then building up the protruding features of your scenery with an armature of chicken wire or wads of newspaper taped to the flat. Make sure to secure the papier-mâché you add by stapling.

Hints:

    For a finer working medium, use a special mixture of papier-mâché made exclusively from tissue or toilet paper and paste to add special details to your regular creations.

    For an unusual finishing touch to a mask or piñata, try pressing leaves and feathers in overlapping patterns to the mixture while it is still wet.

Yield: 28 ounces papier-mâché

Cost of Ingredients: $2.26
Comparable Purchased Product: Celluclay
    Instant Papier-mâché, 1 pound, $3.75 ($6.56)
Savings: $4.30

Sewing Cards

    This toy can be made ahead by an adult and then used to teach a child how to sew.

    White shirt cardboard or bristol board
    Nail
    Felt-tip markers or crayons
    Short lengths of colored yarn
    Large-eye tapestry needle

1. Trace a simple design from a child's coloring book or allow your child to draw freehand designs on the shirt cardboard. Outline the design with bright colors—this outline will be your final stitching line.

2. With the nail, puncture the design at regular intervals along the outline. Make sure your holes are not too close together—leave at least a 1/4-inch space between.

To Use:

    Cut brightly colored yarn into 1-foot lengths. For a younger child, you will have to stay close by to thread the needle and knot and untangle the yarn. Show the child how to sew along the outline using a simple running stitch.

Yield: 10 to 15 cards

Cost of Ingredients: $.55
Comparable Purchased Product: Muppet
   Babies Sewing Cards, $3.85
Savings: $3.30

Decorated Sweat Shirts

Here are three techniques for creating truly individual, one-of-a-kind garments for your child. The ideas for decorating the sweat shirts that are described here can also be used for other items—jeans, jackets, knapsacks, even doll clothes.

However, these projects are messy and the results aren't always predictable, so it's a good idea to start with something simple and not too expensive until you get the knack of painting and decorating.

> **Sweat shirt, or other garment**
> **Opaque acrylic paints**
> **White glue**
> **1/2 cup sand**
> **Buttons, snaps, fringe, assorted trimmings**
> **Paper doilies**
> **Popsicle sticks**
> **Sponge, fat paintbrush**
> **Crocheted lace with large loops**
> **Newspapers**

Dribble Painting

1. Spread the newspapers out on the work surface and place the sweat shirt, carefully spread out, on the newspapers. Choose the colors of acrylic paint that you wish to dribble across the garment and dip the Popsicle stick into the paint. Gently wave it over the sweat shirt, letting small drops and long streamers of paint fall in a random pattern.

2. For special effects, try mixing a small batch of textured paint by squeezing a teaspoon of white glue into a sandwich bag and adding a few drops of paint and a tiny bit of sand. Squish the bag around a bit and then cut a tiny hole in the corner. Squeeze your textured paint on in a swirly pattern.

3. Allow the garment to dry for 24 hours before wearing. Buttons, trim, fringe, and snaps can also be added if desired.

Doily Stencil

1. Cut a paper doily in half and arrange the two pieces on the shoulders of the sweat shirt. Another full doily can be added to the front and back of the sweat shirt, if desired.

2. Dip a sponge or fat paintbrush into the acrylic paint and gently sponge it over the doily. Remove the doily and allow the garment to dry for 24 hours before wearing.

Charm Sweat Shirt

If your child collects plastic charms, this sweat-shirt idea will allow her to show them off.

1. Sew lace trim along the front of the sweat shirt, along the seam allowance of the lace. The charms are attached to the loops in the edging.

Hint:
         To set the paints on a stencil or dribble design, mix a solution of:

> **1/2 cup vinegar**
> **1/2 cup water**

1. Lay painted items on an ironing board. Dip a clean dish towel or washcloth into the solution and lay it directly on top of the painted area. Press with a warm iron to steam-set the designs.

Yield: 1 decorated sweat shirt

Cost of Materials: $6.79
Comparable Purchased Product: Childcraft
   Charm Sweatshirt, $18.95; Unique Clothing
   Warehouse Spatter Paint Sweatshirt, $24.95
Savings: $18.16

Big Picture Puzzles

Select one of your child's favorite photos and once you've had it enlarged, you have the base for a very special puzzle. Other pictures can be used for the base, as well as blank paper that you might use for secret messages or party invitations. In each case, remember the age and skill of the child as you determine the size and difficulty of the puzzle pieces.

> **White glue or Gooey Glue (page 327)**
> **8-inch-by-10-inch photo, magazine**
>   **illustration, or drawing**
> **Shirt cardboard or bristol board**
> **Acrylic fixative (optional)**
> **Sharp scissors or X-Acto knife**

1. Glue the picture or drawing of your choice onto the cardboard. If you plan to make an invitation, a letter, or a special message your puzzle base, write directly on the cardboard. Spray or brush the photo or picture with acrylic fixative if you expect it to have heavy use.

2. Turn the cardboard over and draw puzzle shapes to suit the skill of your child. Keep the pieces large and easy to handle, as well as simple to cut out, if a small child will work on the puzzle.

3. Carefully cut around the shapes you've drawn with a pair of small, sharp scissors or an X-Acto knife.

Secret Message Puzzle

To make a special secret message puzzle, first write on the blank cardboard with a fountain pen or cotton swap dipped in lemon juice. Then proceed as above to make the puzzle. To put this puzzle together, you have to hold each piece under a light bulb until the secret writing appears.

For an especially puzzling puzzle, try writing your message in only a small portion of the entire puzzle, leaving the rest of the pieces blank.

Yield: 1 to 10 puzzles

Cost of Ingredients: $.22
Comparable Purchased Product: Care Bears
   Puzzle, $.93
Savings: $.71

Giant Chalkboard Wall

This is one of the most creative ways to decorate a wall in your child's room. Once you've spent a few hours creating this giant drawing space, your child will have endless hours of fun and learning at hand.

> **4-foot-by-8-foot sheet of Masonite**
> **Quantity of newspapers**
> **8-ounce can of blackboard spray paint, green or black**
> **8-foot length of wood trim**
> **Chalk**
> **Felt eraser or soft cloth**

1. Lay the Masonite facedown on spread-out newspapers and spray the blackboard paint thoroughly over the entire surface. It's a good idea to cover your nose and mouth with a bandanna and leave the windows open for adequate ventilation in the room.

2. When the first coat is completely dry, spray on a second coat and allow it to dry for 24 hours.

3. Attach the board to the wall at a height comfortable for the child. Nail the trim piece to the bottom to hold the chalk and eraser.

Hint:
> *It is a good idea to clean the board once a week or so with plain white vinegar to keep it shiny and looking new. Let the blackboard dry completely before using it again.*

Yield: 4-foot-by-8-foot chalkboard

Cost of Ingredients: $16.89
Comparable Purchased Product: Harry's
Custom-made Wall of Blackboard, $25.00
Savings: $8.11

Old-fashioned Computer

For the true math whiz, an abacus is a revelation—it can be as fast as a pocket calculator and just as accurate. Since I still use my fingers for adding, I must confess that the best use such a toy would see in my house would be to teach basic counting skills.

However, after you go to the trouble to make a nice, convenient counting toy like this for your child, you really should look into some advanced work with it. You'll know you have succeeded if your child insists on bringing her abacus with her to college.

> **10 empty thread spools or large beads**
> **Paint**
> **Large drapery hanger from the dry cleaner's**
> **Wire snips**
> **Electrician's tape**
> **Yarn**

1. If you are using empty wooden or plastic thread spools, paint the spools bright colors. If you are using colorful wooden beads, you can add your own decorations or perhaps your child's initial.

2. Open up the hanger with the wire snips at one end of the lower bar and slide the spools or beads on. Tape the hanger closed securely with the electrician's tape.

3. Add a pretty bow of yarn and hang the abacus on the back of your child's door on on a hook at his or her height.

Idea:
Make more than one abacus and teach advanced math. Or, make a double-decker one from two hangers taped together.

Yield: 1 abacus

Cost of Ingredients: $1.00
Comparable Purchased Product: Milton
   Bradley, $10.00
Savings: $9.00

Sticky Fingers Catch

*This game teaches dexterity and skill in catching,
aiming, and throwing and it's also lots of fun. Make as many
catching mitts as you need—any number of children can play
this game. This is a great way to finally find a use for the one
large adult glove you might find on the ground in winter or left
behind at your house after a party. If you're the type who loses a
glove or two each winter, your kids will thank you for your
forgetfulness if you make them a catching mitt from your
orphaned glove.*

   3 to 4 oven mitts or several adult gloves
   12 inches hook-and-loop tape
   6 inches elastic tape
   Cotton batting or cotton balls
   Large-eyed needle and thread or white glue
   1 light foam ball

1. Keep in mind the size of the child's hand who will be playing
this game. The glove should be considerably bigger than the
child's hand, with some room left inside to wiggle and bend his
or her fingers. Lay the child's hand over the glove and mark
off the tops of fingers. Stuff a bit of cotton batting into each
finger or into the top of the oven mitt down to the mark where the
child's fingers begin.

2. Sew a strip of elastic tape around the wrist so the glove will
stay on securely; glue or sew the receiving side of the hook-and-
loop tape across the palm of the glove.

3. Glue the sticky side of the hook-and-loop tape around the
foam ball.

Yield: 1 game

Cost of Ingredients: $1.24
Comparable Purchased Product: Popples
   Deluxe Toss-up Catch Mitt, $5.97
Savings: $4.73

Bowling in the Living Room

Set this safe and quiet game up anywhere in your house and your kids, no matter how small, will be able to play it with little supervision provided they stick to bowling with the soft rubber ball. If you fear throwing or hurling, try playing this game in the garage or even on the deck or patio. For the younger child, choose bottles bigger than the 1-liter size.

> **1 cup dried beans**
> **Ten 1-liter soda bottles**
> **2 cups sand**
> **Plain, large sheet of cloth, paper, or oilcloth**
> **Index cards**
> **Small pencils**

1. Preheat oven to 200 degrees.

2. Spread the beans out on a cookie sheet and heat for 1 hour to be sure the beans won't sprout. Allow beans to cool thoroughly before using.

3. Wash the soda bottles carefully and allow them to dry overnight.

4. Weight the bottles by pouring in a mixture of about 1/2 inch or more of sand and dried beans.

5. Set the bottles up in bowling formation on a large piece of sturdy cloth or paper and mark the outside edges as a guide to setting the bottles up.

6. If the set is being used by older children, draw lines for the different frames on the index cards to use for scoring and provide pencils for the scorekeepers.

Yield: 1 bowling set

Cost of Ingredients: $.88
Comparable Purchased Product: Empire
  Junior Bowling, $3.68
Savings: $2.80

Bean Bags

These little toys are soft and cuddly and give a satisfying thunk when thrown around. You should personalize them—make cute and huggable ones for one kind of child, make smart and gritty bean bags for another kind of child, and then make a fun target to toss them into.

Just remember to keep in mind the size of the child's hand that the bean bags are meant for: don't make them too big and heavy for a tiny child.

> **1 pound navy or pinto beans**
> **1 yard colorful closely woven fabric such as cotton, terry cloth, corduroy, felt, or gabardine**

1. Preheat oven to 200 degrees.

2. Spread beans on a cookie sheet or shallow baking pan and bake for 1 hour to prevent beans from sprouting. Let beans cool completely before using.

3. Fold your fabric in half lengthwise, with right sides together. Create a simple pattern from an illustration from a child's coloring book or create a pattern of your own design and cut two pieces for each bean bag. With right sides together, sew twice around the suggested design along the dotted lines or 1/2 inch inside of your own design, using a small machine stitch or, if sewing by hand, a sturdy lock stitch. Leave a 2-inch opening for pouring in the beans.

4. Turn the bag right side out and press. If you are creating an animal character, add the features and details. Feel free to improvise and add your own ideas, especially if you are letting a child help with this project. Just make certain that you don't add any details that can be chewed off by a very small child, and don't sew on any plastic or hardedged trinkets that may hurt someone if the bean bag is thrown astray.

5. Fill the bean bag with the cooled beans until the bag is 1 to 2 inches thick and still soft and flexible. Sew up the hole left for the beans.

Variations:
> *Create a simple target-toss game by making small round bean bags and decorate an oatmeal box or a small carton for the target, if desired.*
> *Or, if you really feel that you have no sewing talents at all, pour the beans loosely into a small, woolen mitten or glove and decorate. Your kids will never know the difference and they will still like their bean bag toy, even if it's not a work of art.*

Yield: 4 to 6 bean bags, depending on size

Cost of Ingredients: $2.98
Comparable Purchased Product: Fisher Price Fozzie Bear Bean Doll, $3.90
Savings: $.92

Cheap Trick ....

If your child has accumulated a large collection of stuffed animals, bean bags, and soft cuddly toys, you may run out of room for the items long before the child outgrows the urge to collect. Here is one clever way to solve the problem of where to put all the stuffed animals and still have room for the child in the room.

One method to try for the smaller items is to sew or glue the sticky side of hook-and-loop tape on the animal's back and the receiving side anywhere in the room you want to secure the animal: on the back of the door, high up on the wall, arranged under a window, or near the bed. The child can easily position the animals at any of the hook-and-loop points and the animals help to decorate, rather than mess, the room.

Soap Crayons

Here's one way to lure any child into the bathtub—even the most dyed-in-the wool-scaredy-cats. These crayons are fun to make and fun to use, and then, easy to clean up. Let budding artists paint the sides of the tub, the tile walls around the tub, and then let them create self-portraits by coloring all over their bodies with these nontoxic crayons. Then, just wash everything down and do it again tomorrow.

1 cup soap flakes
2 tablespoons hot water
Food coloring or Nature's Colors (page 367)

1. Have ready one large bowl and several small bowls, one for each color. You will also need an ice cube tray with different sections or containers to act as small molds. The segmented plastic dividers used to pack ravioli or fancy cookies will also work.

2. Put soap flakes in a large bowl and drop the hot water into the soap flakes, stirring constantly. The mixture will be extremely thick and hard to stir.

3. Spoon some of the soap into each of the small bowls and color each separately, adding the color by drops until the soap has the consistency of a very thick paste.

4. Press spoonfuls of the paste into your molds and set the crayons in a dry place to harden. They should take a few days to a week to dry completely.

5. When dry, remove from the molds and allow to dry for a few more days before using.

Note:
*If these crayons will be used by very small children who might put them into their mouths, use only the natural dyes in **Nature's Colors** on page 367. Otherwise, it is safe to use regular food coloring from the kitchen.*

Yield: 20 crayons

Cost of Ingredients: $.64
Comparable Purchased Product:
  Rub-A-Dub Magic Soap Crayons, 36 crayons,
  $4.95 ($2.75)
Savings: $2.11

Rock Candy

*Here is a project and a treat for one of those days when your
children have had their share of natural foods and this frankly
sweet treat can at least be considered as an easy chemistry
lesson. In this case, you will be able to eat the crystals that
form.*

> **4 cups sugar**
> **1 cup water**
> **Food coloring or Nature's Colors (page 367)**
> **Clean glass jar**
> **String, cut into 6-inch lengths**
> **Pencil**

1. In a medium saucepan, heat 2 cups of the sugar and the
water. Stir until the sugar is completely dissolved. Gradually
add a few drops of the food coloring of your choice and the
additional sugar, stirring continuously until all the sugar is
dissolved.

2. Pour the solution into a clean glass jar and tie the pieces of
string to the pencil and suspend them across the mouth of the
jar so that the ends hang into the sugar water.

3. Crystals suitable to eat will form in an hour and continue
for several days to a week. Pieces can be broken off and eaten
after the first hour.

Yield: 12 ounces

Cost of Ingredients: $.68
Comparable Purchased Product: Barricini
  Rock Candy, 16 ounces, $3.50 ($2.62)
Savings: $1.93

Crystal Garden

This is a project for the older child—and it should still be supervised carefully, especially if you have younger children in the house. The chemical reaction is pretty to watch but dangerous to touch.

> 1 red brick
> Hammer
> Heavy cloth or newspaper
> 4 tablespoons noniodized salt
> 4 tablespoons laundry bluing
> 4 tablespoons water
> 1 tablespoon ammonia
> Food color or Nature's Colors (page 367): 1 drop
>   each of red, yellow, green, and blue

1. Wrap the brick in the heavy cloth or newspaper and hit with a hammer until you have walnut-size chunks. Pour chunks and brick crumbs into a glass bowl or baking dish.

2. Mix salt, bluing, water, and ammonia together until salt dissolves. Pour mixture over brick chunks.

3. Carefully apply one drop of each of the food colors at different places on the wet surface. Colored crystals will begin to sprout in several hours.

Variations:

For a slightly different effect, try using crushed charcoal instead of brick as the surface, or intermix both brick and charcoal in the same bowl.

Yield: 1 crystal garden

Cost of Ingredients: $.28
Comparable Purchased Product: Instant
    Egg, $1.98
Savings: $1.70

Birdy Gourds

Almost any variety of gourd can be transformed into an interesting birdy for a centerpiece at a party or for just admiring. There birdies won't last forever, unless you poke thin holes into the gourds first, let them dry out, and then coat them with clear fixative when you are done.

> **Gourds**
> **Acrylic paint**
> **Movable animal eyes**
> **Toothpicks**
> **Construction paper**
> **Thin wire or pieces of coat-hanger wire**
> **White glue**
> **Small piece of cork, bark, or stone**

1. Choose an interesting gourd, study it, and determine just what kind of bird it might become. Then paint on appropriate features, glue on two movable eyes, and either a toothpick or little half circle of construction paper for a beak.

2. Dip two pieces of wire or two toothpicks into the glue and then into the bottom of the bird for legs. Bend the bottom of the wire and glue the bird onto the rock, or press the legs into cork or bark. You might add a bit of moss to the rock and a little string worm to the beak for special effects.

Gourd Bird Feeder and Nest

Make a pleasant and pretty home for the birds by using available materials—you can even fit the gourds out with nesting materials or customize your nests for a purple martin apartment house.

> **1 or more gourds**
> **1/2 cup High-protein Bird Treats (page 291)**
> **Straw, soft lint, strings, or thread**
> **Wire for hanging**
> **Wooden dowel or pencil**
> **Wire clippers, sharp knife**

1. Carve out a circle on the front of the gourd and scoop out all the insides. Reserve the pulp for **Liquid Fertilizer**, page 298. Let the gourd dry thoroughly overnight.

2. If you are making a feeder, make a hole for the wooden dowel or pencil just below the larger opening.

3. Fill the gourd with the bird food if you are making a feeder and with the nesting materials if you are making a nest. Hang with the wire from a branch.

Yield: 1 to 10 birdy gourds; 1 bird feeder or nest

Cost of Ingredients: $2.45
Comparable Purchased Product: Agway
   Bird Feeder, $5.00
Savings: $2.55

Super Bubbles

These bubbles are the biggest ones you'll ever see—and they last, too, thanks to the glycerin. Since you will be using a regular bottle of bubble formula to start with, it is a good idea to buy an extra bottle and blow lots of small bubbles to accompany the giant ones. Then you will have big whale bubbles and small schools of guppie bubbles to swim together through the air.

> **1 bottle of regular bubble solution**
> **2 tablespoons glycerin**
> **2 tablespoons Soft Soap (page 278) or dishwashing liquid**
> **1 wire coat hanger or 12-inch length of thin wire**

1. Combine first three ingredients and pour the liquid into a deep cookie sheet or long, wide pan with high sides.

2. Make a giant blowing loop by untwisting the coat hanger completely and then reforming it into a big loop with a handle. Other shapes such as spirals and squares can be made with a length of thin wire. Remember to leave a bit of wire for a handle.

To Use:
    Dip loop into the bubble solution until it is completely submerged and then slowly lift it up and then gently stroke it through the air to form the big, big bubbles.

Hint:
    For longer-lasting bubbles, try storing the finished mixture overnight in the refrigerator before using.

Yield: 8 ounces

Cost of Materials: $1.41
Comparable Purchased Product: Baby Gee Bubbles Big Bubbles, 8 ounces, $1.49
Savings: $.08

Monster-be-gone

This is a silly idea—unless your child is awake nights worrying about the monster in the closet or under the bed. Sometimes you may have to use this product with a cup of warm milk with cinnamon if there is a nightmare problem as well. After the patient has slowly sipped the milk and is ready for sleep again, remember to turn the pillow over, thus changing the channel to a happier dream.

    1 tablespoon lemon juice or extract
    1 teaspoon allspice
    1 cup water

1. Blend ingredients and pour into a spray or pump-type container. Label, and keep in a safe place for emergencies.

To Use:
    Whenever there is a fearful worry about a monster under the bed, shoot several spurts of the mist into the trouble spot. As everyone knows, monsters can't tolerate the smell of yellow.

Yield: 1 cup

Cost of Ingredients: $.16
Comparable Purchased Product:
   Anti-Demon and Monster Spray, 7 ounces,
   $3.59
Savings: $3.43

Live, Organic Disco Lights

On a warm and calm summer night, you can temporarily replace your child's night-light with one of these magical lanterns. Go out and enjoy the evening with your child as you gather the tiny twinkling fireflies. Just remember to let the creatures out as soon as the child is asleep or no later than morning. Then, you can make a fresh light jar the next night.

> **2 clean, clear jars with lids**
> **Hammer**
> **Nail**
> **Short twigs, 2 leaves, lettuce**

1. Punch a few small holes in the lid of one jar with the hammer and nail. Add the twigs, leaves, and lettuce and take both jars and lids out on a summer night just as twilight approaches.

2. Carefully and gently catch some fireflies with the jar without the air holes. As soon as one is caught, drop it into the other jar. Keep the lid on the night-light jar except when you are adding fireflies.

3. Catch between 10 and 20 fireflies for a wonderful display in a darkened room.

Yield: 1 night-light

Cost of Materials: $.00
Comparable Purchased Product: GE Night
   Light, $2.49
Savings: $2.49

E-Z Ant Farm

Place your finished ant farm in a spot where you can observe the ants at work and play. Take good care of the ants: feed them small bits of bread, birdseed, dog food or doggie biscuits, and be sure that the sponge inside is always kept moist.

> **Small shovel**
> **Large, clear jar with lid**
> **Hammer**
> **Small nail**
> **Small jar with lid**
> **White glue**
> **Small sponge**
> **Sheet of black paper**
> **Masking tape**

1. Make sure all your jars are clean and dry. Screw the lid on the smaller jar and glue the sponge on top. Place the small jar in the center of the bigger one. Hammer tiny holes in the lid of the big jar. Make sure your holes are smaller than one ant.

2. Find an ant hill and observe it for a day or two to see how the ants come and go. Bring out your clean jars when you are ready to move the ants. Carefully dig up the hill and ants with a shovel and place them in the space between the small jar and the sides of the bigger container.

3. Moisten the sponge with a few tablespoons of water. Put the lid on the bigger jar and cover the sides with the black paper. Secure with masking tape.

To Use:

Keep the black paper on at all times, except when you are observing the ants. If you have captured the queen with the ant hill, your ants will tunnel and create a whole environment. If you have no activity after a week, you will have to start over and keep looking for a queen.

Yield: 1 ant farm

Cost of Ingredients: $1.50 (assuming you find a
   queen)
Comparable Purchased Product: Uncle
   Milton's Ant Farm, $6.97
Savings: $5.47

Nature's Dolls

*Probably ever since there was a cave mommy and child,
there have been dolls for the young ones to hold. They can be
fashioned out of anything on hand—twigs, grasses, bits of
cloth. Some of the most charming are the simple ones that allow
the child to add special features and details. The following doll
ideas are classic ones, and you will probably devise more after
you begin with these.*

Corn-husk Doll

*For a rough, simple doll, you can use corn husks just as
you take them from the corn, moistened to make them pliable.
For fancier dolls, you can bleach, soften, and tint the corn
husks in delicate colors to suggest skirts, shawls, and hats.*

> **Inner corn husks**
> **2 cups water**
> **2 tablespoons bleach**
> **Paper towels**
> **Nature's Colors (page 367) or fabric dye (optional)**
> **Cotton ball, wooden bead, or small styrofoam ball**
> **Twist ties or thin wire**
> **Corn silk**
> **White glue**
> **Felt-tip markers**

1. If you want to make a fancy doll, place the corn husks in a
pan of water to which 2 tablespoons of bleach have been added.
Let soak for 30 minutes. Remove, rinse, and let drain on paper
toweling.

2. To tint corn husks, dip into the dye of your choice and let the husks remain until a desirable color tint is achieved. Remove, blot on paper toweling, and keep moist by storing in a plastic bag until needed.

3. To make a doll, fold several long strips lengthwise over a cotton ball, bead, or styrofoam ball to make a head. Tie at the neck with a thin strip of husk, wire, or a twist tie.

4. Right beneath the neck, insert a few husks horizontally for arms. Tie off the ends and puff out the arms to suggest full sleeves.

5. Tie off a waist below the arms, and shape the bottom of the doll into two pantaloons, if desired. Otherwise, let the husks remain gathered in a skirt.

6. Braid some of the corn silk and glue it on the head. Cut a triangle of corn husk as a kerchief or a cap, and another for a shawl, if desired.

7. Add facial features with felt-tip marker.

Hollyhock Doll

This is a delightful, transitory doll that will charm a child with its delicate beauty.

> **1 large, open hollyhock blossom**
> **1 leaf**
> **Several toothpicks**
> **1 seed case, closed**
> **1 seed case, with calyx**
> **Tiny twigs**

1. Begin with a large, open hollyhock, held upside down, to form the skirt. Fasten a leaf over the skirt with a length of broken toothpick.

2. A closed seed case makes the upper torso, and a seed case with calyx intact will form the head. Attach one on top of the other with toothpicks.

3. Attach tiny twigs to the side of the middle seedcase for arms.

Yield: 1 doll

 Cost of Materials: $0.00
Comparable Purchased Product: House of
    Glass Cornhusk Doll, $1.29
Savings: $1.29

Delicate and Fancy Easter Eggs

*Try these techniques for an Easter egg decorating session
that is made possible entirely with materials from your
kitchen pantry and hall closets. The colors are natural, the
ideas are simple, and if you feel especially artistic, you can
blow some eggs out of their shells and make permanent
decorations.*

Lacy Eggs

**Lacy leaves: parsley, dill, fern, doilies, or bits of lace
6 eggs
Used pantyhose or cheesecloth
Twist ties or rubber bands
Outer skins from 4 or 5 yellow onions
4 cups water**

1. Arrange bits of lacy leaves, lace, or doily designs around
each egg and wrap the egg and designs in a piece of pantyhose
or cheesecloth. Secure the cloth tightly around the egg with a
rubber band or twist tie.

2. Arrange the eggs in a glass or an enamel pan with the onion
skins and cover with water. Bring the water to a gentle boil and
simmer eggs and onion skins for 15 minutes. Remove the pan
from the heat and allow the eggs to cool in the pan before
unwrapping.

Variations:

Some of the other color treatments described in
Nature's Colors *(page 367) can also be used to boil the eggs.
Avoid any of the colors that come from flowers, especially
unknown species which might be poisonous—it's safe to boil the
eggs with the cabbage, red onion leaves, berries, or beets for a
variety of colors.*

Yield: 6 decorated eggs

Cost of Ingredients: $.32
Comparable Purchased Product: Paas
Easter Egg Dye, $1.89
Savings: $1.57

Kids' Gift Wrap

*These wraps are especially colorful and suited to kids' art
and kids' tastes. No grandparent will be able to tear into these
without first complimenting the child—it's almost like giving
two presents at once. Stay close at hand to supervise this project,
even for older children, because a hot iron is required.*

Crayon Melt

Newspaper
Aluminum foil
Absorbent paper
Vegetable peeler or penknife
Bits and pieces of broken crayons
Iron, medium-hot

1. Cover ironing surface with several layers of newspaper and
a sheet of aluminum foil. Lay the sheet of paper you will use for
wrapping paper on top of the foil. With the vegetable peeler or
the carving knife, whittle off shavings of different colors of
crayon until the surface is covered.

2. Fold the paper in half, top with another layer of aluminum
foil, and slowly draw the iron over the foil. Unfold the paper
and let it cool.

Paint-blot Paper

Absorbent paper
Newspaper
Several colors of acrylic or tempera paint

1. Fold a piece of absorbent paper in half and place it on several layers of newspaper.

2. Open the paper and squeeze or drop several colors of paint along the fold. Close the paper and press the ink around with your hands. Open and let dry.

Yield: 10 to 12 sheets of paper

 Cost of Ingredients: $1.50
Comparable Purchased Product: Christmas
  Kingdom Wrapping Paper, 40 feet, $2.99
Savings: $1.49

Chapter 12

Craft, Holiday, and Decorating Items

The following craft items are meant for adults or older children who are closely supervised by adults. Even handy adults should exercise normal caution, particularly if working with craft materials is a new experience for you. For example, an X-Acto knife is one of the tools you will need and although it's sometimes called a craft knife, some artist friends of mine use a regular surgical scalpel instead of the familiar X-acto. You can imagine, therefore, just how sharp it can be and what kind of cuts it can inflict.

There are not a great many craft projects included here because people who are out to save money don't necessarily look to their crafts and hobbies as the proper place to do so. Accordingly, I've chosen crafts made with materials that are either extremely cheap or even free, and most of these crafts can be created and used with some of the other items in the book. Try using your rubber stamp creations and your paper-making projects to create nifty labels and gift tags for the goodies you make for gift basket items.

> **Nature's Colors**
> > *Red*
> > *Yellow*
> > *Blue*
> > *Purple*
> > *Green*
> > *Brown*
> **Baker's Craft Dough**
> **Fine Crafty Clay**
> **Christmas Tree Preservative**
> **Christmas Snow**
> **Padded Picture Frame**
> **Homemade Paper**

Custom Rubber Stamps
Dried Flower Wreaths
Gift Baskets for Cheaper & Better Gifts
 Gourmet's Delight
 Christmas Alone Cheer-Me-Up
 Bridal-Shower Basket
 Summer Camp Send-off
 Bon Voyage Basket

Nature's Colors

These colors have all the softness and variety of the colors you find in nature—and they are all safe and nontoxic for any use. The colors will fade with time, however, so if you want a dye to be permanent you will probable want to work with either food coloring, tempera paints, or acrylics, depending on the project.

*If you would like to try natural colors for dying yarns or woolens, refer to the **Hints** that follow for information about making these colors last.*

Red

> **1 cup beets, fresh or canned**
> **Water to cover**
> **2 teaspoons vinegar**
> *or*
> **1 cup cranberries**
> **Water to cover**

1. If using fresh beets, cover them with water and boil in an enamel or a glass pan until barely done. Remove the beets and peel, slice, and chop them, reserving the juice. Return beets to the juice and soak them for 4 hours. Strain liquid and measure out 3/4 cup. Add the vinegar to the liquid.

2. If using canned beets, strain out 3/4 cup of the liquid and add 2 teaspoons of vinegar.

3. If using cranberries, cover with water and boil for 2 hours, mashing the cranberries as they soften. Strain liquid.

Yellow

> **Outer skins of 5 yellow onions**
> **1 cup water**
> *or*
> **1 cup daffodil, acacia, or crocus blossoms**
> **Water to cover**

1. Boil the dark, dry outer skins from the yellow onions in a

covered glass or enamel pan for 10 minutes, or until the liquid is dark yellow. Strain the juice.

2. If using flower blossoms, cover with water in an enamel or a glass pan, bring to a boil, and simmer, covered, for 2 hours. Strain liquid.

Blue

1/2 head red cabbage, chopped
1 cup water
or
1/2 cup blueberries, fresh or canned
Water to cover

1. Simmer the cabbage and water in a covered enamel or a glass pan until the cabbage turns dark green and is just tender. Strain the juice, which will be blue.

2. For a darker shade of blue, cover the fresh blueberries with water and simmer for 30 minutes. Mash the berries and strain the juice. If using canned blueberries, strain the juice.

Purple

1/2 cup fresh-frozen blackberries

1. Use the pulp directly by allowing the frozen blackberries to soften at room temperature for 30 minutes and then blending for 30 seconds.

Green

Outer skins of 5 red onions
1 cup water
or
1 cup grass clippings, spinach, or moss
Water to cover

1. Boil the outer skins of the onions in the water in a covered enamel or glass pan for 10 minutes. Strain the juice.

2. If using grass, spinach, or moss, cover with water and boil in an enamel or a glass pan for 1 minute and then simmer, covered, for 10 minutes. Strain the liquid.

Brown

1 cup coffee grounds or 10 tea bags
1 cup water

1. Cover coffee grounds with water or add tea bags to water. Simmer, uncovered, in an enamel or a glass pan for 30 minutes. Strain the liquid.

Hints:
>   *If you plan on using any of the above colors on fabrics, you will have to boil the fabric in a fixer or **mordant** before adding the colors. There are several different types of mordant you can use, and each will give a different shade when mixed with the dye. You will have to experiment to get the exact shade you like.*
>   *You can choose either 4 tablespoons of potassium alum mixed with 1 tablespoon cream of tartar, or 1 teaspoon of chrome mixed with 1 1/2 teaspoons cream of tartar.*
>   *To apply mordant to fabric, first dissolve the mordant you have chosen into 1 cup of water. Add this mixture to a large pot containing at least 1 gallon of water. Use the above measures of mordant for each 8 ounces of fiber. Add the fabric, making sure there is enough water to cover, and simmer for 1 to 4 hours, depending on the color intensity that you want to achieve. Turn off the heat and let the fabric rest for another 4 hours; rinse, and dry.*
>   *There are many other mordants, flowers, and leafy materials that you can boil for color. Experiment with flowers you have on hand; interesting little rocks, berries, twigs, and even insects all yield pretty colors.*
>   *Just be careful working with plant materials that are unfamiliar to you—make sure no child or pet tries to eat or drink the materials. Refer to one of the books, magazines, or sources for materials for wool or fabric dying in the **Resources** section for more information about dyeing techniques.*

Yield: 1 cup of each color

Cost of Ingredients: $.87
Comparable Purchased Product:
   McCormick Red Food Color, 1 ounce, $.85
   ($6.80)
Savings: $5.93

Baker's Craft Dough

This craft dough is very pliable and simple to make and use. Some of the ingredients listed are not strictly necessary—just nice. The powdered alum retards spoilage and the cooking oil makes the dough a little easier to work with, but if you don't have these items handy, or if you're just beginning to experiment with this craft form, just go ahead and make up the dough with flour, salt, and water.

4 cups unsifted flour
1 cup salt
1 1/2 cups water

Optional Ingredients

1 tablespoon powdered alum
1 tablespoon cooking oil
1/4 teaspoon food coloring or Nature's Colors (page 367)
1/4 teaspoon oil of cloves or peppermint extract

For Finishing

Acrylic paints
Spray acrylic fixative
Clear or orange shellac

1.   Mix together flour, salt, and alum if you are using it. With a big wooden spoon, slowly stir in the water, oil, coloring, and scent. Keep mixing until the dough follows the spoon around the bowl and then knead with your hands until smooth. The initial kneading will only take a minute or to to get the dough going and to make it pliable. After that, you will knead as you work with smaller pieces and the dough will stay soft.

2. Store dough in the refrigerator until ready to use. It will remain in good condition for up to 4 weeks. Let it warm to room temperature before using.

To Use:

Generously flour the work surface and pinch off just enough dough to mold with. Leave the rest in a plastic bag until needed. Fill a small bowl with water to use as glue when you want to stick two pieces together.

When you have made an item you want to keep, place it on a floured cookie sheet and bake in the oven at 250 degrees for at least an hour. Baking time varies considerably depending on the thickness of the object. It's a good idea to check for doneness by inserting a toothpick into the thickest part of the item. If you think your ornaments are getting too brown, cover them with aluminum foil, turn down the oven, and compensate by cooking a bit longer.

After the item is completely dry, you can paint it with acrylic paints and then either paint it with shellac or spray it with several coats of acrylic fixative.

Ideas:

This dough is used quite successfully for creating homey-looking Christmas ornaments. When my kids were little, I helped them make their own creations each year for the tree and now I treasure these ornaments.

Try helping children create their own handprints by outstretching their hands on a 1/2-inch-thick layer of dough while you carefully cut around their fingers with a dull paring knife. Or, the children can press their handprints into a plaque-size circle of dough.

All sorts of kitchen implements can be used to give interesting textures to the dough. By far the most interesting effects can be created by forcing the dough through a garlic press. The resultant threads can become a bird's nest, hair, animal fur, and of course, spaghetti. Just remember to "glue" the strands together with water as you go. Add teeny little eggs to a nest or roll out some meatballs for a bowl of spaghetti.

Another natural creation for Baker's Craft Dough is to make a bread basket, bagel, or pretend muffins out of it. To make a basket, roll out and cut thick strips of dough. Drape several, close together, across an inverted, heavily floured loaf pan or baking dish. Weave strips in the opposite direction through the original ones. Create a lattice-work design and finish off the edges as if you were creating a fancy pie. Bake your creation, pan and all, in the oven and lift the basket off the pan when it is completely cool.

Hints:
A rolling pin is extremely useful for flattening the dough, but if you have many little hands around the table at once, cans of soup or vegetables will work just as well.

You can finish the smaller items by coating them with clear nail polish. Or try brushing them with evaporated milk if you want your creations to look brown and golden, like baked goods.

If you want to add a hanger for a Christmas ornament or wall plaque, push a paper clip almost all the way into the top of the ornament.

To create a hole for threading a pendant, take a cocktail straw and carefully drill out the hole just before you are ready to bake.

Yield: 40 ounces

Cost of Ingredients: $1.66
Comparable Purchased Product: Rose Art
  Modeling Clay, 3.35 ounces, $3.39 ($40.47)
Savings: $38.81

Cheap Trick . . . . ✂ . . . .

In the hands of a real craft artist, the various dough mixtures described in this chapter can turn into true works of art. Meanwhile, here is an easy project that can turn into a nice conversation piece. Remove the crusts from a slice of white bread and place the bread in a shallow bowl to which you've added 2 teaspoons water, a drop of red food color, and a squirt or two of white glue. Mush and knead the bread and break off a small piece. Mash and smush it between your fingers until you have a flat piece that looks like a rose petal. Continue and make enough petals for a complete rose; let them dry, glue them together, and glue on a little ribbon loop and you have an interesting, hanging pendant.

Fine Crafty Clay

*This mixture creates the finest texture of all the doughs. It also hardens by air drying rather than baking, so features created will not puff up in the oven. Interesting effects can be created by coloring this clay before working with it—see **Ideas** for more details.*

2 cups baking soda
1 cup cornstarch
1 1/2 cups water

Optional

Food coloring or Nature's Colors (page 367)
Oil of cloves or peppermint extract

For Finishing

Matte acrylic varnish

1. In a saucepan over medium heat, stir together the baking soda and cornstarch and add the water, stirring constantly. Mixture will become thin and smooth at first.

2. Cook, stirring constantly, until mixture is too thick to stir. Turn the mixture out onto a cookie sheet to cool, covering with a damp cloth. When cool, knead until smooth.

3. Store the mixture in a tightly closed plastic bag in the refrigerator for up to 2 weeks.

To Use:
Items can be molded from this clay by either shaping with your hands, rolling out and cutting with a cookie cutter, or pushing through a cookie or garlic press.
Clay will harden at room temperature, depending on the size of the object. Most items are dry after 24 hours, and if necessary, you can preheat the oven to 350 degrees, turn it off, and put the clay in to dry, turning the pieces occasionally.

Ideas:
Consider tinting the Crafty Clay with different spices

from your kitchen for a simple, earthy look. Try using dry mustard for a creamy color, or cinnamon and allspice for darker tones.

Hints:

Smooth off any rough edges after drying with an emery board.

Because this clay is especially absorbent, more than one coat of varnish or shellac will be necessary. Experiment with a trial piece to see how many coats you will need—I've used as many as five coats on a thick figure.

Yield: 20 ounces

Cost of Ingredients: $.77
Comparable Purchased Product: Roma Pastilina, 32 ounces, $3.50 ($2.18)
Savings: $1.41

Christmas Tree Preservative

If you use a fresh tree at Christmastime, or if you bring fresh-cut greens into the house, try spraying them with this solution before you bring them in.

When you decorate with the greens and put the tree up, make sure to locate them away from heating ducts or other sources of heat such as fireplaces, heaters, or bright light bulbs. Keep the tree's water container filled with the solution, and your tree will have a happy, safe holiday.

> **1/2 cup ammonium sulfate**
> **1/2 cup boric acid**
> **2 tablespoons borax**
> **1/4 cup hydrogen peroxide**
> **Warm water**
> **1 teaspoon pine oil**

1. In a clean plastic gallon jug, combine all ingredients except the water and pine oil. Shake gently until combined.

2. Add pine oil to the solution and add enough warm water to

fill the gallon jug. Label the solution and pour into a spray bottle. Solution will last for 4 weeks in a cool garage. Discard unused portion after the holidays.

To Use:

> Prop cut tree and greens against a tree outside and spray thoroughly. Turn and spray all sides, and let dry for 30 minutes before bringing into the house.

Yield: 1 gallon

Cost of Ingredients: $2.70
Comparable Purchased Product: Frosty Christmas Tree Saver, 16 ounces, $1.29 ($10.32)
Savings: $7.62

Christmas Snow

> This frankly fake touch to your tree or greens is a lot of fun to make and apply. If you have children around to help, their suggestions will undoubtedly run to different colors for the "snow" as well as any number of glittery additions to sprinkle on.
> This snow looks terrific with white sparkles added minutes after you've painted on the snow.

> **1/3 cup liquid starch**
> **1 cup soap flakes or detergent granules**
> **1 to 2 tablespoons water**
> **Blue food coloring or Nature's Colors (page 367)**

1. Mix the liquid starch into the soap flakes, add the water, and beat with a rotary beater until the mixture has the consistency of marshmallow fluff or thick meringue.

2. Beat in the blue food coloring drop by drop to achieve a white, icy effect.

To Use:
> Using a clean paintbrush, dab the snow onto the tops of your green branches in various artistic patterns.

Variations:
> You can certainly experiment with different colors of snow to match your decor and your mood, or try a rainbow effect of many different colors at once.
> Sprinkles to try on top of the snow include candy sparkles from the cookie shelf, sequins and glitter from your sewing basket, or confetti.

Yield: 16 ounces

Cost of Ingredients: $.68
Comparable Purchased Product: Snow Bliz, 13 ounces, $.99 ($1.21)
Savings: $.53

Padded Picture Frame

> This pretty but expensive item can be found in all sorts of speciality stores. You can make custom frames in just the sizes you need and in just the right colors for your rooms by following the simple directions, here.
> Or, you make the job even easier for yourself by covering a purchased frame with cotton batting and the fabric and trim of your choice.

> **2 pieces of sturdy cardboard,** approximately 1 inch larger than the finished piece
> **X-Acto knife or scissors**
> **1 to 2 yards of cotton batting**
> **1 to 2 yards of fabric for cover**
> **1 to 2 yards of trim: ribbon, lace, bias binding, or cord**
> **White glue**
> **Small pieces of cardboard for stand**

1. Choose the size frame you would like to make by first laying the photo or art to be framed on one of the pieces of cardboard.

Carefully draw an outline around the art and put the art or photo aside.

2. Decide on the shape and width you would like the finished frame to be and draw a second outline around the outline of the art. Cut out the frame and the opening for the picture with an X-Acto knife or sturdy scissors. Cut out a second piece of cardboard for the frame's back.

3. Trim a piece of cotton batting to fit the front of the frame and glue the batting to the cardboard. Cut out fabric to cover the batting and to wrap around to the back of the cardboard. Stretch the fabric over the batting, cutting out notches so that the fabric fits smoothly into corners or curved shapes.

4. Cover the back of the frame with fabric, bringing the edges to the wrong side and gluing securely. Cut a rectangle for the hinge from cardboard. Score the hinge near the top, cover with fabric, and attach a piece of ribbon to the back at the bottom. Glue the top of the hinge and the other end of the ribbon to the back of the frame.

5. Glue the front of the frame to the back at the bottom and sides, leaving the top open to insert the picture. Add trim, if desired.

Yield: 1 padded picture frame

Cost of Ingredients: $4.76
Comparable Purchased Product: Purchased
  padded frame, 8 inches by 10 inches, $9.99
Savings: $5.23

Cheap Trick . . . . ✂ . . . .

Use the same materials and the same skills you've acquired for your Padded Picture Frames and make padded, fancy fabric covers for regular loose-leaf binders and use them for notebooks, address books, and for gifts. I use old ones that the kids have tired of after the school term is over, and I cover them with scraps and bits of fabric and padding and then beads, ribbons, netting, feathers—whatever I have on hand.

Homemade Paper

I've always loved fancy and unusual papers, but I was surprised at how easy it is to master the basic skill of making some of my own for special occasions. I've even found that "mistakes" that are too coarse or crumbly to write on have a place in art projects—I've kept all the bits and pieces of my experiments and found interesting ways to include them in other designs, or at the very least, I've shredded them back into new paper.

The type of paper you shred will determine the shade and consistency of the final product, so choose tissue paper, old wrapping paper, interesting mail, and other odds and ends of paper with the final look in mind. Don't worry about any writing or ink on the papers—you can bleach the pulp if you think the ink darkens the color too much.

This is a somewhat involved project that requires you to be superorganized and work quickly once you've processed your paper pulp in the blender.

Therefore, I've listed the equipment you will need, as well as the raw ingredients. By all means, organize your workspace and invite any children who might be milling about the house to lend a hand. They will love helping with this project.

> **4 cups shredded scrap paper**
> **Food colors or Nature's Colors (page 367)**
> **2 tablespoons liquid laundry starch**
> **Laundry bleach (optional)**
> **Newspapers**
> **Iron**
> **1 window screen**
> **2 large sheets of blotting paper**
> **Quantity of paper toweling**

1. Put the shredded paper into a blender, 1 cup at a time. Pour between 1 and 2 cups of hot water and 1 tablespoon of laundry starch over the paper. Cover, and process until you have a thick pulp. Add extra color, if desired, or a few drops of laundry bleach if the color seems too dark.

2. Pour the pulp into a large bowl and process the rest of the paper, adding the additional pulp to the bowl until all the paper

is processed into a pulpy mush that is the consistency of thin
oatmeal or gruel. Mix more hot water into the pulp if it seems
too thick, and make sure you add color at this stage if you don't
like the shade of the pulp.

3. Organize your work space next to the bowl by first covering
the area with several thicknesses of newspaper. Plug in your
iron and turn it on the woolen or warm setting. Place the
screen directly over the newspapers and spoon some of the pulp
onto the screen. Smooth it around evenly and let some of the
moisture drip out of the paper. Press the pulp gently with the
back of the spoon.

4. Cover the pulp on the screen with a piece of the blotting paper,
flip the screen, pulp, and paper over onto fresh newspaper
covered with paper toweling, and carefully lift off the screen,
leaving the pulp sitting on the blotting paper.

5. Cover the pulp with another piece of blotting paper and
change the newspaper underneath if it's too wet. Iron the
blotting-paper sandwich, moving the iron slowly and gently
over the blotting paper. Lift a corner every now and then to see
how well your paper is coming along—the paper is ready when
you can lift off the top blotter and peel the new paper off the
bottom blotter. Iron until the paper is dry enough to peel.

6. Let the blotting paper dry out completely between ironings
(about 1 hour) and spoon out more pulp onto the screen. Repeat
Steps 4 and 5 until all the pulp is used.

Variations:
        *Try adding exotic items to the shredded paper in your
blender. My children have made paper from celery, banana
skins, and scraps of blue jeans that have soaked overnight in
1/2 cup of laundry bleach.*

To Use:
        *You can use the variously shaped patches of paper just
as they come from the blotting papers, but you can and should
trim the papers with a paper cutter or scissors for a more
refined look.*
        *Try adding a deckle edge to your paper by marking a
straight line where you want the edge to be and then dabbing*

along that line with a brush or Q-tip dipped in water. Once the line is nice and wet, you can work it apart with your fingers. Let it dry completely before using. You can tint the edge another shade by using watercolors in place of plain water.

Many artists are making whole constructions from homemade paper. Try draping a piece of still-damp paper over an interesting shape and letting it dry for a special effect.

Yield: 10 to 20 sheets

Cost of Ingredients: $.50
Comparable Purchased Product: Hallmark
Premium Paper, 25 sheets, $15.00
Savings: $14.50

Custom Rubber Stamps

No craft gives me more pleasure than making up my own rubber stamps. You can find designs to carve from greeting cards, wrapping paper, magazine illustrations—anything as small as an eraser that catches your eye and has a simple shape to it will work, and a simple stamp pad completes your stamp set.

Several pink, white, or gum-type erasers
X-acto knife
Pencil

1. Plan your design before beginning to carve and then draw the design directly onto the flat side of a soft pink eraser with a pencil.

2. Outline the design to a depth of about 1/4 inch with the tip of the X-Acto knife. Cutting away from the design, remove about a quarter-inch of eraser from around the design.

Cost of Ingredients: $1.54
Comparable Purchased Product: Bizzaro
Rubber Stamps, $2.50 to $10.00
Savings: $.96

Dried Flower Wreaths

The beauty of dried flowers can be enjoyed year-round, each and every year. You can gather most of the raw materials for your dried-flower arrangements from the fields and roadsides near your home, or you can purchase most of the materials from the florist shop or craft store.

However, it's very rewarding to find your own treasures as you garden or take your daily walk because what you find will likely be unique and special to your family.

You can be as inventive or as practical as you like when making your own wreaths. For example, you can gather your own grapevines and willow branches and weave them into circles, or you can purchase ready-made wreath bases of straw, styrofoam, or grapevine; you can grow and dry your own materials or purchase them all from the store.

You will save the most money, of course, if you make everything, from scratch, for yourself and you can decorate your house with as many wreaths as you like.

> **Generous quantity of dried materials: pods, pinecones, statice, strawflowers, baby's breath, berries, twigs, moss**
> **Purchased wreath forms or a quantity of grapevine, honeysuckle, or other flexible vines or branches**
> **Trimming material such as ribbon, lace, yarn, silk flowers, or tiny birds and other figurines**
> **Florist's wire, florist's picks, pipe cleaners, long twist-ties, string, florist's tape**
> **Wire clippers, scissors**
> **White glue**
> **Hot glue gun (optional)**

1. Gather and store your dried materials so that you have easy access to them when you begin to assemble your wreath. Plastic shoe boxes let you see what you have; or try arranging your materials, by size, in clean cut-off paper milk cartons.

2. Prepare your pods, flowers, and pinecones by twisting florist's wire or the specially prepared floist's picks around the base of the material and leave a tail to attach to the wreath. Wrap exposed ends with green or brown florist's tape or use pipe cleaners in colors to match the materials.

3. If you are making your own wreath bases from vines, you should plan on soaking the vines overnight in a basin of warm water to soften before you weave them. Or, you can weave them as you cut them—I've had good luck with just cutting, wrapping with wire, and weaving the vines as I walk along—and the finished circles are easier to carry than a grocery bag full of vines.

4. If you are going to attach ribbon in long loops or put a fancy straw or dried-seed vine in with the base wreath, arrange it around the base before attaching any smaller, individual items. Attach the long ribbon loops at strategic points to the base with white paste or spots of glue from the glue gun.

5. Try to visualize what the major accents for your wreath will be before you begin to attach your ornaments or flowers because it is much easier to attach than detach. Place the biggest items in a pleasing fashion and finish your design with little items until the wreath looks balanced and pretty.

6. Once you are satisfied with the look of your wreath, use a pipe cleaner for a hanging loop and attach it at the back of the wreath by looping it through and twisting off the ends. Test the hanging loop before trusting it to your door to make sure it is secure. Use two loops if your wreath is particularly heavy.

Yield: One 8-inch-diameter wreath

 Cost of Ingredients: $3.46
Comparable Purchased Product: Country Notebook Single Cottage Wreath, $36.00
Savings: $32.54

Cheap Trick . . . . ✂ . . . .

As you go about gathering your materials for drying, save a few fresh flowers for pressing: place them on paper toweling, then between layers of newspaper, then weight with books. Use your pressed flowers to decorate some of the plainer jars you've saved—simply glue the flowers by using a small amount of white glue and fill the jars with your creams from Chapter 6.

Gift Baskets
for
Cheaper & Better Gifts

*The following suggestions for gift baskets use many of the recipes from **Cheaper & Better**. You can purchase inexpensive baskets and paint and decorate them in a style appropriate to the type of gift you are giving—try pretty pastels for a baby, dried flowers and ribbons for a woman, or tiny toys and candies for a child. You can use containers other than baskets, of course, such as painted tins, small wooden boxes, almost anything that will hold a few surprises or treasures. Ideas for types of containers, as well as suggested contents, are given here.*

*I've described a few typical gift basket ideas, including ideas for alternate containers and suggested contents. Then, I've made a long list of other gift giving ideas you might want to try. You will certainly get the hang of this type of gift, and each and every recipe in **Cheaper & Better** would fit into one basket or another.*

Gourmet's Delight

A bottle of fine vintage wine is always welcome. If you are not sure of your wine selecting ability and want to leave the choosing to the wine store salesman, specify exactly how much you wish to spend.

In your best penmanship, write out a favorite recipe or two that you have enjoyed making.

Container Suggestion:
An earthenware cooking container or antique soup tureen.

Items to Include:
  Pear Cordial (page 186)
  Quick Chicken Liver Pâté (page 155)

Boursin Party Spread (page 154)
French Herb Butter (page 105)
Herby Vegetable Crackers (page 112)
Raspberry Vinegar (page 148)
Marinated Mushrooms (page 151)

Christmas Alone Cheer-Me-Up

If you know that someone you love will be spending Christmas alone, try gathering a basketful of goodies, each wrapped separately, with instructions to open each gift one day at a time.

Container Suggestion:

One of a pair of festive holiday-colored woolen stockings or socks. Enclose the mate, and you will have another gift.

Items to Include:

A paperback book
A favorite album
Record-cleaning Kit (page 317)
Holiday Fruitcake (page 157)
Mulling Mix (page 176)
Cranberry Liqueur (page 188)
Soothing Bath Salts (page 225)
Sweet Potpourri (page 282)
Super Bubbles (page 356)

Bridal Shower Basket

A treasured gift I received at my bridal shower was a big basket filled with all the little things you need to set up house with—the measuring spoons and wire whisks and clothespins and sponges—none glamorous, all necessary and welcome.

Container Suggestion:

A wicker laundry basket or pretty clothing hamper would be very appreciated.

Items to Include:
      A copy of *Cheaper & Better*
      Measuring cups and spoons
      Never-fail Pastry Mix (page 60)
      Healthy Whole Wheat Baking Mix (page 73)
      Spaghetti Sauce-from-Scratch Mix (page 102)
      Spiced and Fancy After-dinner Coffee (page 178)
      Ultra-bubble Bath (page 226)
      Soft Soap (page 278)
      Houseplant Potting Soil (page 297)

Summer Camp Send-off

If you have a camper in your family, especially a first-time camper who may experience a bit of homesickness, here are some comforting items to send off to camp with your loved one.

Container Suggestions:
      A box that the camper can lock up and hide private treasures in will be most appreciated. Make sure you include a lock and key if the child is not old enough to remember a combination, and keep an extra copy of the key at home.

Items to Include:

      Silly Saturday Cereal (page 118)
      A supply of stamped, home-addressed envelopes
      Pretty or snazzy letter paper
      Happy Trails Mix (page 121)
      Fruit Leathers (page 130)
      Beef Jerky (page 131174)
      Creamy Hot Chocolate Mix (page xx)

Bon Voyage Basket

When friends or family plan a trip, they don't always think about the comforting little things that can make their time away from home special. Here is a collection of ideas for travelers.

Container Suggestion:

A small carry-on-size piece of soft luggage that you can fold and pack for coming home would be appreciated.

Items to Include:

A travel game set for the plane trip: checkers, backgammon, chess, or playing cards
A few dollars' worth of currency for the destination country (to spend on cab fare, drinks, emergencies)
Rose Beads (page 232)
Bloody Mary Mix (page 177)
Soothing Bath Salts (page 225)
Delicate Care Soap (page 274)
A paperback book or novel
A blank journal
Film and developing-service envelopes
Stamped and home-addressed envelopes

Additional ideas for gift-giving baskets are only as limited as your gift list, your budget, and your imagination. They might consider some of the following themes to get you started using items created from **Cheaper & Better:**

New Apartment Warming
First Housewarming
Retirement
Pet Pampers
Children's Play Box
Roughing-It-in-the-Woods
Herb Basket
Summer Bounty Basket
Wine Basket
Women's Bath Basket
Men's Grooming Basket
Car Care Basket
Gardener's Basket
Arts and Crafts Basket
Grandparents-Are-Nice Basket
Congratulations to the Proud Parents (or Grandparents)
Mother-to-Mother Basket

Get-Well Basket
Picnic in the Park for Two
Baby Shower
College Care Basket
Child's Birthday

Yield: 1 basket

Cost of Ingredients: $10 to $20
Comparable Purchased Product:
Bloomingdale's Parent Congratulations
Basket, $70.00
Savings: $50

Resources

When it comes to mailing away for things, there are those who love to and those who never do. It's conceivable that if you live far, far away from specialty stores and shopping malls, gourmet outlets, sewing and craft centers, garden supply emporiums, computer stores, toy stores, and health food stores, you could still make all the items in **Cheaper & Better** by ordering from the following pages.

If you believe you don't get enough mail or enough interesting offers through the mail, you can place your name on a master list to receive lots of catalogs and free offers as well as plenty of junk mail. If you would like to receive more mail, write to:

Direct Marketing Association
Mail Preference Service
6 East 43rd Street
New York, NY 10017

You can request their **Great Catalog Guide** listing over 700 companies offering services and items by mail for $2.00.

The companies and suppliers listed on the following pages offer their services, goods, or at least helpful information through mail order.

Chapter 1

Canning Supplies

Ball Corporation
345 South High Street
Muncie, IN 47302
Recipes, hints, rules, and regulations from the home-canning authority; the Blue Book is a canning bible.

Dover Publications, Inc.
180 Varick Street
New York, NY 10014
Publishes the United States Department of Agriculture's **Complete Guide to Home Canning, Preserving and Freezing***; $3.95, as well as an incredible selection of books on other subjects; catalog: free.*

Cooking Equipment

See the listings under Chapter 4, gourmet items, for speciality cooking and preparation equipment.

Chapter 2

Dehydrators

The following manufacturers produce dehydrators that vary in price from under $100 to over $200. Write for additional information:

Bee Beyer
1154 Roberto Lane
Los Angeles, CA 90024

B & J Industries
514 State Street
Marysville, WA 98270

Excalibur Products
6083 Power Inn Road
Sacramento, CA 95824

Ideal Harvest
PO Box 15481
Salt Lake City, UT 84115

Solar Dehydrator

The Storage Room
Route 1, PO Box 229
Belen, NM 87002
Build-it yourself; write for information.

Chapter 3

Snack Foods

Also see the catalogs listed under Chapter 4, gourmet items, for companies that make fancy snack products, especially in large quantities for gifts and parties.

Trombly's Peanut Butter Fantasies
80 Boylston Street, Suite 450
Boston, MA 02116

Chapter 4

The companies listed here specialize in gourmet cooking supplies and food items. Although many of these purchases may be too steep for a stict budget, you can consider these items for special occasions and gifts. In addition, the containers that many gourmet foods are packed in are worth saving and reusing.

The Chef's Catalog
3215 Commercial Avenue
Northbrook, IL 60062
Professional restaurant equipment for home cooking; books, food; catalog: $2.00.

Pierre Gerardaux
300 Chestnut Street
Middlesex, NJ 08846
Supplies, specialty foods; catalog: free.

Williams-Sonoma
PO Box 7456
San Francisco, CA 94120
Kitchenware, household articles, and gourmet food; catalog: $2.00.

The Wooden Spoon
Route 6
Mahopac, NY 10541
Specialty cookware; catalog: free.

Chapter 5

Tea Supplies

Grandma's Spice Shop
RR 10, PO Box 448-E
Burlington, NC 27215

Meadowbrook Herb Garden
Route 138
Wyoming, RI 02898

New Discoveries
PO Box 39333
Phoenix, AZ 85069

Taylor's Herb Garden
1535 Lone Oak Road
Vista, CA 92084

Winemaking

Amateur Enologist
PO Box 2701
Vancouver 3, British
Columbia
Canada
*A quarterly magazine
for the home beer and wine-
maker; 4 issues a year: $2.00*

Great Fermentations
87F Larkspur
San Rafael, CA 94901
*Supplies, equipment,
books; catalog: free.*

Cask & Keg
24182 Red Arrow Highway
Mattawan, MI 49071
*Supplies; catalog:
free.*

Chapter 6

*Also see the listings for
Chapter 8, clothing care, for
additional potpourri and
sachet sources, and the
listings for Chapter 9, gardens, for seeds to grow your
own herbs. The cooking
supply and gourmet food
catalogs listed for Chapter 4
will provide additional
sources for ingredients.*

Aphrodisia Products, Inc.
282 Bleeker Street
New York, NY 10014
*Potpourri supplies,
essential oils; catalog: $1.00.*

Autumn Harvest Natural
Foods
1029 Davis Street
Evanston, IL 60201

Caswell-Massey Co., Ltd.
111 Eighth Avenue
New York, NY 10011
*Natural and personal-
care products.*

Crabtree & Evelyn, Ltd.
PO Box 167
Woodstock Hill, CT 06281
Toiletries, oils.

Ellon (Bach) USA
PO Box 320
Woodmere, NY 11598
*Herbal remedies, herb
guide.*

Indiana Botanic Gardens,
Inc.
PO Box 5
Hammond, IN 46325
*Potpourri supplies,
sachets, castile soap powder;
catalog: $.25.*

InterNatural
PO Box 463 E
South Sutton, NH 03273
*Natural personal-care
products.*

Nature's Herbs
281 Ellis Street
San Francisco, CA 94102
        Potpourri supplies.

San Francisco Herb Company
250 14th Street
San Francisco, CA 94103
        Bulk herbs, teas;
wholesale catalog: free

Chapter 7

General Household Tools and Equipment

Cumberland General Store
Route 3
Crossville, TN 38555
        General supplies;
catalog: $3.75.

Chapter 8

*Also see the listings for
Chapter 6, Health and Beauty
Aids, for additional sources
for potpourri.*

Potpourri, sachet materials

The Carolina Perfumer
PO Box 1115
Southern Pines, NC 28387
        *Potpourri by the
pound; brochure: $1.00*

The Country Sampler
PO Box 2179
Evansville, IN 47714

Faith Mountain Country Fare
102 Main Street
Sperryville, VA 22740
        *Old-fashioned
hanging herbs; catalog: $2.00*

Tom Thumb Workshops
PO Box 332
Chincoteague, VA 23336
        *Dried materials, orris
root, fragrances, books;
catalog: $1.00.*

Chapter 9

Gardening, Outside Living

Agway
239 West Service Road
Hartford, CT 06101
        *Catalog of supplies,
tools, seeds, chemicals;
catalog: free.*

Yankee Books
PO Box C3F5
Depot Square
Peterborough, NH 03458
        *Publishes a library of
"forgotten arts" including
information on building a
stone wall, gardening, and
canning. Write for free list;
books are $4.95 each.*

Pet Supplies

Bird 'n Hand
40 Pearl Street
Framingham, MA 01701
Catalog: free.

Seeds and Flower Supplies

Catnip Acres Farm
Christian Street
Oxford, CT 06483
Catalog: $1.00

Park Seed Company
Highway 254 North
Greenwood, SC 29648
Catalog: free.

Sandy Mush Herb Nursery
Route 2
Surrett Cove Road
Leicester, NC 28748
*Herb seeds and
plants; catalog: $1.00.*

Stark Bro's Nurseries
Louisiana, MO 63353
Catalog: free.

Stokes Seeds, Inc.
PO Box 548
Buffalo, NY 14240
Catalog: free.

White Flower Farm
Litchfield, CT 06759
*Flower bulb
specialists.*

Chapter 10

Computer Equipment and Supplies

Beagle Brothers, Inc.
3990 Old Town Avenue
Suite 102C
San Diego, CA 92110
*Software and tips for
Apple computers*

Connections Catalog
5221 Central Avenue, Suite 205
Richmond, CA 94804
*Colored, continuous-
feed paper, envelopes, labels;
catalog: free.*

Global Computer Supplies
45 South Service Road
Department 64
Plainview, NY 11803
*Discounted computer
equipment, peripherals,
furniture; catalog: free.*

Lyben Computer Systems
1050 East Maple Road
Troy, MI 48083
*Computer supply
discount items; catalog: free.*

General Office Supplies

Also see the listings under Art Supplies, Chapter 12.

Quill Corporation
100 South Schelter Road
PO Box 4700
Lincolnshire, IL 60197
General office and computer supplies at a discount; catalog: free.

Chapter 11

Rubber Stamps

See Chapter 12.

Stencil Crafts

See Chapter 12.

Toys

Childcraft Education Corp.
20 Kilmer Road
Edison, NJ 08818
Children's books, toys; catalog: free.

Government Printing Office,
Washington, DC 20402
Booklet about toymaking: free.

Hearth Song
2211 Blucher Valley Road
Sebastapol, CA 95472
Toys, books, educational toys.

Judy Horn
42 Brechinridge
Asheville, NC 28804
Cornhusk dolls and flowers; catalog: free.

The Nature Company
PO Box 2310
Berkeley, CA 94702
Gifts, tools, some natural and scientific toys.

Playper Corporation
PO Box 312
Teaneck, NJ 07666
Makes covers for home-made Big Blocks (see page 331.)

Chapter 12

Art Supplies, General

Arthur Brown & Bro., Inc.
2 West 46th Street
New York, NY 10036
Catalog: $2.00.

A.I. Friedman
25 West 45th Street
New York, NY 10036

Bookbinding and Paper

American Paper Institute, Inc.
260 Madison Avenue
New York, NY 10016
Brochure on paper-making.

Basic Crafts Company
1201 Broadway
New York, NY 10001
Bookbinding materials, fine papers.

Dried Flower Materials

Changing Seasons
63 East Main Street
Westfield, NY 14787
Price list: free.

Flower Press, Publishers
RFD 1, PO Box 222
Warner, NH 03278
Plant list, illustrated guide to wreath-making; brochure: $.25.

Fabric Supplies

The Fabric Barn
PO Box 576
Plymouth, MI 48170
Waverly fabrics; fabric swatch: $4.00

The Fabric Center
521 Electric Avenue
Fitchburg, MA 01420
Discounts on decorator fabrics; price folder: free.

Rubber Stamps

Bizzaro
PO Box 16160
Rumford, RI 02916
Catalog: $1.00

Rubberstampmadness
PO Box 168
Newfield, NY 14867
A really nifty newletter; 6 issues: $15

Stencil Crafts

Adele Bishop, Inc.
PO Box 3349
Kinston, NC 28501
Catalog: $2.50.

Plaid Enterprises, Inc.
Box 7600
Norcross, GA 30091
Stencils, books, supplies; catalog: $3.00.

Stencil Artisans League, Inc.
5780 Peachtree-Dunwoody
Road, Suite 460
Atlanta, GA 30342

Textile Crafts

Soft Touch Handspun Yarns
13119 NE 129th Street
Kirkland, WA 98034
Catalog: $3.00.

Straw into Gold
5533 College Avenue
Oakland, CA 94618
Fiber materials:
woolens, weaving supplies,
dyes, and mordants.

Index

G

M

O

P

Waffles, Quick, 72
   See also Blintzes; Crepes;
      Pancakes.
Walker's Honey Whip, 104
Wall
   Cleaner, 250
   Giant Chalkboard, 346
Wash, Iodine Antiseptic, 231
Washer Fluid, Windshield,
   313
Washing
   Machine Soap, Automatic,
      276
   Solution, Safe Car-, 310
Wassail, Christmas, 196
Water
   Hard, Mix, 276
   Soft, Mix, 276
   Test, Soft-Hard, 270
Wheat
   Creamed, Cereal, 13
   Germ, and Cornflake
      Topping Mix, 92
   Whole
      Healthy Baking Mix, 73
      Honey Muffins, 74
      Nutty Biscuits, 74
*White Lily Pore Reducing
   Solution, 213*
*William Sherrel Natural
   Garlic in Oil, 25*
Windex, 253
Windshield Washer Fluid,
   313

Wine, Dandelion, 189
Wise Potato Chips, 135
*Wishbone Chunky Bleu
   Cheese Salad Dressing,
   33*
Woolite, 274
*Workman's Scrub Hand
   Cleaner, 201*
Wrap
   Crayon Melt, 363
   Kids' Gift, 363-64
   Paint-blot Paper, 364
Wreaths, Dried Flower, 381
Wright's Brass Polish, 264

Yago Sangría, 179
Yellow (coloring), 367
Yellow Brick Toad
   Custom Party Sangría, 180
   Dandelion Wine, 190
   Herb Butter, 107
   Pippins and Port, 195
   Rum Coffee, 178
   Sugar Flowers, 166
   Wassail, 197
Yogurt
   Frozen Fruiti, 141
   Homemade, 121
   Mud Pack, 208
   Sipping, 172
   See also Gelato; Ices; Ice
      Cream; Pops
Young Man's Citrus Splash,
   213

NOTES

NOTES

NOTES